SCOTTISH
PREHISTORY

SCOTTISH PREHISTORY

Richard D.Oram

Birlinn

This edition published in 1997 by
Birlinn Limited
14 High Street
Edinburgh EH1 1TE

British Library Cataloguing-in-Publication Data
A Catalogue record of this book is available from the British
Library

ISBN 1 874744 69 6

The publisher acknowledges subsidy from

towards the publication of this volume

Maps drawn by Jim Renny

Printed and bound in Finland by Werner Söderström OY

CONTENTS

Acknowledgements

The genesis of this book can be traced back to the early 1980s and my days as an undergraduate student in Medieval History with Archaeology at St Andrews where, despite the mainly historical bias of my degree, I developed a deep and abiding interest in the prehistory of Scotland. For that, I owe a great debt of gratitude to my tutors and lecturers in prehistoric archaeology – James Kenworthy and Nick Dixon – and to Colin Martin, whose lectures on the Roman period in Scotland raised many of the questions about the relationship between Roman and native expressed in the later stages of this book. Together, they instilled in me an understanding that it is impossible to divorce the world of the historic era from its long roots stretching deep into the prehistoric, and that interdisciplinary research was the only key to understanding of the shadowy interface between the prehistoric and early historic periods.

Many other debts have been amassed during the writing of this text, all of which are gratefully acknowledged. But in particular I must thank the endurance and forbearance of my long-suffering wife, who once again became a computer-widow while I disappeared for nights on end to tap away at the keyboard.

LIST OF FIGURES, MAPS AND PLATES

PREFACE

THE PAST holds a particular fascination for many people. It is something deep-rooted in us, which has seemed to grow stronger as the constantly changing world of the 20th century has opened wider and wider chasms between the old certainties and modern instabilities. There is something reassuring in knowing where we come from, even if there is less certainty about where we are going. It is relatively easy in our modern, literate society to trace our descent back several generations, using records of births, baptisms, marriages or deaths for the most part, or possibly even in some cases more detailed family records. But recorded history can only take us so far back, for we eventually reach the barrier of the prehistoric, where a cloak of anonymity shrouds our ancestors.

Anonymous the prehistoric may be, but inaccessible it is not, for archaeology can take us far beyond the point where the historical record fails. In many ways, unencumbered by the restrictions imposed on historians and archaeologists of the historical era, the prehistorian can get closer to the voiceless societies with which he is dealing, drawing on the powers of analogy and inference. Social anthropology and ethnology have added insight to our study of early cultures, where the responses and approaches of modern primitive societies are used to explore the possible practices and beliefs of our earliest ancestors. But it is easy to overstep the mark in the pursuit of social reconstruction, and let imagination take over where hard fact gives out.

Lack of hard fact was one of the central weaknesses in early schemes which attempted to trace the path of human development. For long, our understanding of the prehistoric in Europe and Britain was tied to chronologies which were based largely on inference and opinion, and on typologies of structures and implements which sought to trace the slow diffusion of ideas from an epicentre of innovation to a culturally backward periphery. Ideas and the equipment which they spawned were seen as travelling outwards in ever-widening circles from a point of origin, slowly changing in form with the greater passage of distance and time. Thus the chambered tombs of Orkney were seen as the cultural descendants of an idea which had originated in the eastern Mediterranean, tracing its origins to the beehive tombs of Mycenaean Greece, and ultimately to the pyramids of Egypt. The slowness with which these ideas were assumed to spread meant that by their arrival at the cultural terminus in the extreme north of Scotland they had been overtaken by major new technological innovations which had occurred back in the spawning-grounds of the Middle East. Thus, the prehistory of Scotland was compressed into a relatively short time-span, to allow space for all the various changes which were evident in the archaeological record to have occurred before the beginning of recorded history.

Our understanding of the prehistoric has been revolutionised since the 1950s by the development of scientific techniques – largely as a spin-off from atomic weapons research – which permit us to provide more accurate dating for excavated sites. The most valuable for the period covered by this book is radiocarbon or C-14 dating. This is based on the principle of atomic decay, where unstable radioactive isotopes of common elements, such as carbon, lose electrons until they become stable. C-14 is a radioactive isotope of carbon, having an atomic weight of 14 as opposed to normal carbon's 12, and it will decay progressively until it stabilises as nitrogen. The loss of electrons occurs at a steady rate, permitting the calculation of the point where half the radioactive content remains (the so-called half-life). In C-14's case this is roughly 5500 years. As C-14 is present naturally in the atmosphere, it is absorbed into all living organisms during their lifetime. This absorption ends on the death of that organism, at which point the C-14 which it contains begins to decay at the known rate. In theory, the level of the surviving radioactive content can be measured and expressed as a calendar date.

C-14 dating was not, however, the perfect technique which it was claimed at first to be. In the first place, whilst described as an 'absolute' dating technique, radiocarbon dates can be expressed only as a statistical probability that the date of a site or object falls between two extreme points. More far-reaching was the discovery that C-14 years and calendar years were not synchronous, and that the further back in time one went, C-14 years deviated in a constant – but irregular – curve, giving 'younger' dates than was in fact the case. Salvation came in the form of an incredibly long-lived North American tree, the Bristlecone Pine. Samples from its annual growth rings, taken from both living and preserved dead timbers extending over some 8000 years, revealed that there were fluctuations in the levels of C-14 absorbed, reflecting variable levels of atmospheric C-14. It therefore proved possible to work out 'calibration tables', where C-14 dates could be re-calculated in accordance with the data provided by the bristlecones. These tables have been revised and refined over the years, permitting a degree of fine-tuning. The use of C-14 dates, however, can often prove misleading to the non-specialist, as the dating systems used are frequently expressed in a confusing variety of forms. For example, in Britain, some archaeologists make use of lower case *bc* or *ad* (as opposed to BC and AD for absolute calendar years) to express uncalibrated C-14 dates, but this is not an internationally recognised system. In some cases *bp* is used, meaning *before present*, but that 'present' is 1950, the year in which the C-14 principle was first set out. In this book, all dates are expressed in absolute calendar years for consistency.

The development of this new technique which offered a means of dating which was independent of typologies and the guesstimates implicit in the old chronologies shattered the traditional view of Scotland as a cultural terminus at the end of the technological distribution network. Structures for long seen as the late and debased successors of forms which had developed thousands of miles away in an earlier period were now shown to long pre-date the monuments from which their builders supposedly drew their inspiration. Ideas could still be transmitted and adopted, but there was now greater scope for understanding how that process came about, and also for acceptance that ideas could have multiple points of near-simultaneous development. The ancient Near East, while always a major seed-bed of innovation, no longer needed to be seen as the fount of all wisdom. More comfortable chronologies which gave breathing space for the development of ideas could now be constructed, and the prehistory of Scotland pushed its boundaries rapidly backwards. C-14 dating, in fact, continues to permit us to push the origins of human settlement in Scotland still further into the past.

1

THE FIRST PEOPLES:
HUNTERS AND GATHERERS

In the Beginning

'WHEN DID the first human settlers arrive in the area that is now Scotland?' It is a question often asked of archaeologists, one which invites a casual answer, but which also reveals all too starkly the limitations of our knowledge of the origins of human settlement in northern Britain. The most truthful answer would be that we do not, and probably will never, know in even relatively general terms the date at which human colonisation began in these lands. But then there is always the temptation to speculate, based, of course, on the best available evidence currently to hand. That evidence, and our ability to interpret it, has expanded and changed dramatically in recent decades, and a glance over the archaeological literature of the last fifty or so years will soon demonstrate how movable the archaeological milestones have become. The past, it seems, is still growing, not simply in terms of the passing years, but also in the sense that we are able to push our supposed starting date further and further back in time. Only sixty years ago, when V. Gordon Childe published his *Prehistory of Scotland*, the beginnings of human settlement were placed in general terms in 'the Atlantic period', a phase of climate development roughly assignable to *c.*5000 to *c.*3000 BC. By the early 1970s, with the advent of new scientific dating techniques, that general date had been firmed up and pushed back to *c.*6000 BC. The discovery and excavation of yet more sites, and the recovery of further dating evidence, has allowed the starting-line to be set yet further into the past, with *c.*7000–6800 BC being the dates given for the earliest settlement at Kinloch on the island of Rum. Kinloch is currently the *earliest* settlement yet excavated in Scotland for which a date can be given with confidence, but it is unlikely to be the *oldest*. Indeed, human settlement in Britain is without doubt considerably older.

A mere 9000 years is but a short step in time in comparison to the 300,000 or so years since the earliest of modern man's ancestors first moved into the parts of north-western Europe which eventually became Britain. These settlers were quite recognisable as human, but they had several characteristic physical differences which would distinguish them from the modern population. Generally shorter than today's average, they had stocky, 'robust' bodies and more prominent facial features, especially around the jaws which were quite heavily muscled. They are usually labelled as hominids to distinguish them from 'true' men in the modern sense, and assigned the genus homo sapiens, from which we – homo sapiens sapiens – ultimately developed. Most importantly, they were tool-users, shaping and sharpening stone and bone to form weapons with which they hunted then butchered their prey. The name Palaeolithic – Old Stone Age – is given to these earliest tool-users, often divided into lower, middle and upper phases distinguished largely by variations and developments in the types of tool used and, in the upper Palaeolithic commencing some 30,000 years ago, by the emergence of a clearly 'modern' element in the population.

For most of its duration, the upper Palaeolithic coincided with the last major phase of glaciation in what is popularly referred to as the Ice Age, an era of several hundred thousand years which had seen successive periods of dramatic cooling and warming of the climate. This last glaciation lasted from about 70,000 BC down to about 8000 BC, but should not be thought of as an unchanging era of a land locked in perpetual winter, frozen under a deep ice sheet. Instead, for much of the time Britain was a treeless sub-arctic tundra, similar to northern Canada or Siberia above the treeline. Only from about 25,000 BC down to shortly before 8000 BC were glaciers and ice sheets present, but except at the peak of such periods most of the region which became southern and midlands England, and the southern coast of Wales, remained free from the ice. Even there, in what is called the periglacial region on the fringes of the ice, the land was barely habitable. Nevertheless, it was accessible from the adjacent parts of mainland Europe for, with so much water taken up in the ice, Britain was connected to the continental lands by broad, shallow valleys lying in the areas now occupied by the North Sea and English Channels, while Ireland, too, was joined briefly by a land bridge to the southern Hebrides.

The archaeology of all phases of the Palaeolithic is fraught with difficulties. Not only were there probably always very few settlement sites – the population was both small in numbers and highly nomadic – but evidence for human activity of this age is often difficult to recognise. In addition, there are serious complications stemming largely from the glaciation, for the ice and, subsequently, the melt-waters, have radically altered the shape of the land, scouring out valleys and dumping the detritus elsewhere. Much is probably buried beneath deep layers of boulder clay, sand and gravel, or lies in the lowland areas subsequently flooded by the re-advancing seas. The majority of excavated Palaeolithic sites in Britain lie in the south and east, beyond the limit of the ice sheet, but this is a deceptive distribution for we must admit of the probability that in periods of better climate, especially before 25,000 BC, nomadic bands could have moved into the then ice-free zones, but evidence for their activity has been removed by later phases of glaciation. Such upper Palaeolithic sites as do survive should, then, be viewed as perhaps typical of the style of life elsewhere in Britain during the inter-glacial phases.

What are these sites? There is a growing body of evidence to show that Palaeolithic settlement occurred both in the shelter of natural caves – such as at Kent's Cavern in Dorset, Robin Hood's Cave in Derbyshire, or the many caverns which honeycomb the cliffs of the Cheddar Gorge – and in open country, where shelters of scrub and brushwood, or skin tents, would have afforded protection from the elements. Sites of this type have been excavated at Hengistbury Head in Dorset, and are scattered across the south of England from Dorset and Gloucestershire to Norfolk. Cave sites were probably especially favoured in periods of poorer climate. That at Paviland in Glamorgan, for example, was occupied around 16,500 BC at a time when the ice sheet extended almost to the Bristol Channel.

Artefacts recovered from these sites represent almost our only evidence for the lifestyle of these early peoples. Tools, and the waste from their manufacture, however, can go a long way towards illustrating a way of life for which all other evidence – clothing, wood, plant remains – has long since perished. Flint was the main raw material from which tools and hunting-weapons were made, but other stone types as well as bone, ivory and antler were also utilised. Bone in particular was used in the production of fine, harpoon-like heads for hunting-weapons, some decorated with engraved designs. The stone tools include ranges of blades for butchering meat, and scrapers, awls and borers used in the preparation of skins which, using bone and ivory needles, would have been sewn into clothing.

By about 13,000 BC the ice was in what, apart from a few brief and localised re-advances, was its final retreat. In this period, the later upper Palaeolithic, evidence for human activity has been identified much further to the north than in earlier times, with settlement sites found in southern Cumbria and the Yorkshire Dales. This represents the generally-accepted northernmost limit of Palaeolithic settlement, although it must be stressed again that most archaeologists would not nowadays rule out the possibility that settlement for which no firm evidence now survives may have occurred much further to the north in better periods of climate. There is, in fact, some slender and also controversial evidence which may point to upper Palaeolithic settlement in Scotland. A scattering of artefacts – two handaxes and several so-called tanged flint points – hardly constitutes firm proof, particularly as the circumstances of the handaxe finds are poorly recorded, and the dating of tanged points open to question. Debate surrounds the only excavated site of supposedly Palaeolithic date in Scotland, at Inchnadamph in Sutherland, where examination of a cave in 1926 produced what appeared to be evidence – in the form of the remains of upwards of 900 reindeer antlers and what was identified as an ivory spear point – of settlement dating from the latter end of the last phase of glaciation. Modern radiocarbon dating of the antler has established its earlier upper Palaeolithic date (deposited between 22,000 and 44,000 years ago), but serious doubts have been raised over whether it arrived in the cave through human or natural action.

Whether or not the antler at Inchnadamph was brought to the cave by human hunters, their settlement would have soon been abandoned as the climate deteriorated in the period down to about 16,000 BC. About three thousand years later conditions began to warm and the ice to melt, until by about 10,000 BC Scotland was probably ice-free, its landscape cloaked in largely featureless grasslands over which roamed herds of reindeer and now extinct species such as giant fallow deer and elk. Hunters may have moved north to exploit these new grazing-lands, but no evidence for their presence has yet been discovered. This warm spell proved to be short-lived, the climate deteriorating rapidly with two periods in which glaciers once again edged down from ice sheets over the Scottish mountains into the lower lands, which had reverted to bleak tundra. But the deterioration was, unlike earlier periods, to be a relatively brief episode and by 8500 BC the climate had warmed once more and vegetation returned. This time, it was no false dawn.

The Mesolithic, *c.*7000 BC to *c.*4000 BC

A climate milder than today's, rich grasslands interspersed with thickets of birch and hazel scrub, abundant game and teeming rivers drew nomadic bands of hunters and gatherers into the land which is now Scotland. People had been moving northwards across the land bridge into Britain once more as the ice had retreated, re-occupying old hunting-grounds in southern and midlands England after about 12,000 BC, and continuing to follow the game herds north as the climate improved. These people were still using tools and weapons of later upper Palaeolithic types, but by around 8500 BC, while older types continued to be produced and used by some groups, clearly new forms began to emerge. The change is most noticeable in terms of size and shape: blades and scrapers become smaller; tiny backed blades – called microliths by archaeologists – were used to produce arrowheads of a new form, with groups of the bladelets set into the shaft rather than a single large head; scrapers become rounder; new forms of axe – the 'tranchet flaked axe' – appear; and bone and antler were put to a much wider range of uses. It is not a sudden change, and probably should not be seen as evidence for the arrival of a wholly new wave of colonists, but resulted from continuous adaptation to ever-changing environmental conditions. Nevertheless, it marks the opening of a new chapter in the story of human development, where people were pursuing a lifestyle significantly different from that endured during the ice ages, and to highlight the change it is awarded a new archaeological label. This is the *Mesolithic*.

As with the Palaeolithic, it is probably wrong to think of the Mesolithic as an era marked by unchanging cultural traditions. The Scottish Mesolithic spans a period of some 4000 or more years, centuries which were distinguished by the continuing evolution of the Scottish landscape and environment. The changes were quite marked, especially as the climate continued to warm towards its post-glacial peak around 6500 BC. The grasslands which had soon developed

Map 1: Mesolithic Scotland

Key to numbered sites:- 1 Loch Scresort; 2 Oronsay; 3 Lussa Wood; 4 Oban Bay; 5 Ulva; 6 Redpoint; 7 Shieldaig; 8 Bettyhill; 9 Freswick Links; 10 Camster Long; 11 Inverness; 12 Caysbrig; 13 Little Gight; 14 Newburgh; 15 Nethermills; 16 Banchory; 17 Stannergate; 18 Morton; 19 Kinneil; 20 Corse Law; 21 Rink Farm; 22 Dryburgh Mains; 23 Barsalloch Point; 24 Low Clone; 25 Auchareoch; 26 Seatter; 27 South Ettit; 28 Wideford Hill; 29 Valdigar

MAP KEY

●   Main named sites
O   Others

as new soils formed in the ice-scoured landscape were quickly colonised by tree species which had survived beyond the southern edge of the ice. Birch came first, followed by hazel, which may have thrived in the rather arid conditions which prevailed at the time. Then, between about 6500 and 6000 BC came first elm then oak, producing dense forest cover over all but the highest mountain areas. In the far north-west, pine established an early dominance and by *c.*5500–5000 BC was spreading throughout the Highlands. Forms of wildlife also changed, their habits and movement affected by such dramatic developments in the land cover, and their human hunters would have had to adapt to meet the changing patterns. Similarly, with the spread of trees came other plant species – edible herbs, berries and roots – which increased the range of resources to be exploited by both animal and human populations. Such responses have not made a clear imprint which we can recognise in the cultural thread which gives continuity and identity to the Mesolithic, even though it was probably a thread that underwent continuous metamorphosis along its length. While it retained its general characteristics, the cultural luggage of tools, weapons, settlement forms etc., which it carried with it may have changed subtly in response to the slowly shifting environment through which it runs.

We shall probably never know when the first Mesolithic hunters and gatherers moved into the open lands of Scotland. The earliest settlement yet discovered – leaving aside Inchnadamph – lies at Kinloch at the head of Loch Scresort on the east side of Rum in the Inner Hebrides. Excavated in the early 1980s, it has been identified as the encampment of a group of hunters and dated to shortly before 7000 BC. Certainly, however, it is not the site of the' first Mesolithic settlement in Scotland for, with the land suitable for exploitation from over 1000 years earlier, it is unlikely that bands of hunters had not ventured north long before that date. Indeed, although the next oldest identified sites are nearly 1000 years younger, they are distributed widely over the country in a manner which suggests that the whole of Scotland was already well-explored, and by soon after 5000 BC it is clear that the country was extensively penetrated by colonists. Sites dating from around 6000 BC have been identified throughout the southern Hebrides and adjacent mainland areas, in particular on the east coast of Jura, in Islay, and in caves above the old shoreline overlooking the sheltered waters of Oban Bay. Similar dates apply to sites in Galloway and along the Solway coast in the south-west, to Morton in north-east Fife, and only slightly later to the Castle Street site in Inverness.

Our image of these Mesolithic people is gradually expanding as more of their settlements are recognised and excavated and, as archaeological techniques for recovery and interpretation of the evidence improves, so our focus sharpens. Settlements in the Hebrides speak of navigational skills and seamanship for which no physical evidence remains. It points to an ability to construct craft capable of withstanding quite lengthy sea-voyages, which in turn would suggest a capability to exploit marine resources in deep waters rather than just the shallow inshore fishings. The siting of the settlements often indicates exploitation of a wide environmental range. Kinloch on Rum, for example, has the shore and sheltered waters of Loch Scresort, opening onto the deeper reaches of sea towards Skye and the mainland to its east, while to the west rose the hilly hinterland of the island, rich in game. Morton, on Tentsmuir in Fife, enjoyed similar diversity. Although the site here is now nearly 2km inland, in the Mesolithic it formed a sandy islet joined to the mainland at first by tidal spits and, as the sea-levels dropped and coastal deposits accumulated, by expanses of salt-marsh. Situated close to the estuaries of the Tay to the north and the Eden to the south, it was ideally located to maximise on the rich fisheries in the shallower coastal waters, but more important may have been the great masses of migrating wildfowl which continue to over-winter in Tentsmuir. It also lies only a kilometre or so from the rising ground of north-east Fife, offering opportunities for hunting in the easternmost outliers of the Ochil Hills.

A more restricted natural range was offered to the Mesolithic inhabitants of Oronsay in the Inner Hebrides. This is a small island, joined to its larger neighbour, Colonsay, by a tidal strand, and consists largely of an undulating landscape of sand-dunes and grassy machair with only the rocky outcrop of Beinn Oronsay at the north-west rising to any significant height (93m). Evidence for Mesolithic settlement here takes the form of great mounds of shells, the accumulated middens of the island's ancient inhabitants. There are at least six of these, first explored at the end of the nineteenth century, lying close to what was the highest reach of the post-glacial sea. While the shell-mounds certainly show that shell-fish formed a major element in the Mesolithic diet here, some was destined for use as bait – fish-hooks were recovered from the middens – and bones mainly of saithe and coalfish have been identified amongst the shells. So, too, have crab shells and bird bones, but no remains of larger animals, such as seals. Larger and hillier Colonsay may have offered more scope for hunting, but the diet on Oronsay seems to have been limited largely to the produce of the shallow coastal waters.

To talk of Mesolithic 'settlement sites' may give a misleading impression of the nature of the encampments. As with the earlier Palaeolithic hunters, these people lived a nomadic life. While they may have returned year after year to the same general spot, their occupancy was only temporary, perhaps just a few days, certainly no more than seasonal. As a consequence, the remains of the settlements are very insubstantial, and it is largely the mounds of midden-debris which accumulated over generations of use rather than remains of structures which survive to indicate the former presence of these early hunters. The most substantial remains so far located were found at Lussa Wood on Jura. There, three linked rings of stone, each some 1.5m in diameter, formed a line in the centre of a broad scoop dug into a gravel terrace above the River Lussa. The scoop, it has been suggested, may represent the site of a large tent-like shelter. At both Kinloch and Morton, and the site at Low Clone on the Wigtownshire coast, arcs of stake-holes have been interpreted as positions of wind-break shelters, probably affording some protection for outdoor work, while scooped hollows again point to the outlines of larger covered, but still lightly constructed, tents or shelters. The hollow at Low Clone measures some 13.7m by 5.5m.

Our image of Mesolithic life as illustrated by the settlements which have been explored by excavation is severely limited by the narrow range of materials which have survived down to the present. Essentially, with the exception of bone, antler and ivory items, or the chance survival of recognisable elements of carbonised wood – often little more than carbonised hazelnut shells – it is mainly the stone implements, of flint, chert, bloodstone and the like, which survive. This completely distorts our viewpoint, for the loss of most organic remains, i.e. wood, skin, wicker, leads us to adopt a rather negative opinion of Mesolithic material culture. Although it was aceramic – non pottery-using – it is

Figure 1: Mesolithic Settlements

1 Morton, Fife:– period II occupation (after Coles, J.M., 'The early settlement of Scotland: excavations at Morton, Fife', *Proceedings of the Prehistoric Society* 37.2 (1971), 284–366).

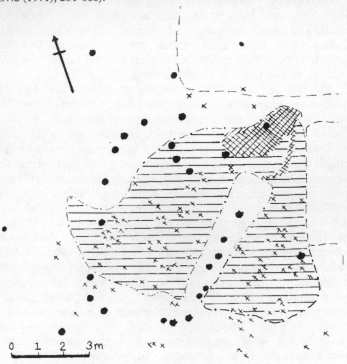

Key: Stained sand ≡
 Hearth ▨
 Artifacts ✕

 Stake-hole •
 Limit of disturbed area – – –

2 Lussa Wood, Jura:– stone rings (after Mercer, J., 'Lussa Wood I: the late glacial and early post-glacial occupation of Jura', *Proceedings of the Society of Antiquaries of Scotland*, 110 (1978–80), 1–31.

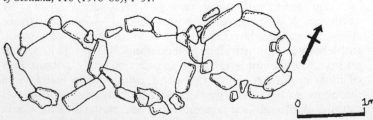

probable that wooden or birch-bark containers, skins, baskets and the like were used instead for carrying and containing. The use of skins for clothing, for shelters, for boat-coverings, must be imagined. Also, we must remember that what archaeologists find is basically the discarded rubbish, food waste – bone and shell – broken implements, tool-manufacturing debris, and the charcoal from the hearths. Effectively, it would be like trying to reconstruct a detailed picture of late twentieth-century life from the contents of the average household rubbish-bin.

It is only rarely that the presence of Mesolithic settlement is betrayed by massive midden-heaps, as at Oronsay. Instead, their discovery often results from chance observation, usually of the characteristic flints which they utilised for tools and weapons. These are known as lithic scatter sites, where a dispersed area of discarded implements, or the waste flakes from their manufacture, are detected on the present ground surface. Often, they occur in farmland where ploughing has disturbed archaeological deposits, or in areas of windblown sand erosion. Many have been identified, but few have been excavated and as a result can only be given very general dates based on the types of implements recovered. This is a particular problem in some areas where early settlement could be expected, but for which no firm radiocarbon dates are available. One such is the Tweed Valley. There, particularly in the middle reaches of the valley between the Tweed's confluences with the rivers Ettrick and Teviot, several seemingly important sites – Rink Farm overlooking the confluence of the Tweed and Ettrick from the north, or Dryburgh Mains across the river from St Boswells – have been identified. It could perhaps be expected that these represent amongst the earliest areas of Mesolithic settlement in Scotland, marking the movement north from England of groups of pioneering hunters, and flints recovered from the area show strong similarities of style to northern English types, but this hypothesis has not been tested by modern excavation.

Lithic scatter sites occur widely throughout Scotland. From those which are known, even without excavation, it is possible to identify what made a particular location attractive to the Mesolithic people. This allows archaeologists to suggest where settlements may lie in areas where there is as yet no firm evidence, by focusing their attentions on similar kinds of location. Of course, the evidence is imbalanced, for many of the recorded lithic scatter sites occur in areas of modern arable farming – ploughing being the main means by which remains are brought to the surface – which tends to draw attention away from the upland zones. This has shown that the Mesolithic hunters exploited the valley floors of the major river systems: the Tweed, the Clyde, the Forth and the Dee have all produced such evidence, as have the valleys of the Annan, the Nith, and the Ken and Dee in Galloway.

Upland zones have also proven fruitful for chance discovery of sites. In the Carrick and Galloway highlands, particularly in the areas around Loch Doon, Loch Dee, Clatteringshaws Loch and the upper reaches of the Ken Valley, fieldwork connected largely with projects to determine the nature of the ancient environment has resulted in the coincidental identification of a large number of sites which would have been bases for the exploitation of an environment quite different from the lowland valleys. Many chance discoveries have been made in areas of forestry ploughing and peat erosion, often in what we would now regard as quite remote and inhospitable inland locations. In Ardnamurchan, for example, artefacts have been recovered from the bottoms of the deep furrows produced by forestry ploughing in the interior of the peninsula. In both Galloway and Ardnamurchan, coastal sites have also been identified, and although the relationship between the coastal, valley floor and upland sites has not been determined, it is probable that these mark the passage of people who were moving between coastal, lowland and upland zones, and exploiting the different ranges of natural resources in each, perhaps on a seasonal basis. The material recovered from Ardnamurchan includes evidence which points towards a widely-ranging body of people. Bloodstone, whose nearest natural source to Ardnamurchan is 30km to the north-west on Rum, had been used in place of flint to make tools. This could point to the movement of one group over a wide area, involving lengthy sea crossings, or to contact between different groups with over-lapping zones of movement. However we view it, it underscores the high level of mobility of the early hunter-gatherers.

This mobility raises the question of from where and how did the first Mesolithic people enter what is now Scotland. The most logical answer is that they moved up from the south, following the natural routes from England. This was certainly the major point of entry, but it was not the only possible access route. If we take the English evidence, we could expect that the range of tools found on sites in Scotland – at least the more southerly ones – would parallel those found in northern England, where sites such as Star Carr in the Vale of Pickering in North Yorkshire, or Whitburn in Co. Durham, have yielded a wide range of distinctive artefacts. These include microliths for mounting in arrowheads or utilised for cutting-edges, scrapers, awls, flaked axes, and bone harpoon heads. Similar material is found widely throughout Scotland. Northern English-style microliths, for example, occur on lithic scatter sites in the Tweed valley, and from excavations at Banchory on Deeside, Morton in Fife, Shewalton in Ayrshire and from three of the Jura excavations. Harpoon heads comparable to those found at Whitburn have been recovered from Oronsay, from Risga in Loch Sunart, the Oban Bay caves and Shewalton. This might seem conclusive, but the quantity of the material recovered says otherwise. Microliths of English type, which are quite broad backed, are a minority amongst the artefacts identified, and occur alongside microliths of a different form. Scottish microliths are generally longer and narrower, pointing to a different cultural tradition. Even Tweed valley sites do not yield northern English forms alone. Perhaps most damning is that they are found on none of the earliest sites for which radiocarbon dates are available. Even allowing for vagaries of survival, site identification, excavation and dating, no Scottish site appears to represent settlement by a population which brought their cultural traditions intact northwards from England. Future discoveries may change this perspective, but at present all we can say is that if Mesolithic settlers were moving north, their cultural tradition changed rapidly as they moved.

There is an alternative source of colonisation, especially for the Hebrides and south-western mainland. Ireland appears to have been populated at an earlier date than Scotland after the last phase of glaciation. At present the earliest dated site in Ireland lies at Mount Sandel on the River Bann in northern Ulster, where a community had established itself before about 7000 BC. From here, and from other potential sites along the Ulster coast, it is but a short sea-step to the clearly visible islands and peninsulas of the Hebrides and western mainland. None of the southern Hebridean or south-western Scottish sites have produced radiocarbon dates as old as Mount Sandel, but some have yielded artefacts which are close in form to those manufactured on the Irish sites. Furthermore, as archaeologists have pointed out, surely there is some significance in the fact that the earliest radiocarbon dates yet obtained in Scotland all come from the western seaboard and islands. It is an attractive possibility, but it has yet to be established beyond doubt.

A yet more intriguing possibility implies colonisation from the north-east. A scattering of arrowheads of a form referred to as tanged points has been found in locations spread as widely as Orkney, Fife, Tiree and Islay. These may date from the upper Palaeolithic, being of a form popular in parts of northern Europe towards the end of the last glaciation, but it is doubtful that later upper Palaeolithic hunters were operating in northern Scotland when it was still largely ice-covered. Instead, they may represent cultural descendants in the Mesolithic of later Palaeolithic traditions. Tanged points are also common on Mesolithic sites in northern Scandinavia, but this is not an argument for long-distance colonisation across the North Sea in the post-glacial era. Rather, it may be that Palaeolithic hunters were active on the plain which formed in the southern North Sea basin during the last major phase of glaciation when much of the water was taken up in ice. It was an inhospitable landscape, but it was probably itself largely ice-free for part of the time. Scandinavian material indicates that human populations moved into the region quite soon after the landscape was freed from its icy covering, and it is possible that movement also occurred out of the North Sea basin into parts of northern and eastern Scotland which were freed from ice earlier than other parts of the country. This movement to east and west stemmed from a common root which quickly diverged into separate branches, but cultural similarities persisted – the tanged points – to indicate the old relationship. The evidence is tantalisingly slim. The chance discovery of a flint scraper in a core sample taken from the sea-bed 150km north-east of Shetland raises the stakes. While it could represent the remains of some ancient tragedy at sea, it is also possible that it marks the site of an encampment, for some 18,000 years ago this area, now 143m below sea-level, was dry land. Later upper Palaeolithic bands in the North Sea plain may have abandoned traditional hunting lands as they grew first wetter then flooded, and entered the ice-free fringes of what became Scotland. As the environment changed, they, like their cousins further to the south, adapted to new circumstances and developed their own distinctive Mesolithic culture.

A greater amount of work is necessary before more satisfactory answers can be given to the question of the origins of Mesolithic settlement in Scotland. A major obstacle in the path towards clearer understanding is the limited amount of work which has been undertaken, and the quite restricted distribution of the known sites. The large gaps on the distribution maps of Mesolithic settlement sites – such as Tayside and the country between Buchan and Inverness – as opposed to the major concentrations of discoveries in Galloway or Tweeddale, do not mark areas where there was no settlement, but rather areas where fieldwork has been limited or non-existent. Recent discoveries around the mouth of the River Naver in northern Sutherland, for example, highlight the great void in knowledge of Mesolithic settlement in the hinterland of the north coast. The recognition of shell-middens on the old raised-beaches around the Laich of Moray, which was a shallow, sheltered lagoon in the Mesolithic period, might begin to fill the great gap between Inverness and the Deeside sites, while recent discoveries at Little Gight near Methlick in Buchan extend the evidence into the north-eastern corner of the country. Only when more of the missing pieces of the Mesolithic jigsaw have been recovered can we begin to address the many key questions which remain unanswered. Only then can we realistically hope to offer firm answers to the problems of when the Scottish Mesolithic began, from where did the settlers come, and how did their culture(s) respond to four millennia of continuous environmental change.

2

THE EARLIEST FARMERS:
THE NEOLITHIC –
c.4000 BC TO c.2500 BC

NO CATACLYSM brought the Mesolithic to an end. There is no cultural decline and fall, as with say the Egyptian, classical Greek or Roman civilisations of the ancient world. Instead, it is archaeological convenience which draws an arbitrary line in the sand to mark the end of one era and the dawn of another. It is a line, however, whose relevance is as questionable as the many other divisions which have been set down on paper to break the past into nicely digestible chunks, for, although we can recognise the beginnings of a sea-change in the underlying basis of prehistoric culture around this time, it is a change which is blurred into a pattern of continuity from the Mesolithic past rather than a new departure taking off from a sharp break with the old ways. Gradually, however, and we cannot answer how long it may have taken, the new traditions – farming rather than hunting and gathering as the basis for subsistence, permanent settlements, beliefs and rituals which resulted in the erection of tombs and 'temples', new techniques and forms in the manufacture of flint and stone implements, and the introduction of pottery – became dominant and a world which was radically different from that of the Mesolithic emerged. With the emergence of this new world we enter the *Neolithic*.

Culture Clashes?

It is easy to fall into the trap of thinking that the settled farming lifestyle of the Neolithic was so diametrically opposed to that of the nomadic hunters and gatherers that confrontation must have resulted. Our perspective here is dominated by more modern clashes of dissimilar cultures, particularly by the tragic encounter between European 'civilisation' and the North American Plains Indians. There, two largely incompatible cultures collided, their impact heightened by the wide disparity in technological development, material sophistication, and by the supposed moral, intellectual and cultural superiority of the one over the other. Even before the days of new 'political correctness', it was difficult to argue that the meeting of Mesolithic and Neolithic cultures would have resulted in the same violent reaction on which the world of the Wild West thrived, for nowhere have we found evidence for the forcible replacement of one culture by the other, or of physical resistance to the new ways. The passage of time may have removed the detailed record, allowing us to gloss over individual tragedies and triumphs, but the general picture which emerges is one of slow, peaceful transition.

Adaptability was one of the cornerstones of Mesolithic success, and it is likely that they adapted and adopted aspects of the new Neolithic culture which were of use to them. Although it is possible to recognise the development of larger and more permanent Mesolithic encampments, they are still far removed from the idea of established farming communities. Those entailed an end to the mobility and the flexibility to respond to the environment around them, and a commitment to settle and await the ripening of crops. It involved also a major commitment of communal effort to clear and prepare land for cultivation. Aspects of this are traceable in earlier Mesolithic society. Woodland, for example, may have been cleared or burned, both to encourage new growth, perhaps of particularly desirable plants, and to create open spaces where game animals may have come to browse on the young shoots. There are suggestions, too, that the Mesolithic people encouraged the growth of certain varieties of wild herbs and berry-bearing bushes, returning to 'harvest' their crop at suitable times of the year. This is still a far cry from settled agriculture, but it is a step along the road in that direction. Some aspects of Neolithic technology might also have been attractive to the hunters. Pottery was probably not one of these, its bulk and weight unappealing to a still highly-mobile people. But new techniques in the manufacture of flint tools and weapons, and in the grinding of other types of stone to produce better cutting edges, probably quickly found favour. We must also remember that aspects of Mesolithic life continued to play a central part in that of the Neolithic. Although cultivated crops and domesticated livestock formed the linchpin of survival for the new way of life, hunting, fishing and the gathering of wild resources still supplemented the agricultural produce.

For a long time, possibly for several centuries, the two ways of life must have co-existed. Although the clearance of land for agriculture probably interfered with traditional patterns of hunting and wilderness exploitation in some parts of the country, it was still a vast and largely empty landscape. At first, the new communities would have formed only tiny islands of cleared and cultivated ground in a wilderness of trees and grasslands, allowing traditional Mesolithic ways of life to continue largely undisturbed. Finds of Mesolithic material datable from well within what we would regard as the fully-developed Neolithic show that some hunter-gatherer communities continued to pursue ancient ways of life, perhaps evidence for a few die-hard traditionalists clinging to ancestral beliefs, but we must assume that the majority had been absorbed into the expanding agricultural societies of Neolithic Scotland. Intermarriage and slow assimilation were probably the chief mechanisms for change, processes which are reflected in the slow fading out of Mesolithic culture and the gradual blurring into the Neolithic.

The Earliest Farming Communities

Of the many developments which marked the arrival of a new age, agriculture and the establishment of permanent settlements had probably the greatest long-term significance. The appearance of these two features marked another arrival: people. While the Mesolithic culture was probably gradually changing over time as the product of natural evolution, there can be little doubt that the radical break with much of the past in Scotland that Neolithic society represented was brought about by the arrival of groups of colonists bringing with them cultural luggage of quite different form. It is a society which was beginning to exert controls over nature – selection of growing crops, domestication of animals – that were wholly alien to the Mesolithic people. For the first time, we can see the undoubted evidence for human impact on the land as our ancestors altered its shape and appearance to meet their needs, clearing forests and scrub to create open areas for agriculture and grazing. Human fingerprints in the landscape, imprinted nearly 6000 years ago, are still there to be read today.

The origins and spread of Neolithic culture in Scotland present many problems, but these difficulties stem largely from the limited range of sites which have yet been excavated and securely dated. Furthermore, our knowledge is restricted by the geographic range of survival of sites, for it is recognised that much evidence from those parts of the country which are still highly prized as arable, or which have experienced a major spread of urban settlement in the last two hundred years, has been obliterated, a particular loss as chance finds of pottery and artefacts suggest that some of the earliest settlement occurred in those regions. Large areas, too, have suffered marine flooding and coastal erosion, particularly in the Hebrides and Northern Isles. As a result, most evidence for early farming communities comes from sites in what are now regarded as remote areas of the country, especially from Orkney, Shetland, the Western Isles and the far north of Scotland. Orkney especially is littered with an incredible array of prehistoric monuments, including some of the most impressive in the whole of Britain. Not only is there a staggering number of sites, but their range of diversity and high level of preservation combine to make this one of the most important archaeological landscapes in Scotland. This, though, has resulted in a top-heavy concentration of archaeological research in Orkney to the relative neglect of other parts of the country (in the 40 years after 1945, for example, there were 12 research excavations on Neolithic sites in Orkney, as opposed to only four in all north-eastern Scotland between the Tay estuary and the Spey, six for central Tayside, Fife, Central Region, Clydesdale, Lothian and the Borders, and eight in Dumfries and Galloway), an imbalance underscored in the standard literature, which is dominated by discussion of Orcadian sites.

The initial impact of these pioneering farmers can only be guessed. Few in number, it took centuries for any significant changes to become apparent in the landscape at large, but from the first they would have been clearing land not only for arable cultivation, but also to provide grazing for their flocks and herds. Using axes made from flaked flint or ground down from hard grained stones, such as hornfels, mounted in wooden hafts, clearings were hacked out of the forests and thickets. Such axes were amongst the most important items in the pioneers' tool-kits, and demand for good-quality and durable stone for the axe-heads stimulated a developing trade and primitive manufacturing industry as the Neolithic progressed. While many were produced locally from the best available stone, major production centres emerged at sites such as Creag na Caillich on the southern flank of Meall nan Tarmachan to the north of Killin in Perthshire. Some 29 axes of stone from Creag na Caillich have been identified on sites scattered from southern England to Lewis, but the greatest concentration lies in north-eastern Scotland, mainly Tayside and Grampian. The main centres of production, however, were at Great Langdale in Cumbria, (whose products are found scattered mainly throughout northern England and southern Scotland, but also as far afield as the Hebrides), and Tievebulliagh in Antrim. The spread of Tievebulliagh stone axes, however, may also point to movement of settlers out of Antrim into Scotland. The axes were the main tool used in the felling of timber, modern experiments suggesting that blows were aimed at roughly waist height of the wielder, leaving tall stumps standing proud. Once the trees had been felled, timbers and off-cuts that were surplus to domestic requirements were burned where they fell and the ash would then, coincidentally, have been dug into the soil as the ground in between the stumps was prepared to take seed. Equipment for the breaking of virgin soil was limited probably to seed-sticks for scratching and disturbing the surface, hoe-type implements, or simple ploughs of *ard* type which consisted only of a point for breaking up the ground, but lacking coulter or mould-board for turning the soil.

Whilst traces of early cultivation, usually pointing to slash-and-burn techniques, have been identified widely around the country, much of our evidence for the early spread of Neolithic settlement into Scotland comes, not from the sites on which the farmers lived, but from the tombs in which they buried their dead. Quite logically, where there are tombs there must also be settlements, but often we have not been able to establish such a link, or indeed even to identify the location of the settlements. The tombs are the most numerous type of monument to survive from the Neolithic and amongst the most prominent in the landscape. They are sophisticated structures, and regional variations in plan and constructional techniques reveal much about the origins of their builders. For example, in large parts of eastern Scotland at least as far north as the Moray Firth, the preferred early tomb-building tradition was for burials within massive, elongated or circular mounds of earth – *long* or *round barrows* – or similar mounds of stones – *long cairns* –

21

which, together with a distinctive form of pottery, suggests that the settlers who built these monuments were possibly colonists from communities based in Yorkshire and north-east England. On the west coast, there is similar evidence in the form of what are referred to as *chambered tombs*, where burials were placed within a stone-built chamber beneath a cairn of smaller stones, for a movement of colonists from the western districts of southern mainland Britain into south-western Scotland, the Hebrides and beyond.Dating evidence from these barrows and chambered tombs implies that colonisation of Scotland had commenced before 4000 BC –

Figure 2: Neolithic Burial Sites

1 Lochhill, New Abbey, Kirkcudbrightshire: long cairn.
2 Maes Howe, Orkney: Maes Howe Chambered tomb.
3 Balnuaran of Clava, Inverness-shire: Clava-type chambered tomb.

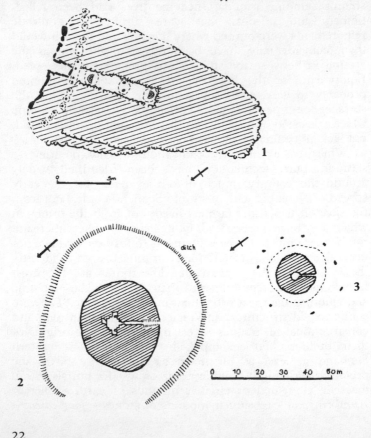

the chambered tomb at Monamore on Arran has yielded C-14 dates of around 3950 BC for its earliest phases — and was well advanced by the early 4th millennium BC, by which time it had reached as far as Orkney and Shetland.

Megalithic tombs, so called on account of the massive stone construction of the burial chambers which they contain, have long been the focus of antiquarian and archaeological enquiry. They are, in fact, the most intensively studied of all the classes of prehistoric monument in Scotland, and the only one which has been comprehensively researched and published in modern times. One of the main results of this work has been the identification of clearly defined regional traditions of tomb-building, from which it has been possible to suggest patterns of colonisation, cultural interchange and influence, and long-distance communication. Until the 1960s, however, it was the norm for excavation of chambered cairns to focus on the burial chambers and entrance passages to the neglect of the main body of the cairn proper. As a result, while excavators frequently recovered a large amount of skeletal material and associated pottery or flint grave-goods, little was actually known about the processes by which the tombs were built or, indeed, about structural development and chronology. Excavation of cairns ranging from Tulach an t-Sionnaich in Caithness to Mid Gleniron in Wigtownshire, however, radically altered this situation. Work here under the direction of the late John Corcoran demonstrated complex processes of development spanning long periods, usually involving elaboration and enlargement of originally simple burial cairns.

Considerably less work has been focused on long and round barrows. As recently as 1963 only ten monuments of the former class had been recorded in Scotland, and it is only since the identification of the long barrow at Dalladies in Kincardineshire and its excavation in 1970–1, and the excavation of the cairn at Lochhill near New Abbey in Galloway, coupled with increasing levels of aerial reconnaissance, that the so-called non-megalithic burial monuments of eastern and southern Scotland have been recognised as widely distributed phenomena in a landscape that had hitherto been seen as largely – and inexplicably – devoid of Neolithic burial sites. A date of *c.*3700 BC obtained from Lochhill, moreover, underscores the importance of this form of monument as indicators of the earliest spread of

Neolithic culture into Scotland. At present, around 20 such monuments have been identified. Still less work has been undertaken on non-megalithic round barrows, but excavation at sites such as Pitnacree in Perthshire or Boghead near Fochabers in Moray have demonstrated that these monuments are also amongst the earliest Neolithic burial sites in Scotland, dating from at least the middle of the 4th millennium BC.

Until very recently, the long barrows represented our only structural evidence for the earliest farming communities in most of eastern and southern Scotland. Evidence for an early settlement had been identified during the excavation of the barrow at Boghead in Moray, but here the barrow-builders had largely cleared the former habitation area prior to the construction of the burial mound, leaving only a spread of debris and a disjointed scatter of postholes, hearths and pits. Our ideas about the appearance of their actual settlement sites was, as a consequence, largely moulded by experience of the well preserved, but somewhat later, Neolithic settlements to be found in Orkney and Shetland, such as Skara Brae, Knap of Howar or Scord of Brouster, where families occupied individual houses which either stood alone, as at Knap of Howar, or were clustered into 'villages', as at Skara Brae. The superbly well preserved buildings of Orkney could be represented as the survival in stone of what had probably largely been a tradition of timber building elsewhere in Scotland. This picture was revised radically in the late 1970s by excavation of a site at Balbridie in northern Kincardineshire. What was believed to be a Pictish timber-built hall was located through aerial reconnaissance, but excavation revealed it to be over 4000 years older, dating from around 3500 BC, thus making it the oldest Neolithic settlement excavated to date and approximately contemporary with the barrow at Dalladies. The Balbridie structure was what is known as an aisled timber long-house, that is where the roof is supported internally on two parallel rows of free-standing posts. It measured roughly 26m by 13m, with straight side walls and slightly bowed ends, and appears to be related to house forms found on early Neolithic sites in Holland and Germany. Since the discovery of the Balbridie site, similar sites have been located nearby at Crathes, and at Monboddo in the Mearns, but neither can be definitely labelled as Neolithic without excavation. It is unlikely that Balbridie is unique, and it is probable that in the early

Figure 3: Neolithic Burial Sites

1 Camster Long, Caithness, Orkney–Cromarty long cairn.
2 Carn Ban, Arran, Clyde-type chambered cairn.
3 Rudh'an Dunain, Skye, Hebridean-type chambered cairn.

1

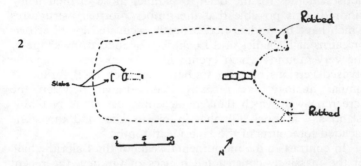

2

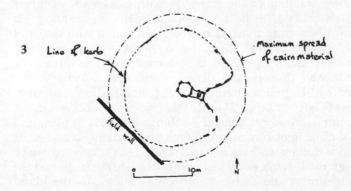

3

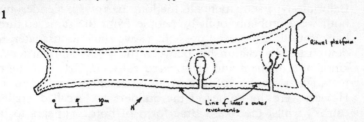

centuries of forest clearance for agriculture, settlements of this type were common in the timber-rich districts of eastern Scotland.

At present the evidence for the relationship of the Balbridie-type settlements to the long barrows is slender, but both were probably built by people from the same cultural background. It has been possible, as we shall discuss later, to demonstrate a relationship between the builders of particular kinds of settlement and chambered cairns in Orkney. There, rectangular houses of the type represented by Knap of Howar, were the homes of the builders of so-called 'stalled cairns', whilst the Skara Brae form of house appears to be associated with the 'Maes Howe' class of chambered tomb. In both cases, the tombs seem to be stylised models of the houses; homes for the dead to parallel those of their living kindred. It is possible that the timber mortuary structures which have been identified beneath excavated long barrows or cairns at Dalladies and Lochhill – or indeed the shape of the very mounds which eventually covered these – may be stylised versions of great timber halls such as Balbridie. A similar analogy has recently been drawn between the screening wall which flanked the entrance to the Neolithic island site at Loch Olabhat in North Uist and the stone façaded forecourts of the Hebridean tombs.

In contrast to the monumental scale of the Balbridie hall, or the massively constructed houses of Orkney, the recent excavation of Eilean Domhnuill in Loch Olabhat has shown that the Outer Hebrides possessed their own distinctive local building tradition in the earlier Neolithic. The site occupies what is believed to be a man-made islet – or crannog – a form of structure more commonly associated with the Iron Age, linked to the shore by a timber causeway. The causeway led to an elaborate, in-turned entrance formed by a low wall of vertically placed slabs, reminiscent of the façades of Hebridean tombs, above which had been a timber palisade or screen. Within this stood a succession of structures, mostly rectilinear or elongated ovals in plan, and all of quite light construction. One was certainly a house, its interior dominated by a massive hearth, but others may have represented roofless stock enclosures. After a period of abandonment caused by the flooding of the site, the island was re-occupied, still in the earlier Neolithic, when the timber causeway was replaced by one of stone, a simpler screening palisade was constructed to either side of the entrance, and two substantial rectilinear buildings with walls of earth and rubble stood within the enclosure.

While the Balbridie and Dalladies excavations provide general pointers towards early Neolithic activity in north-eastern Scotland and Loch Olabhat to the west, it is to Orkney that archaeologists still largely turn for detailed evidence for the material culture and lifestyle of the first farmers. At Knap of Howar on Papa Westray, excavation revealed substantial remains of two adjacent stone-built structures, identified as houses linked by a short passage. Radiocarbon dates from animal bone show that the houses had long life-spans, extending to some 500 years from c.3600 BC to 3100 BC. Both structures are rectilinear with rounded ends, entered via external doors in one narrow end, or through the short linking passage. Internally, both are divided into compartments by upright slabs, the larger into two rooms, the smaller into three. There are hearths in the middle compartment of the smaller structure – which appears to have served primarily as a storehouse and workshop – and in the compartment of the 'house' placed further from the door.

Finds from excavations in the 1970s allow detailed insight on the lifestyle of the people who lived here, and of the local environment in which they moved. Amongst these were sherds of pottery of a style known as Unstan Ware, named after the chambered cairn at Unstan on Orkney's mainland where such pottery was first identified. The style is typified by round bottom bowls which have a pronounced shoulder, above which there is a decorated collar. Although Unstan pottery is found most commonly in Orkney, this may be due to the greater amount of archaeological work undertaken in the islands than elsewhere in Scotland, for it has also been found as far afield as the Hebrides and north-east Scotland. Indeed, pottery of Unstan type was found at Balbridie. Studies of Unstan Ware show that it is related to styles in use amongst early communities in Yorkshire, Ireland and Wessex, pointing to directions of colonist movement and also to possible continuing cultural contacts. The sherds from Knap of Howar included portions of fine, decorated vessels intended for display, and plain, coarsely made containers which probably served as storage-jars, all of which are believed to have been manufactured on the site.

Most of the material from Knap of Howar was recovered from the midden on which the houses had been built, and which subsequently accumulated around them. The presence of midden material below the house walls showed that the surviving buildings were not the earliest houses on the site, but only slight traces survived of their predecessors. The midden material contained animal, bird and fish bones, and shellfish remains, as well as fragments of pottery and discarded flint, stone and bone implements. Also found in the deposits were the tiny shells of land-snails. The nature of the soil at Knap of Howar meant that no pollen remains survived to permit a reconstruction of the plant environment around the house, but the snail shells offer an alternative source of evidence. Snails are highly sensitive to their environment, different species favouring different vegetational and landscape types. Those from Knap of Howar, which now lies above the foreshore on the west side of Papa Westray, show that in Neolithic times the houses lay far back from the sea in open grassland. There were probably dunes to the west, and there were standing pools of fresh water dotted around the grassland. This open landscape had replaced an earlier one covered by light woodland, probably of alder and birch, which may have been cleared by a combination of agricultural action and changing weather conditions. The shellfish from the midden also indicate radical change in the local environment. Amongst shells found were those of large oysters, which favour sheltered waters quite different from those of the island's modern exposed west coast, pointing to severe erosion and marine encroachment over the last 5000 years. Papa Sound, which separates Westray from Papa Westray, is quite shallow, and it is suggested that the islands were once linked by low-lying sandy ground between sheltered bays.

Most of this midden material demonstrates the continued importance of exploitation of natural resources – through hunting and beach-combing – to the Neolithic incomers. The sea in particular provided an important supplement to the diet, but most food was obtained from farming. The absence of pollen evidence from the site does not allow us to gain a complete picture of the farming activity, but the survival of a few grains of barley show that at least some cultivation was practised. The snail-shells, however, point to a largely grassland environment which, together with bone remains from the midden, suggest that the Knap of Howar farm depended mainly on the rearing of sheep and cattle rather than on arable cultivation. Knap of Howar's occupants also manufactured all the domestic equipment which they required. As well as producing pottery, they worked in bone and stone, using locally available materials. Whalebone, probably from stranded animals, was used to make spatulas, vertebrae serving as mallet-heads.

Yet more detail of Neolithic domestic life has been recovered from what is regarded with justification as one of the finest prehistoric sites in Britain, Skara Brae. The settlement here is younger than Knap of Howar, radiocarbon dates indicating that it flourished between about 3100 and 2600 BC, and it presents a substantially different image to that provided by the earlier site. The houses here are of quite different form to those at Knap of Howar, being generally square or rectilinear one-room structures with central hearths and alcoves in the walls, probably for beds. Also, while Knap of Howar appears to have been home to at most an enlarged family, Skara Brae could be described as a village made up of several family units. The houses currently visible at the site represent only the latest phase in the development of the community and overlie the remains of earlier structures. These, however, appear to be of the same general plan as the existing buildings. Massively built of stone, the latest houses survive to eaves level, above which were probably roofs of timber and turf, or possibly of stone flags (such flags have been found at the Skara Brae-type house at Rinyo). The chief features of the houses noted by most visitors are the stone furnishings, including recessed or free-standing box-beds, and large farmhouse-style dressers, probably for storage and display of pottery vessels. The central hearth was used for cooking – as well as heating-fires, and in the excavations at Rinyo the base of a clay oven was found alongside the hearth area, providing some insight on cooking techniques.

The pottery also points to considerable differences between the inhabitants of Knap of Howar and those of Skara Brae. Instead of Unstan Ware, the inhabitants of Skara Brae were using a style referred to as 'Grooved Ware'. This is a rather heavy-looking pottery made from coarse and gritty clay, its surface decorated with zones of grooved, cut or applied raised decoration (of pellets or strips pressed onto the side of the vessel), usually of geometric style. The commonest Grooved Ware forms are jars, some of which had diameters up to 0.6m, and are characteristically flat-based and often heavily decorated. Such large vessels were probably

Figure 4: Neolithic Settlement Sites

1 Knap of Howar, Orkney.
2 Rinyo, Orkney.
3 Balbridie, Kincardineshire.

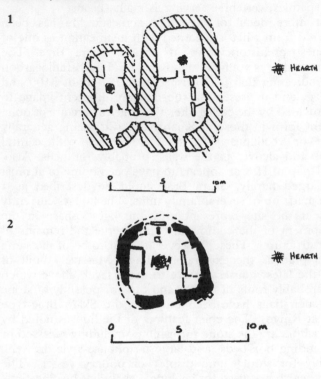

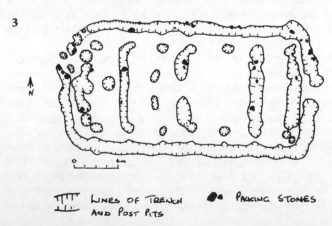

used mainly for dry-storage of produce, perhaps grain. Grooved Ware occurs extensively throughout Britain on later Neolithic sites, but the relationship between Orkney – where the earliest radiocarbon-dated Grooved Ware sites lie – and southern locations is unknown at present.

Midden material at Skara Brae provides most evidence for lifestyle and environment. As at Knap of Howar, coastal erosion has brought the shore to Skara Brae's doorstep, but originally it lay back from the sea in what was probably grassland interspersed with patches of cultivation. In addition to the growing of cereal crops, bone remains show that cattle, sheep and pigs were being reared. Farming, however, continued to be supplemented by fishing, collecting of shellfish from the nearby shore, some limited hunting, and by the gathering of naturally occurring plants and fungi. Waterlogged midden deposits have preserved quantities of wood, plant and other organic remains, including pieces of heather rope. It is in artefact remains, however, that the site is richest, with an abundance of flint, stone, bone, ivory and antler items. Flint is rare in Orkney, unless imported, and most of the Skara Brae flints were small items such as scrapers. The majority of stone implements were made from local fine-grained stones. These include axes and a form of blade known as Skaill knives formed from pebble flakes, as well as quite spectacular ceremonial or decorative pieces. These latter include a macehead, several carved balls, and weird spike-covered objects. Bone was used for a wide range of tools, including adzes, awls, knives, needles, pins and shovels, and also for items such as beads, bowls and small pots for holding pigments. Many of the items are enriched with decoration, and several carved slabs are built into the house-walls, indicating that life was not simply a relentless struggle for survival, but there was time for artistry and an interest in personal adornment.

Detailed though the insights onto Neolithic life provided by the major Orkney sites are, they are but tantalising glimpses of a living society which remains largely unknown to us. Indeed, we are better acquainted with it through evidence for the Neolithic way of death. In comparison with the bare handful of excavated early Neolithic settlement sites, there are over 360 known chambered tombs of this period, many of which have been excavated at least in part in the last 100 or so years, to which number has to be added the long and round barrows, and other Neolithic funerary monuments, bringing the total to considerably in excess of 400. Study of burial practices, however, is not simply an end in itself, for much can be learned about the living society from the manner in which it deals with its dead.

Chambered tombs are the most prominent – and most studied – class of Neolithic burial site in Scotland, but represent only one general approach to disposal of the dead. A wide range of burial customs are known, many perhaps sharing common cultural roots, but diversifying down different paths over time. The evidence for both prolonged use and structural development throughout the functional life of some chambered tombs has added further complications and makes it difficult to argue for one preferred model of burial on the basis of the remains found within them: practices may have changed but evidence for that change has been obliterated. Bones and grave-goods were clearly inserted and removed from the tombs at stages throughout their functioning lives, and most probably the remains recovered by archaeologists represent only the latest in a long succession of burials. A large number of the chambered tombs, for example, contain bone from interments, which has come to be regarded as the most common burial practice. Inhumation seems also to have been the preferred burial custom in the long barrow at Dalladies. In some areas, however, cremated bone was placed in the chamber. Cremation, too, occurs at Pitnacree in Perthshire and Boghead in Moray, where the burials were covered by round barrows. At Cairnpapple Hill in West Lothian, cremated bone was simply placed in holes in the ground to form a cemetery unmarked by a raised mound.

Preparation of the dead for burial also varied. In some of the chambered tombs it is possible to identify the complete skeletons of individuals who were clearly deposited as fully-fleshed corpses. At Midhowe on Rousay, for example, the latest burials in the cairn are represented by complete skeletons laid on their sides in crouched positions on stone shelves along the sides of the tomb. In some cases, however, the skeletons had been gathered into piles in the centres of the shelves, while more bone lay on the floor beneath them. It would seem that earlier burials had been pushed aside to make space for fresh interments. Elsewhere, it is clear that earlier burials and the grave-goods interred with them were removed completely, while at some sites only parts of skeletons can be accounted for. At Torlin on Arran, for example, the bone remains had been deliberately positioned around the chamber, and were comprised largely of skulls in the corners and long bones, such as femurs, laid along the side walls: no complete skeletons could be identified. John Hedges' excavation of the cairn at Isbister on South Ronaldsay in Orkney likewise showed evidence for sorting and arranging of bone. There, skulls were arranged along the side walls of the main chamber, each with a pile of other bones, but again in no case could a complete skeleton be identified. Furthermore, in two of its side chambers were groups of skulls alone.

While it is possible that the incompleteness of most of the skeletal remains in the tombs stemmed from the removal of bones – perhaps for ritual use – to make way for subsequent burials, it is equally possible that only selected parts of the body were interred in the first place. There are strong arguments in favour of excarnation, the process of defleshing the bones by exposing the body to the elements and to natural scavengers, either in a 'mortuary house' or raised on a 'mortuary platform' in a manner similar to the burial rites of some North American Indian tribes. Such mortuary houses have been identified at Dalladies and Lochhill, in both cases having apparently been burned deliberately at the end of the process. At several sites in Scotland – for example at Balfarg in Fife, Inchtuthil in Perthshire and Douglasmuir in Angus – there are large, timber-built rectilinear enclosures which, on excavation, have been shown not to be associated with settlement, but appear to have had a ritual function. These have been interpreted as 'mortuary enclosures' where the corpses of the dead were exposed for excarnation.

In most cases, whether cremation or inhumation was the preferred custom, the burial site was marked by the raising of a covering mound; the cairn or barrow. The construction of such monuments was no small enterprise and would have required the outlay of considerable labour over a long period. To a society which depended largely upon the product of its labour in the fields, that represented a considerable commitment. The barrow at Dalladies, for example, needed turf for its construction stripped from an area of at least 0.6 ha, and took over 6000 man-hours to erect. The level of commitment becomes yet more impressive when it is borne in mind that the communities which laboured to erect these monuments were formed by no more than a handful of extended families, estimated at between 25 and 50 individuals with half that number under the age of 15. While it is clear that they were built through communal effort and were intended for collective burials, it is not clear that all members of the community were buried within them. This, of course, begs the question of how the society which built these tombs was organised. There is little sign of social stratification in settlements like Skara Brae, which has led to suggestions that Neolithic society was relatively egalitarian and lacked obvious social leaders. Such societies could certainly account for the smaller and simpler early tombs, but the monumental chambered cairns like those of Maes Howe, Quanterness or Quoyness in Orkney, or Camster in Caithness, argue for an ability to control and direct labour resources which sits awkwardly with ideas of primitive communism. Here instead, it has been argued, we can see the guiding hand of individual chieftains, priests, or ruling elites.

Burial rites which involved the periodic insertion and removal of bone from tombs makes it difficult to be certain one way or the other. In Orkney, for example, the Isbister cairn contained the remains of some 338 individuals and that at Quanterness of 157, in both cases representing a full cross-section of the population in terms of age and sex. There is no obvious elitism here, and the numbers involved suggest interment of most members of their respective communities over several generations. In the Kilmartin Valley in Argyll, however, there appears to have been greater selectivity as to who received burial in the chambered tombs there, leading to arguments in favour of a more hierarchical society. In view of the wide range of burial rites used throughout Scotland, however, it is probably safest to assume that practices governing who was buried within the tombs also varied from region to region and changed over time.

Within all the various burial customs are hints of some form of ancestor worship. In a society where, as the bone evidence from Isbister or Quanterness shows, 50 per cent of the population was aged under 15, where average life-expectancy reached only the mid-20s, and where just over 10 per cent of the population was aged over 25 – with the oldest aged 50 years – the older individuals must have been vital repositories of knowledge and ideas, and the ever-present dead would have offered the only link with even the relatively recent past. The strong ties between the living and dead members of the community are emphasised in some cases by parallels between the designs of houses and tombs. The similarity in plan between the so-called 'stalled cairns' of Orkney, for example, and Knap of Howar-type houses is striking. Like the houses, the tombs are rectilinear with rounded ends, are divided internally into compartments by upright slabs projecting from the side walls, and are entered via a passage in the middle of one of the narrow ends. The identification of stalled cairns as 'houses of the dead' for people of the same culture who were building Knap of Howar houses is confirmed by the presence in the tombs of Unstan Ware pottery.

Deposits of pottery form just one piece of evidence for ritual activity within the tombs. Other artefacts, often scorched by fire, or deposits of midden material were placed in the chambers. Fires played an important part in the rites, still traceable as patches of burning or scorching on chamber floors and walls. Along with human bone, excavators often unearth animal and fish remains, some of which arrived by natural means – owls and otters, for example, are known to use tombs as their lairs – and others perhaps brought in the earth deposits from middens. Most were perhaps food offerings brought to the dead, joints of mutton and beef being recognised at Quanterness. In some tombs, quantities of bones of particular species, often not of birds or animals favoured for their meat, are found. The most famous case is Isbister, where the so-called 'Tomb of the Eagles' derived its modern name from the quantities of bones and talons of white-tailed sea-eagles found within it. Elsewhere, bones of dogs, fish or deer occur. These creatures may have been the 'tribal' totems of the tomb-builders, while fish or deer remains may represent an attempt by the living to secure the aid of the dead in preserving or increasing food stocks, but such interpretations are not accepted universally.

Ritual activity seems also to have occurred outwith the tombs. In the cases of several of the different classes of chambered cairns, as the plans grew more elaborate the cairns developed particular external features. For example, the tombs are often aligned axially on major solar events, such as midwinter or midsummer sunrise or sunset. In some cases, the entrance passage is aligned in such a way as to permit the sun's rays to penetrate into the burial chamber. In certain tomb styles, such as the Clyde Cairns of south-western Scotland, or the Cromarty and Hebridean forms, elaborate façades were formed to either side of the entrance, their outer ends often curving forward to form a shallow forecourt area. Few forecourts have been examined in detail, but those which have produce evidence for ritual activity in the form of fires and the apparent smashing of pottery. Some of this activity may have been connected with the final sealing of the tomb, when not only was the chamber and passage blocked with material, but the forecourts, too, were infilled. At Camster in Caithness, however, the long cairn was developed from two small round cairns. The chambers were entered from the southern flank of the cairn and the forecourt at its north-east end had an unbroken façade. Here the excavator found a raised platform, or stage, fronting the façade, suggesting that the dummy forecourt still held ritual importance although the tomb entrance lay elsewhere.

As collective burial-places, the chambered tombs were designed from the first to be entered and resealed at intervals to allow fresh interments to be made. We have little clear evidence as yet for the lifespan of most of the tombs, but some continued in use for several centuries. New cairns continued to be built throughout the 4th millennium BC, indicating perhaps the steady growth of the population, with new communities splitting off from older ones and providing themselves with separate tombs to mark their individuality, or perhaps serving as a replacement for an earlier tomb which had somehow come to the end of its functional life. Tombs of the so-called Clyde style, for example, were built and developed over 1500 years from about 4000 BC down to around 2500 BC, but with apparently diminishing frequency after c.3000 BC. By the middle of the 3rd millennium BC many of the tombs had been blocked, and while the cairns and barrows which covered them continued to be the focus for burials and some ritual activity – in some cases for thousands of years after – it appears that by about 2500 BC the tombs of the ancestors had lost their place as the main foci for the rituals and beliefs of the farming communities.

Henges and Stone Circles

While burial monuments may have served as the spiritual foci for local communities, other types of site appear possibly to have formed the social or religious centres for much wider areas. Amongst such sites are henge monuments, a class of structure whose exact function remains unknown. The term, henge, is usually associated in the popular imagination with great circles of stone like Stonehenge in Wiltshire, but in fact it refers to the banked and ditched enclosures in which such circles occasionally stand. They take the form of a central platform enclosed by a deep ditch, the upcast from which is thrown up on its outer lip to form a bank. There are two basic classifications of henge (Class I and Class II) which refer to the number of entrances across the ditch: Class I have a single causeway, Class II have two diametrically opposed entrances. In Scotland, henges are distributed mainly in the east of the country, with concentrations in the Don valley in Aberdeenshire and in Strathconon in Easter Ross. Amongst the most impressive of such sites are Cairnpapple Hill in West Lothian (Class II), Balfarg in Fife (Class I), the two Orkney examples at Ring of Brogar (Class II) and the Stones of Stenness (Class I). The labour expenditure on such monuments points clearly to their being the product of more than just one or two farming communities, suggesting rather an ability to command the resources of a wider geographical area. At Stenness, for example, it is estimated that the digging of the rock-cut ditch and construction of the bank alone would have required over 20,000 man-hours of work.

Detailed excavation of Scottish henges has been limited, but a series of important projects has thrown considerable light on their construction, development and use. Three Class I sites, Balfarg, Pict's Knowe in Galloway and the Stones of Stenness, have been excavated under modern conditions. Balfarg, which lay at the heart of an extensive complex of major Neolithic monuments including mortuary enclosures and a barrow, originally had a 25m-diameter circle of massive timber uprights, concentric and apparently contemporary with its enclosing ditch, as the focus for activity in its central area. Radiocarbon dating of material from the sockets which had held the timbers provided a date for construction of c.3000 BC. At Pict's Knowe, the interior of the henge had been devastated by rabbit-burrowing, but excavation of the water-logged ditch deposits produced some remarkable evidence for what appears to have been ritual offerings, including the earliest known plough of ard type. At the Stones of Stenness the main focus for ritual at the site appears to have been a rectangular arrangement of recumbent slabs in the centre of the embanked ditch. This stone setting was associated with deposits of cremated bone, charcoal and pottery. In place of the timber ring at Balfarg, at Stenness, where there was a shortage of suitable local timber, there was a concentric stone circle. Other structures were identified on the central platform of the henge, principally a small timber building with upright slabs at its entrance. Excavation of the ditch to either side of the entrance causeway unearthed deposits which included the bones of domestic ox and sheep, interpreted as the debris of

Figure 5: Balfarg, Fife, henge monument

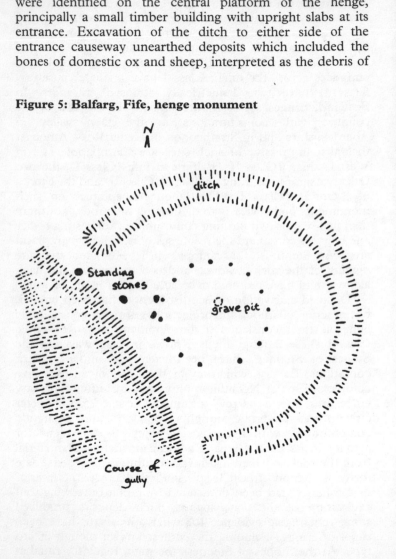

ritual feasting. Radiocarbon dates from the ditch and from the central setting of stones were roughly comparable, indicating that the henge had been constructed in the early 3rd millennium BC, which makes it contemporaneous with the building of the Maes Howe type tombs. The association of the henge with the builders of Maes Howe is also indicated by the presence of Grooved Ware pottery at the Stones of Stenness.

Excavation of Class II henges has produced roughly similar dating to that for Class I monuments, suggesting that the two forms are roughly contemporary rather than the one being a developed form of an earlier, plainer type. There is also evidence for early use of both timber and stone in the construction of the settings which ringed the internal platform. At Strathallan in Perthshire, the henge, whose entrances were aligned on a large round barrow, contained a ring of massive posts set in deep pits, but at Cairnpapple Hill, where construction is dated to c.2800 BC, the centre of the platform appears to have contained a rectilinear setting similar to that found at the Stones of Stenness, and an oval arrangement of standing stones. At Cairnpapple, the henge developed around what had earlier been a Neolithic cremation cemetery, and an inhumation in a rock-cut pit had formed a central feature of the newer enclosure. Burial seems to have been a central function of this henge, and Cairnpapple preserved an important role as a major funerary monument through the Bronze Age and into the Iron Age, with the stone setting being dismantled and reused as the boundary kerb of a large round cairn. Cairnpapple, however, is so far unique in its evidence for burial activity focused on the henge and, while burials are not unknown within other henge monuments – e.g. Balfarg – this does not appear to have been their primary role.

But what *was* the function of henges? Excavation on several very large henge sites in southern England revealed the presence of substantial timber buildings within the earthworks, which has given rise to the suggestion that these should be viewed as secular sites rather than ceremonial centres. In particular, the large quantities of domestic refuse – pottery, stone and animal bone – have been used to argue for their use as secular sites which contained important 'public buildings', or which functioned as the settlements of a newly emergent governing class of priest-chieftains. Grooved Ware appears to be particularly associated with these sites. In Orkney, it was suggested that settlements such as Skara Brae were the residences of such a new theocracy which had established some form of dominance over the earlier Unstan Ware users, and that they were able to exercise that dominance for the building of the Maes Howe type tombs and the great new ritual centres of the Stones of Stenness and Ring of Brogar. It is an argument which is difficult to prove one way or the other, but the remoteness of Skara Brae from Stenness, and the nature of the domestic evidence from the former, seemed hardly to support such a proposition. The discovery of a major new settlement site at Barnhouse, from which Maes Howe and Stenness are each roughly equidistant, does, however, re-open the debate.

Figure 6: Stones of Stenness, Orkney, henge monument and stone circle.

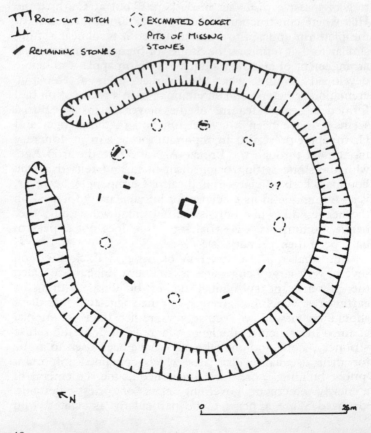

Although the houses are of Skara Brae type, they are free-standing rather than linked by inter-connecting passages. One particular structure, however, points to more exalted status. This was a monumental building measuring 7m square within a 3m-thick wall, standing on a circular platform of yellow clay enclosed by a massive stone wall. The main chamber had a very large central hearth, behind which stood a rear dresser of the type preserved at Skara Brae. Entry to this chamber was through a doorway in keeping with the monumental scale of the rest of the structure. Facing north-west (towards midsummer sunset), it contained a second hearth, and was flanked by upright stones. Interpretations of this site will inevitably differ, for the monumental building could be seen either as a chiefly residence dominating the social landscape, or as a communal meeting-house in a society which continued to display egalitarian characteristics, but what appears clear is that this settlement is linked closely with two of Orkney's major Neolithic ritual monuments.

Whatever the disagreements over their function, there is general acceptance amongst archaeologists that henges held an important place in the development of the tradition of stone circle building in Britain. The timber circles which have been revealed as the earliest structural components of the excavated henges are reflected in timber phases at several excavated stone circles. For example, at Machrie Moor on Arran, excavation of one of the 11 circles (No 1) in this rich ritual landscape revealed that the still upstanding stone monument had been preceded by a timber phase comprising two concentric rings of posts around a central, horseshoe-shaped setting. This timber phase was succeeded by a single circle comprising 11 stones of alternating granite boulders and sandstone slabs. A similar sequence was unearthed at Croft Moraig in Perthshire, where the earliest phase was represented by a horseshoe-shaped setting of posts, subsequently replaced by an oval setting of eight boulders.

It is perhaps significant that while such circles occur widely throughout the country, there are major concentrations in or adjacent to earlier important centres of henge-building. The greatest density occurs in north-eastern Scotland, centred on the Garioch region of Aberdeenshire, where the Don valley has earlier been noticed as one of the main henge-building areas. Other major concentrations lie in the district around Inverness, in Perthshire, on Arran, and in the major river valleys feeding into the Solway Firth in the south-west. There are, however, some surprisingly sparse zones on the distribution map, with relatively few occurring in Lothian, and more interestingly in Angus and Mearns and in Argyllshire, both districts with otherwise clear evidence for important early Neolithic settlement. Here, as with the tomb-building traditions, we seem to be facing evidence for regional cultural variations (perhaps most evident in the strongly regional nature of the form and construction of the monuments), and possibly also for other social and economic factors, such as relative populations, levels of prosperity, and social structure.

With the exception of Callanish on Lewis, the most outstanding of the Scottish stone circles are the so-called recumbent stone circles of the north-east, a group of 99 monuments with a distribution limited entirely to the district north of the Mounth and east of the River Deveron. The great number of these sites within a geographically restricted region lends support to the belief that they were built by the communal efforts of relatively small farming communities, rather than by the collective labour of more extensive localities, but it is difficult to make the additional step – as some archaeologists have done – and argue that this is

Figure 7: Croft Moraig, Perthshire, stone circle

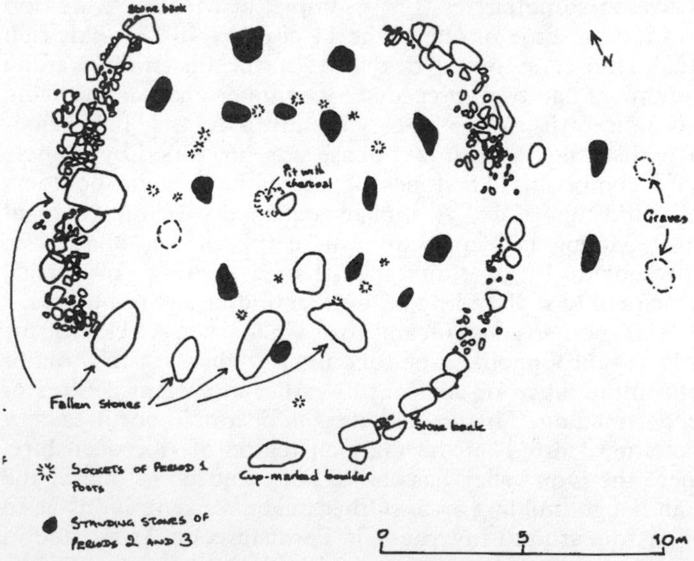

further evidence for the egalitarian nature of these communities. This is a unique class of monument whose relationship with other forms of ritual site in Britain is subject to great debate. Although attributed generally to the 3rd millennium BC, there is no precise dating for their construction, and most of the chronologies offered for them are based solely on archaeologists' opinions of what are probably early features and what may represent stylistic developments. They take the form of a circle of standing stones of between roughly 18m and 24m in diameter, graded in height towards the south-west of the ring where the two tallest stones (referred to as 'flankers') are positioned on either side of a massive slab set on edge (the recumbent). Most recumbent stone circles occupy positions on high ground, usually just below the crests, or on terraces partly up hillsides, but generally commanding wide views to the south. In most cases, the sites appear to have been carefully levelled prior to the erection of the recumbent and flankers. These stones, which it seems logical to suggest formed the focus for ritual at the sites, appear to have been positioned with great care, the recumbent often being chocked up with smaller stones to level its upper surface. By way of contrast, the remaining stones of the circles appear to be haphazardly arranged.

In many cases, the space within the recumbent stone circle is occupied by a low stony mound representing the remains of a type of burial monument known as a ring cairn. Excavation, such as that at Loanhead of Daviot, showed that the building of the cairns appeared to mark a final stage of development, and that while pyres and other ritual fires may have been lit within the circle at earlier dates the main function of the monuments was not as burial sites. This is apparently supported by the discovery that the recumbent and flankers are positioned so as to frame particular episodes of the rising or setting moon in the southern sky when viewed from within the circle, something which would have been rendered difficult had the interior been occupied by a burial mound. The suggestion has been made that the circles, with their emphasis on lunar observation, were the focus for rites connected with the changing of the seasons, perhaps associated with sowing, fertility of crops and animals, and the harvest. An exclusively ritual function for these sites, however, would set them apart from most other Neolithic ceremonial locations where aspects of both ritual and burial functions are evident. Indeed, the death, entombment and rebirth symbolism in fertility rites, might suggest a closer association of the recumbent stone circles with burial than is currently accepted.

The difficulties which archaeologists face in interpreting the function of stone circles are compounded in the case of the recumbent stone circle by uncertainty over the origins and development of the form. There is no clear understanding of the development of ritual and burial sites in the north-east through the 4th millennium BC, which renders it currently impossible to look for the roots of the building tradition in earlier forms in the region. Looking outwith the recumbent stone circle heartlands in Aberdeenshire, there is no satisfactory model from which the north-eastern farmers could have drawn inspiration, and arguments which present the Clava cairn group of monuments in the area round the head of the Moray Firth and in central Strathspey, which share certain characteristics in common, are seen as unconvincing. Indeed, it has been more plausibly argued that the Clava cairns may represent a parallel development to the recumbent stone circle tradition.

The Clava type cairns, where simple ring cairns or more elaborate passage graves are enclosed within a circle of stones graded in height towards the south-west – the entrances, too, are in the south-west – point again to the close association between ritual and burial in the Scottish Neolithic. It is a characteristic which recurs throughout the various regional groups of stone circle in Scotland. At Callanish, for example, recent excavations at the circle have demonstrated that a small passage grave in the inner ring of the setting, previously believed to have been a late insertion into the monument, is part of the original concept and can be dated to c.3000 BC. But excavation, too, is showing that there is no one model for the development and function of the stone circles, nor in any case should we expect there to be one single line of progression for a monument class which remained in vogue for nearly two millennia.

Changes in function at the stone circle sites may be related to deeper changes in the fabric of late Neolithic society as a whole. Amongst the markers of change is a new style of pottery vessel, the beaker, which begins to appear in Scotland from around 2500 BC. These small, highly decorated vessels, more common in eastern and southern Scotland than in the north and west, appear to have been part of the cultural luggage of a new wave of immigrants from the Continent, whose skeletal remains show significant physical differences from those of the Neolithic population: they appear taller, more robust, and had rounder skulls in comparison to the long-skulled earlier peoples. Studies of beaker pottery both in Britain and on the Continent indicate that movement of people or ideas from different areas of the European mainland occurred, with eastern Britain receiving its new arrivals from the Low Countries and western districts from Brittany and Spain. The scale of this immigration is subject to debate, even the more positive proponents of folk movement favouring a limited settlement, but there are those who argue that the skeletal differences are due to long-term genetic development in the indigenous population and that the new pottery styles and associated cultural changes are the product of inter-cultural contact rather than colonisation.

Figure 8: Loanhead of Daviot, Aberdeenshire, recumbent stone circle

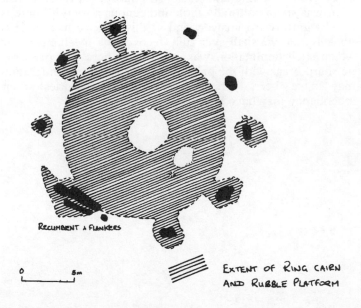

RECUMBENT & FLANKERS

0   5m

EXTENT OF RING CAIRN
AND RUBBLE PLATFORM

As usual in archaeological debates, there is insufficient data to clinch the argument either way, but the profound changes in cultural tradition which appear to have accompanied the arrival of beaker pottery seem to favour more the idea of wholesale immigration rather than just the importation of selected ideas. It is perhaps no coincidence that the end of the functioning life at many chambered tombs was marked by the insertion of a burial accompanied by a beaker, or the inclusion of a beaker in the material used to seal up the chamber. At Neolithic ceremonial centres evidence has also been recovered which appears to point towards the takeover – or possibly deliberate desecration – of the site by the placing of beaker pottery within the monument. At the recumbent stone circles of Loanhead of Daviot, Old Keig and Berrybrae, deposits of beaker sherds in the centre of the circles appear to have been the final acts in the functional life of these sites. Do we here see the incomers placing their stamp of dominance on the sacred places of the earlier culture? But how could what appear to have been small groups of migrants establish cultural supremacy over what was still a culturally virile indigenous society? There is no straightforward answer, and at this remove in time it is unlikely that we shall ever fully recover the mechanisms by which such domination was achieved. There was probably no sharp break with the past and, as the process of migration may have been spread over several centuries, their ascendancy may have been gradual.

3

MASTERING METAL
c.2500 BC TO c.700 BC

Beaker Culture and the
Beginning of the Bronze Age

THE BEAKER-USING incomers followed a lifestyle that was in many ways little different from that of the older communities which they encountered here. Farmers and stock rearers, their interest was in land for cultivation and pasture, and the clearance of woodland which had begun nearly 2000 years earlier continued apace, reaching a peak between c.2000 BC and 1800 BC. There is no evidence, as yet, for conflict over land between the settlers and the older communities, and it seems that the colonists occupied comparatively empty areas on the periphery of the more densely settled zones of the country. In England, early beaker burials were located well away from major Neolithic ceremonial centres, and it may be that there was something in the social organisation of the two groups which made them mutually incompatible. This same separation may be reflected, for example, in the district between the major Neolithic centres in Aberdeenshire and the Laich of Moray, which has yielded traces of early beaker settlement, but where earlier Neolithic activity is scarce. In the west, colonists who may ultimately have moved up the western seaboard from Brittany, settled in the Outer Isles. Remains of one of the earliest Beaker People settlements in Britain yet discovered were excavated at Northton in Harris, where among the dunes had stood two oval-shaped tent-like structures covering scooped depressions in the sand, the sides of which were revetted by low stone walls. Grazing of sheep and cattle, supported by hunting of red deer, seals and fishing was the basis of their subsistence, but there was no evidence from this site for cultivation of crops. In the dunes at Rosinish on Benbecula, however, evidence was found for wheat and barley and the scratch-marks on the old ground surface made by plough cultivation. At a basic level, then, there is little to distinguish between the two groups other than in the styles of pottery used.

Figure 9: Northton, Harris, Beaker-period house

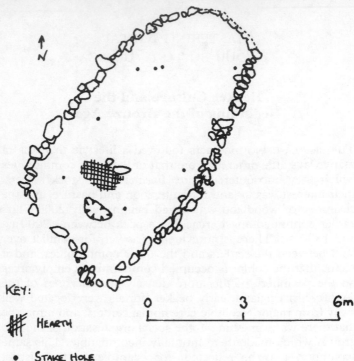

KEY:

HEARTH

• STAKE HOLE

0 3 6m

More fundamental differences appear once we move away from the basics of subsistence. The clearest is in burial traditions, where the collective burial or cremation rites of the Neolithic peoples appear to have been quite alien to the incomers. Their characteristic form of burial is individual interment in stone-lined graves, or cists, usually accompanied by grave-goods (often including a beaker). The individualism of this burial tradition may reflect a contrasting approach to social organisation, suggesting a hierarchical structure that was the very antithesis of the supposedly egalitarian society of the Neolithic farmers. But again, it has been argued that the egalitarian nature of Neolithic society – if it ever truly existed – was in the process of break-down or restructuring in the early 3rd millennium BC, with development of new monumental tomb types and ritual centres marking the emergence of new hierarchies. If, as some archaeologists have argued, the development of beaker culture was achieved more through native adaptation of imported ideas than through introduction by migrants, the hierarchical society of the later 3rd and 2nd millennia BC would be the direct descendant of the earlier Neolithic tradition and beaker domination of society could be explained in terms of continuity of power rather than a takeover. This argument has its attractions, but there is one factor which points to transference of power to an incoming group: it is amongst the beaker users that, by about 2000 BC, we see the first evidence in Scotland for bronze-working technology.

The discovery of metallurgy is, along with the development of agriculture, one of the greatest technological revolutions in human history. Its importance should not be underestimated, for it is more than simply the substitution of one basic material – stone – for a superior one – metal – in the manufacture of tools, weapons and personal items. Transitions from Palaeolithic to Mesolithic to Neolithic are marked by, amongst other things, changes in stone-using technology, but stone remained the principal raw material utilised and the skills involved in the production of stone implements, while being refined over time, remained basically unchanged. Metallurgy, on the other hand, required the acquisition of a whole range of new skills, from the ability to identify ore-bearing rock to the manufacture of moulds in which to cast the new material. It also brought the development of new patterns in human inter-relationships. Trade of a kind, for example, had been known in the Neolithic, where particular kinds of often quite exotic stone for the manufacture of highly-prized axeheads had been transported over long distances. But stone and flint, albeit of relatively poor quality, was basically obtainable in most parts of the country. Metal ores, on the other hand, are far from evenly distributed, and possession of, or control of access to, areas where they were to be found brought a new kind of economics-based power into play. We do not know how relationships between those who controlled ore supplies and those who wanted it were shaped, but we must imagine the development of more sophisticated means of exchange, and perhaps also the emergence of 'diplomatic' negotiation and agreements.

Scotland had several native sources of both copper and gold, two of the principal metals used in the Early Bronze Age. Indeed, it was one of the main sources for these metals in prehistoric Britain, ranking alongside Cumbria and Ireland. Gold occurs, for example, in Upper Clydesdale, western Perthshire and Sutherland. Copper has an even wider distribution, with main production centres in southern Lanarkshire, the Ochil Hills, northern Knapdale, Glen Esk, and Loch Ness-side, and smaller sources scattered from the Southern Uplands to Caithness. The essential ingredient in the manufacture of bronze, however, is tin – bronze being the alloy of copper and tin – and in Britain this occurs only in Cornwall. As a consequence of this single source of supply, there was the establishment of regular communication between northern and south-western Britain, and also a major opening up of links across the Irish Sea.

There appears to have been a delay of at least 500 years in the transmission of knowledge of metallurgy from southern to northern Britain. While bronze technology had arrived in southern England around 2700 BC, it is not until much nearer 2000 BC that there is unequivocal evidence for its arrival in Scotland. In part, the slow spread can be attributed to human factors: reluctance by those who possessed knowledge of metallurgy for that priceless knowledge to pass into other hands; suspicion and distrust towards both the new material and its users (compare this with modern reluctance on the part of some to accept computer technology, or the replacement of the imperial system of measurement with metric); and the initial problems of supply until sources of ores had been identified and exploited. Of course, the fact that we do not find bronze artefacts on Scottish sites which can be dated to before c.2000 BC does not mean that they did not occur in Scotland before that date. It is only when they begin to be buried with the dead that we have our evidence for production. But does the absence of bronze items from burials of the later 3rd millennium BC mean that knowledge of bronze manufacture had yet to reach Scotland, or was it still too highly prized a material to simply 'waste' by disposing of it in a grave?

This basic difficulty highlights one of the fundamental problems with current understanding of the Beaker People and the Early Bronze Age in general. Essentially, most of our knowledge of this period is derived from burials, many 'excavated' in the 19th and early 20th centuries, and we have little corresponding evidence from domestic sites to even out the imbalance. Indeed, most of our ideas about hierarchical society in the Early Bronze Age is based on interpretation of their way of death. Individual burials in separate cists, often accompanied by what are clearly personal possessions – jet buttons and necklaces, fine flint arrowheads or blades, archers' wristguards, and the distinctive beaker pottery – seem in modern eyes to point to a society that took a more individualistic view of its members, at least in death, than that which is displayed by the collective tombs with their scattering of impersonal pot sherds, flint flakes and domestic refuse.

It was 19th-century antiquarian fascination with 'barrow-digging' that yielded the bulk of pottery evidence from burials on which interpretations of beaker culture are based. As early as 1902 typologies showing the stylistic development of beakers had been drawn up, and it is on such typological schemes – which focus on changes in form and decoration – refined over the years, that interpretations are still largely based. The earliest forms, which date from the late Neolithic, are named after their decoration and shape: All-over-cord decorated beakers and European bell beakers. More slender vessels using a wider range of decorative motifs followed. Further development saw the earlier bell-shaped vessels acquire necks, often emphasised by a change in the decoration. The latter stages of the typological sequence see first the accentuation of the neck, followed by vessels where clearly divided neck and body stages have zones of quite different patterning. Finally, there is degeneration into a rather shapeless vessel where division between neck and body has blurred. Opinions vary as to how these changes should be interpreted, but there is general agreement that the earliest forms should be viewed as the products of incoming migrants, while later styles may represent local development. Associated with the beaker pottery is a form referred to as 'food vessels', the name deriving from 19th-century belief that 'beakers' held drink while the 'food vessels' contained just that, as offerings to sustain the dead on their journey to the hereafter. Food vessels are squatter, with a bowl-like appearance, and are decorated with a wide range of distinctive motifs which suggest northern English or Irish sources of inspiration – or of potters.

Despite the longevity of the beaker style, spanning something like 1000 years down to c.1600–1500 BC, it neither altogether replaced other pottery styles, nor predominated in all parts of the country. In general, beaker pottery is most common in southern and eastern Scotland, the zones which probably received colonists direct from the Continent. It is also spread extensively through the south-west, indicating a second major access-point for migration, and has been found at a scattering of locations in the Hebrides, with finds from Bhaltos in Lewis, southwards through Northton in Harris (where thousands of sherds were found associated with the early settlement site), Sorisdale in Coll, to Campbeltown at the southern end of Kintyre. In the western mainland and far north, however, it is rare. Sherds have been recovered as far north as Shetland, and in Orkney a few sherds are associated with the closing of chambered tombs: at Knowe of Yarso and Eday from within the chambers; at Howe and Holm of Papa Westray North from outside the cairn. A single complete beaker was found in a cist burial at Birsay, but this is of a very late type. Beaker pottery from settlement sites in the Northern Isles is equally scarce: a single portion of one vessel was found in the doorway of a house at the Grooved Ware settlement of Rinyo. Northern mainland Scotland is as poor in finds of beaker pottery, with only a thin scattering in the region north of Easter Ross. Limited past work may be partly to blame for the thinness of the distribution, for recent excavations are consistently adding to the total. Excavations at Allt na Fearna near Lairg, for example, yielded one nearly complete food vessel and beaker sherds. Nevertheless, in view of the long antiquarian and archaeological tradition in Orkney in particular, the scarcity of beaker material in the north is quite striking.

How are we to explain this north-south divide? It is probably attributable in part to the original settlement pattern of the Beaker People. Beaker styles would understandably gain a stronger hold in areas where they had settled in greatest numbers and where their descendants exercised a cultural superiority. There is also the avoidance of ceremonial centres of the Neolithic peoples noted earlier. This may explain the near absence of beaker pottery from Orkney, where the ritual centres of the Grooved Ware culture were recent and still functioning features of the cultural landscape, but it is not a satisfactory solution for Shetland, or more particularly, northern Scotland. Nor, too, does it fit the evidence from Lewis and Harris; beaker material has been found at Bhaltos to the west of the Neolithic stone circles around Callanish. Geographical remoteness is probably a factor, but may be less significant than is sometimes suggested. Sea voyages to Shetland are unlikely deterrents to a people who had already displayed their seamanship in the journeys from Iberia to Lewis, or across the North Sea. From about 2000 BC, however, the climate entered a period of long-term deterioration, with wetter and windier weather systems developing: rough seas may have contributed to the comparative isolation of the Northern Isles from the mainstream of beaker and Early Bronze Age trends. This might account for slow transmission of, or receptiveness to, bronze-making technology in Orkney, but it would not of itself account for the relative absence of beaker pottery, a ceramic tradition which had been present in Scotland since about 2500 BC. Also, similar shifts in Atlantic weather systems would have affected the Hebrides in the same manner, but as we have already seen, immigrants were moving into those islands from soon after 2500 BC. Density of already established settlements is another, but largely unquantifiable, factor. Again, this is a more significant element with regard to Orkney, where the spread of Neolithic sites implies high-density settlement in a landscape already divided into territorial blocks upon which individual communities were sustained. This supports the arguments in favour of the arrival of beaker culture with an immigrant population, and it should also be noted that it is in areas with low levels of Neolithic settlement, or peripheral to the main cultural centres of mainland Scotland, such as the central part of the Deveron valley and Buchan, that the greatest concentrations of early beaker material – and early bronze-working centres – occur.

Attitudes towards metalworking, skills which must have seemed potentially sorcerous, were probably crucial in the spread of both beaker pottery styles and bronze implements. The exclusion of both from the two major areas of late Neolithic ritual development – Orkney and the Garioch – could be seen as the response of the established powers in the land to a perceived threat to their authority. To others, however, control of this dangerous new power may have been viewed as a means of either bolstering their existing authority, or of winning prestige, probably on a personal level. It is possible that some communities, or even just some elements within a community, offered patronage and protection to the immigrant metalworkers, while elsewhere they were shunned. Such a position is easier to envisage where the migration was small-scale. It was possibly through patronage or simple co-operation that these first metal-workers became established in Buchan. Control of the production of such high status goods as fine beaker pottery and bronze or gold items, either as patrons or partners, must have brought its own prestige. It would also have brought a power that was both mystical and, on a more mundane level, economic. There is no difficulty in seeing the development out of these circumstances of a new structure of authority where power rested in the hands of the few who controlled metalworking knowledge and supply of the new materials. Perhaps here we can trace the final step in the transition from the egalitarian society of the Neolithic to the hierarchical society evident in the later periods of the Bronze Age?

A link between early areas of beaker settlement and the first centres of metalworking is well attested in the archaeological record. In north-east Scotland, for example, several such areas can be identified stretching through Buchan towards the Spey. The finds include stone moulds for the casting of flat bronze axes found in the valley of the South Ugie Water. From around Aberchirder have come flat axe moulds, flat axes and a bronze halberd, while from the Auchterless area, around the upper reaches of the Ythan, has come one of the earliest bronze daggers found in Britain, its broad tanged blade closely related to examples from the Beaker People's Dutch homeland. Further to the west, the area around Fochabers on the Spey seems to have developed into an important early production centre of both beakers and metalwork, the decoration used on a pair of magnificent gold ear-rings found at Orbliston Junction being closely related to that used on early beaker forms.

The beaker/metalworking link was not the sole means for the transmission of knowledge of metallurgy into Scotland. Ireland was a major early metalworking centre whose influences can be seen quite as widespread in Scotland, and it has even been suggested that Scottish early metalwork finds represent imports from Irish production centres rather than domestic products. Irish copper appears to have been traded extensively throughout Britain, and both finished products and stylistic influences probably flowed along the trade routes also. These influences can be seen in a most striking form in the Bronze Age cemetery strung out along the floor of the Kilmartin valley in Argyllshire, where carvings of flat axes of Irish form are pecked into lid and side slabs of cists at Nether Largie North and Ri Cruin cairns. Irish influence may also be represented in the magnificent gold lunula – a crescent-shaped neck ornament of beaten metal which is found most commonly in Ireland – such as that found with the ear-rings at Orbliston, or the fine pair from Southside in Peeblesshire.

The range of copper, bronze and gold objects being manufactured expanded steadily throughout the early 2nd millennium BC. Dating for many early metal items, and development of typologies which chart stylistic change and technological refinement, relies for the most part on their discovery as grave goods in beaker burials. The lifespan of that pottery style gives a general date for the Early Bronze Age spanning the period down to c.1500-1400 BC. It is interesting to note that there is strong evidence for selectivity in material included with burials. Bronze daggers and armlets predominate, but no beaker burial to date has contained an axe, although carved representations of axe-heads are known. It has been argued that some symbolism attached to axes in the Neolithic – where several clearly high-prestige examples were deposited in the sealing of chambered tombs – and that that symbolism may have continued to be recognised in the Early Bronze Age, rendering them unsuitable for inclusion as grave-goods. Axes, however, often form the most important element of hoards. Excavation in the early 1980s at Dail na Caraidh on the banks of the River Lochy near Fort William, the find-spot of 18 flat axes and 6 daggers, revealed that the objects had been deposited on several separate occasions rather than as a single act, on a site that showed no other evidence for domestic or burial activity. While single deposit hoards may represent the cache of wandering craftsmen, this site is believed to be of ritual significance, which would again stress the possible symbolism of axes. Particularly fine daggers have been recovered from a number of excavations, some, such as that from a cist at Ashgrove in Fife, retaining remnants of hilts made from riveted plates of wood and horn. The Ashgrove dagger had an ivory pommel, but gold examples have also been found. A wider range of metalwork has been recovered from hoards. The finest, from Migdale in Sutherland, comprised eight bronze armlets, a flat axe, an ear-ring, tubular beads of thin bronze-sheet over wooden cores, cone-shaped bronze objects (interpreted as button-covers), and six jet buttons.

Bronze technology continued to be refined and from about 1400 BC innovation brought the introduction of new techniques which allowed production of sophisticated cast pieces. The degree of change, together with the general character of the items produced, is such that the period c.1400-900 BC is sometimes labelled the Middle Bronze Age. Development of two or more piece closed moulds, for example, permitted the casting of socketed implements. New forms of axe-head were devised, with flanges or of the so-called palstave form, which gripped the butt of the blade to give added stability, and in the latter prevented the head from being pushed backwards and so splitting the haft when the axe was used. The flanges, like wings on the upper and lower edges of the axe-head, were progressively extended and folded round the sides until eventually sockets were formed to hold the haft. It was but a short step from there to the hollow casting of fully socketed forms. One of the most notable changes was in the range and quality of the weapon sets being produced. The old short daggers of the Early Bronze Age disappeared, to be replaced by dirks, long-bladed swords (referred to normally as 'rapiers'), and spear-heads, all highly functional weaponry as well as simply the trappings of status. Such specialised weapon sets are far removed from earlier hunting kits, and must have been expensive to produce. In them, we can probably see evidence for a fully developed warrior-aristocracy in control of sources of wealth, and glimpse the smith-craftsmen whom they patronised.

Gold and jet have been prized from earliest times for their beauty and value. Their relatively widespread use in Early Bronze Age society points to an affluent culture, where the power of the newly emergent hierarchies was expressed in material display. Such display is evident in the magnificent archer's wrist-guard with its four gold studs from a cist burial at Culduthel in Inverness, or in the four discs of beaten gold found in a cremation at Knowes of Trotty in Orkney. Jet, too, underscores the evidence for established trading patterns, for it occurs in few places around Britain, yet is found widely in burials and hoards. In addition to the jet buttons, such as those found at Migdale, there are magnificent necklaces of shaped and drilled beads and spacers. The finest included a magnificent three-stranded example from Poltalloch in Argyll, sadly destroyed in a fire, but paralleled by a similar article from Pitkennedy in Angus. Most of the jet necklaces have been found in burial contexts.

As noted earlier, it is such burials that form our chief source of evidence for the Early Bronze Age. As with the Neolithic, a wide range of burial traditions are identifiable, and it is clear that practices changed over time. The most common form was for individual burial within a stone cist set into a pit cut into the ground, often with a cairn raised over the site. Striking examples of such cairn-covered cist burials can be seen in the Kilmartin valley in Argyll, and at Memsie in Buchan. The cists are quite short, and the bodies were placed in them on their side in crouched position. Inhumation was not the only rite used. Cremation had been favoured in some regions in the Neolithic and continued to be practised, but there was a gradual switch generally from inhumation to cremation. The cremated bone was carefully separated from the ash and placed in specialist cinerary urns, occasionally accompanied by small, highly-decorated pottery vessels – usually labelled incense or accessory cups – and also by personal items, such as pins, or jewellery. In most cases, the urns were buried upside-down, indicating that their open tops must originally have been sealed by covers of some perishable material. Burials without urns, for example in pits, were probably originally contained in small bags or sacks. The development of specialist containers to hold the cremated remains appears to mark a deliberate change in funerary tradition in some areas, particularly in eastern and south-western Scotland where detailed typologies have been built from the prolific finds. This regionalised distribution, however, may be something of a red herring, for it is based on studies in areas which have yielded large quantities of material, and where pottery in general can be placed within recognisable style groups. Such typological labelling is less possible in the west and north where pottery sequences are less clear-cut, and where few burials include pottery grave-goods. Here, too, cremation may have been taking over as the dominant burial tradition, as the numerous discoveries of cremations placed 'loose' within small cairns bounded by substantial stone kerbs – prosaically labelled kerb-cairns – point to a general trend in this direction. Cairns of this type are distributed widely throughout Scotland, with excavated examples at Strontoiller near Oban, Fowlis Wester in

Perthshire and Logie Newton in Aberdeenshire.

Excavations in progress at the time of writing on a round barrow in the grounds of House of Dun near Montrose are again highlighting the limitations of our knowledge of Bronze Age funerary monuments and the shortcomings of traditional typological schemes. There, the barrow appears to have developed out of an earthen 'ring cairn', part of the material for which had been excavated from an external enclosing ditch, over which had been piled a stone covering. A burnt surface at the base of the central shaft may mark the site of a pyre, but no primary burial has yet been located. The central area seems to have begun to silt up, or to have been deliberately infilled in part, before the still visible depression was concealed beneath a covering of water-worn pebbles similar to those with which the 'ring cairn' was clad.

Figure 10: Cairnapple Hill, Lothian, henge, cremation cemetery and Bronze Age cairn

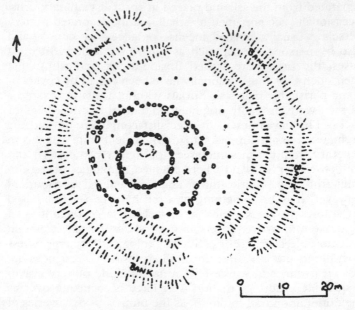

KEY: X PHASE 1 BURIAL PITS

    • PHASE 2 HENGE - SOCKETS OF STONE SETTING

    ⊖ PHASE 3 KERB OF CAIRN

    o PHASE 4 KERB OF ENLARGED CAIRN.

Subsequent to that, and still within the Bronze Age, an extra earthen 'cap' was added to the summit of the barrow, surmounted by a ring of large rounded pebbles. Final Bronze Age activity at the site was represented by the insertion of at least three cremations in large, collared urns. The highly unusual constructional form of the House of Dun barrow may represent a distinct local tradition, echoes of which can be seen in the cairn at West Mains of Auchterhouse north of Dundee where the central cist within a ring of boulders was covered by a turf mound, itself sealed within a covering of stones. Earthen round barrows also occurred closer to Dun, such as the sole surviving mound from the cemetery known as the Three Laws near Logie Pert.

The preference for cremation in some areas is marked also by the appearance of small cemeteries. Several have been located in south-west Scotland, such as Misk Knowe and Ardeer in Ayrshire, Palmerston and Carronbridge in Dumfriesshire. At the last site, excavation of crop-mark features in advance of roadworks in 1989 revealed three cremation burials in cinerary urns, two of which were placed in small stone-lined pits. One of the urns held the cremated remains of three individuals – an adult, a child of between three and twelve years, and an infant. Multiple cremations of this sort are not uncommon: three individuals were represented in an urn-burial from Howford Farm in Aberdeenshire, while the cremation of an adult female and an infant had been placed in a cist inserted into the Neolithic barrow at Boghead in Moray. There are extensive cremation cemeteries on the gravel terraces of the River Clyde in Lanarkshire, and in the vicinity of Leuchars and St Michael's in north-east Fife, pointing to the presence of extensive local settlement. Adjacent to the Loanhead of Daviot recumbent stone circle is a cemetery defined by two arcs of shallow ditch (now marked by bands of rubble) with breaks to form entrances. The focus for the cemetery was a large pyre on which an adult male had been partly cremated, subsequent to which a further 34 individual cremations had been buried in urns or pits.

Several cemeteries and kerb-cairns are associated with impressive pillar-like standing stones, such as those adjacent to the cairns at Strontoiller and Fowlis Wester, or the pair at Orwell in Kinross-shire which marked a small group of cremations. These are clearly memorials, but the function of the many other such monoliths which do not seem to be associated with burial sites remains a matter of debate. Some are truly monumental, such as the 3.4m-high example at Morphie on the skyline above the North Esk north of Montrose, which may have been a way-marker associated with a river-crossing. The massive boulder known as the Wren's Egg in Wigtownshire, however, served as a focus for ritual, and other alignments of stones, such as those at Ballochroy in Kintyre, may have had some role in astronomical observation. The exact relationship between the single standing stones and stone alignments of the Bronze Age and earlier stone circles is unknown, but it is possible that they represent the tail-end of a tradition which commenced with the henges of the later Neolithic.

While burial and ritual monuments of the Early and Middle Bronze Ages are relatively prolific features of the Scottish landscape, settlement sites of these periods, particularly for the earlier, are more elusive in many parts of the country. The fairly impermanent structures from Northton on Harris and Sorisdale on Coll, where tent-like superstructures above stone-revetted scoops in the sand mark the arrival of beaker-using settlers, are now complemented by more substantial free-standing stone-walled houses, such as the oval-plan example from Ardnave on Islay. Survey and excavation in upland zones of sites sealed under blanket peat has added greatly to our knowledge of the spread and density of settlement in the 2nd millennium BC. Large-scale excavation projects, such as those at Kilpatrick and Tormore on Arran, and at Lairg in Sutherland, revealed both actual settlement sites in the form of the remains of individual circular, timber-built house, and extensive areas of field-clearance banks and cairns surrounding them. Several of the houses on Arran showed evidence of having been rebuilt on a number of occasions throughout the 2nd millennium BC.

At Lairg, a series of excavations in the late 1980s in advance of roadworks revealed a Bronze Age landscape in quite striking detail. Some 54 hut circles, representing the stone foundations of timber-built circular houses, were identified within an area measuring 3.5km by 0.3km in Achany Glen. Previous excavation of similar sites at Kilphedir in the Strath of Kildonan in Sutherland had produced radiocarbon dates pointing to construction and occupation throughout the 1st millennium BC, but there had been some evidence to suggest that the dates related to later phases of activity and that earlier occupation was present. Moreover, the 2nd millennium dates from sites at An Sithean in Islay, or Cul a' Bhaile in Jura showed that the circular house form had a greater antiquity than the Kilphedir evidence allowed. The Lairg excavations confirmed this view, with 71 per cent of the hut circles (38 sites) producing radiocarbon dates from the 2nd millennium BC. Indeed, 64 per cent of the total dated from the period 1000–1500 BC and a further 7 per cent to 1500–2000 BC, while only 15 per cent dated from the whole of the 1st millennium BC, suggesting a rapid decline in settlement from shortly before 1000 BC. The remains appear to be those of a rather scattered community, or unenclosed village. The house sites were shown to stand on areas of previous cultivation, and beneath them were plough-truncated remains of earlier Bronze Age houses – 200 or so years older – and traces of cultivation probably extending back into the Neolithic. It has been suggested that the replacement of earlier houses by new ones on different sites, and the giving over of the old settlement area to agriculture, may represent a rotation system where the midden and organic materials from the house structures were ploughed into the ground to raise soil fertility. This would explain the marked contrast in density of occupation between the early and later 2nd millennium, with many earlier sites having been ploughed to oblivion, but does not account for the drop away after c.1000 BC.

Around the huts at Lairg was an extensive area of cultivation. This appears at first to have been an open, tilled landscape, but in the 2nd millennium it was divided into smaller enclosed units by rubble dykes, formed largely by field clearance debris. Cultivation continued throughout the 2nd millennium, but around 1000 BC there is evidence for a change in the site economy, with suggestions of a move away from cultivation of cereals to the raising of stock. In Moray, survey and excavation at the upland site of Tulloch Wood near Forres has likewise revealed an extensive landscape of Bronze Age agriculture, with houses scattered through an area of some 27 ha interspersed with linear field-banks and cairns of field-clearance debris. Here again, cultivation commenced before c.2000 BC and continued down into the later 2nd millennium, when there is a sharp break in activity followed by a prolonged period of abandonment until the late 1st century BC. Similar evidence from a number of sites scattered throughout Scotland points to a major change taking place in the structure of society in the later years of the 2nd millennium BC. Middle Bronze Age society in Scotland appears to have been a society in crisis.

The origins and nature of this crisis are still matters of great debate amongst archaeologists. At the centre of the problem, however, lie climatic changes which had a disastrous impact on a system of agriculture which, in northern and upland districts, appears always to have hovered close to the subsistence level. A general deterioration of the climate had commenced around 2000 BC, seeing a switch to an Atlantic pattern of weather with cooler temperatures and increased rainfall in contrast to the warmer and drier conditions which had largely prevailed since the Mesolithic. With the changing weather came stronger winds, which resulted in tree loss in exposed northern and western districts, and wetter conditions which saw peat growth in upland areas. The practice of agriculture may have become more difficult, but throughout the 2nd millennium BC the acreage under the plough increased and population levels continued to rise, in turn putting additional pressure on agricultural resources. Indeed, it is the rising population levels which probably drove the expansion of agriculture into upland districts where what must always have been marginal land offered a very precarious existence for the farmers. In such conditions, it requires only relatively slight change to precipitate disaster.

That disaster may have come in 1159 BC. In that year a massive eruption of the Icelandic volcano, Hekla, flung masses of volcanic dust, or tephra, into the atmosphere. Carried on the winds, this spread over a wide area – it has been traced as a fine dusting on archaeological sites in northern and western Scotland – and brought about significant changes to the climate. Evidence from the study of tree pollens preserved in peat or lake sediments, or from tree-ring analysis of timbers preserved in bogs, shows how far-reaching the consequences of the eruption were. For example, the growth rings of oak in Ireland reveal that after 1159 BC there were several years of exceptionally poor growing conditions, represented by narrow rings in the timber. Arguments have been put forward that evidence for dramatic declines in the levels of certain tree pollens in northern Scotland, such as pines in Caithness, are attributable either to the volcanic ash fallout, or to climatic deterioration brought about by the eruption, but this decline seems rather to be a result of human activity in the form of further forest clearance for cultivable land. Nevertheless, it is easy to imagine the consequences for a society living on a knife-edge of survival of even a relatively minor change in annual growing conditions.

Rather than a sudden catastrophe bringing about crisis towards the end of the Middle Bronze Age, Hekla's eruption may simply have been the final nail in the coffin of an already crumbling society. There appears to have been, for example, a dramatic drop in population levels throughout Britain commencing in the earlier 12th century BC. Indeed, it has been suggested that the drop might have been in the order of 50 per cent, the kind of level otherwise only achieved during major epidemics such as the Black Death in the mid-14th century AD, and that levels did not recover for some 700 or so years. Further evidence for the crisis has been seen in bronze production, where there is a marked decline in the manufacture of axes after *c.*1200 BC. Around this time instead we see the beginnings of production of a wider and more sophisticated range of weapons – spear-heads, rapiers and dirks – which some have seen as marking the beginning of a struggle for control over resources made increasingly slender by the climatic deterioration, with a warrior-aristocracy contending for possession of the contracted population and agriculture from which they drew their very means of existence.

The Later Bronze Age

Evidence for the contraction of population after 1200 BC is to be seen almost everywhere in upland districts, and especially in northern and western parts of the country. Peat growth, which had been spreading since the beginning of the climatic deterioration in the early 3rd millennium BC, accelerated and encroached upon areas of former cultivation, sealing them beneath a deepening blanket. Abandonment of agriculture, however, did not necessarily imply complete human abandonment of the area and, as the results from Lairg seem to show, the remaining population may have switched from largely arable to mainly pastoral economies. Stock-rearing relies to a much lesser extent on warm growing seasons and suitable levels of rainfall, and was also less labour-intensive. Such a switch, moreover, could indicate efforts to boost soil fertility in smaller areas, as crops were still grown, albeit on a reduced scale.

Evidence for developing pastoral economies is quite widespread in Scotland. The last quarter of the 2nd millennium BC, for example, saw the formation of small communities in the hill-country of Upper Tweeddale and Upper Clydesdale. These took the form of a series of platforms produced by digging a wide scoop into the face of a hill and piling the excavated material on the downslope side to form a level area on which timber roundhouses could be built. Several of these would be strung out in a row along the hillside, forming villages made up of several households. Although traces of cultivation have been found adjacent to some sites, such as those at Normangill Rig in Clydesdale, these are small scale plots, and in general it appears that a largely stock-rearing economy evolved in the Southern Uplands in the course of the 1st millennium BC. At the other geographical extreme of the country, in Shetland, there is likewise evidence for climate-produced change. There, increased rainfall coupled with peat-growth appears to have resulted in the abandonment of many of the older settlement areas in the upland districts of the islands, with a switch instead to low-lying coastal sites. Settlements such as Clickhimmin near Lerwick, where the earliest phase is represented by the remains of a stone-built house of the early 1st millennium BC whose antecedents lie clearly in the Neolithic, may represent such a move. Again, finds of trough querns for the grinding of grain into flour indicate that cereal cultivation continued to play a part in the economy, but sheep and cattle, as well as fishing, appear to have been the basis of subsistence.

These communities are still largely open sites, enclosing walls or fences being more for prevention of stock straying into cultivated plots, or to serve as stockyards. There is no obvious hierarchy of settlement type at this time, but there are hints of something of the kind in the Lairg excavations. By the end of the 2nd millennium BC, all but one of the early hut circles excavated there had been abandoned, one at least having been converted into an unroofed, cobbled stockyard rather than its site being returned to cultivation. The remaining site, a large hut with an internal diameter in excess of 10m, continued in use until well into the 1st millennium BC, but had undergone radical transformation from its original form. From a simple hut circle it had been developed into a substantial raised platform with an outer façade of dry-stone walling, access to which was by a 4m-long ramp which projected from the façade. Quite clearly, this is a prestigious dwelling of high status. There are two smaller hut circles lying to the north-west and south-east of this main site, both of which appear to be houses of contemporary date to that which stood on its raised platform in their midst. It would not be stretching the interpretation of this site too greatly to suggest that here we can see the residence of the warrior-chief and his family who had succeeded in maintaining or establishing their control over the contracted population of Achany Glen, with houses of their dependants scattered around.

It is probably the occupants of such high status sites who should be seen as the chief customers for the high-grade bronze-work and prestige weaponry which developed around the end of the 2nd millennium BC. Although such weaponry was clearly intended for use, its possession may have reflected one's personal status and have had a role that was as much symbolic and ceremonial as practical. The use of gold decoration in the weaponry is one indication of this. For example, the spearhead from Pyotdykes near Dundee, found in a hoard with two swords and datable to roughly 750 BC, has a broad gold band round the base of its socket. Bronze shields, such as the magnificent disc from Auchmaleddie in Aberdeenshire, seem to have been another aspect of the ceremonial role of some weapon sets. These are superb examples of the bronze-smith's craft, but their practicality in battle has been brought into question. Experiments using reproduction shields and weapons have shown that bronze shields are of little effect in absorbing blows from swords, and it is likely that leather versions were used in battle. Indeed, it is possible that bronze shields were produced for ritual purposes, as seems to have been the case with six examples found set out in a circle, sealed beneath peat at Luggtonridge in Ayrshire in the 18th century. In general, however, the weaponry points towards the evolution of an increasingly warlike society, displaying many of the characteristics which we associate with the 'Celtic' cultures of the Iron Age.

Traditionally, much of the bronze-production of this period has been seen as the output of 'itinerant smiths', but it is more likely that most smiths based themselves more or less permanently in at least the larger communities, as at

Traprain Law in Lothian, where they were guaranteed customers for their work. Some more entrepreneurial men may have travelled in search of communities where their skills would be in demand, one such being a smith of apparently Irish background who established himself at Jarlshof on the southern tip of Shetland. Amongst the debris from his workshop were recovered many fragments of clay moulds used for the production of swords, socketed axes, gouges, and decorative pieces including pins of what is referred to as 'sunflower' form, where the head of the pin is extended into a flower-like disc. The smith's workshop here lay amongst the houses of a small farming community, and while it is probable that what appears to have been significant output of high-quality metalwork, including weaponry, would have found a ready market widely throughout what seems otherwise to have been a bronze-starved Shetland society, it has been suggested that his customers were seafarers who used his swords in piratical raids around the coasts of Britain and Ireland.

Hoards of what is clearly scrap bronze metalwork have often been labelled as the collections of itinerant smiths, broken and mis-cast pieces being obtained as raw materials for melting down and re-use. At Peelhill in Lanarkshire, for example, the hoard contained 28 broken or damaged spear-heads and a sword which had been snapped into three pieces, while from Duddingston Loch in Edinburgh came a large hoard of swords, spear-heads and other bronze pieces, many of which had been deliberately bent and some of which had been distorted by heat. Rather than being caches of re-usable material deposited for later retrieval by wandering smiths, however, it has been more plausibly suggested that such hoards represent local collections gathered for transportation to a smith based on one of the larger settlement sites. It is possible that the role of collector was played by a merchant rather than the smith himself, for there are also hoards which contain complete and undamaged pieces which may represent stock in trade. This is the interpretation placed on deposits such as that from Drumcoltran in Galloway, where three differing styles of sword were found in a hoard of twelve blades, but the possible ritual aspect of the earlier axe hoard from Dail na Carraidh points to alternative explanations for the deposition of such collections.

Amongst the Late Bronze Age metalwork finds in

Scotland are styles and items which reveal exotic influences at work. Travelling merchants may have been responsible for bringing new forms and ideas in their packs, but some have seen the material as marking the arrival of new settlers from elsewhere in the British Isles and from the Continent. For example, swords of a style known as Ewart Park (named after an example from a site in Northumberland) have an extensive distribution throughout eastern Scotland and were being manufactured on sites as widely spread as Traprain Law and Jarlshof, but also occur in many hoards throughout the western mainland and the Hebrides. These latter examples, it has been suggested, mark the movement of sea-borne warriors – perhaps customers of the Jarlshof smith. The 'sunflower' class of pins, moulds for which were also found at Jarlshof, and which occur in hoards in the mainland at Tarves in Aberdeenshire and Grosvenor Crescent in Edinburgh, is closely related to styles produced in north Germany. Similar links between northern Germany and the north-east of Scotland are suggested by a localised group of later 8th-century to 7th-century BC items named after the site at Covesea in Moray where they were first identified. Distinctive forms of penannular bracelets and pins, such as those found in Sculptor's Cave at Covesea, or in hoards from Braes of Gight and Glentanar in Aberdeenshire and Balmashanner at Forfar in Angus, have been used as arguments in favour of at least close trading links with the north German plain and southern Scandinavia, if not in a localised movement of colonists. The Glentanar hoard also contained two cast bronze ribbed and handled bowls which both came from the same two-piece mould, and which show strong similarities to Continental forms. Sheet bronze-work, usually in the form of cauldrons or buckets, also has Continental sources. Ireland, too, continued to be both a source of inspiration and design, particularly for fine gold-work.

Amongst the metalwork, items which seem to be linked to the use of horses make their appearance. Some of the bronze rings from the Glentanar and Braes of Gight hoards are probably pieces of horse harness. These, too, indicate Continental influences, perhaps associated with the expansion from about the beginning of the 8th century of that culture to which we give the label Celtic. In central Europe, from about this time, there is evidence for a warrior-aristocracy using horses both to pull chariots and to carry riders into battle, and wealth was lavished on the fine trappings for their mounts. Their appearance in Scotland by about 700 BC may mark the arrival of the first harbingers of the last major prehistoric migration into Britain, and the beginning of the age of the Celts.

4

AN HEROIC AGE
*c.*700 BC TO *c.*500 AD

WHAT IS a Celt? While archaeologists can generally agree that Britain from the second quarter of the 1st millennium BC onwards was 'Celtic' in its culture and society, there is intense debate over what exactly this transformation entailed. Older theories that it was brought about by mass migration of Celtic-speaking tribesmen from the Continent have been largely discredited, but continue to influence some ideas, such as arguments in favour of the political takeover of Late Bronze Age culture by incoming warrior-elites. That there was a degree of migration is probable, and large-scale movement did occur in the late 1st millennium BC with the entry of the tribes whom we know from later sources as the *Parisi* into east Yorkshire and the *Belgae* into south-east England, but it was just one contributory element in a complex process of social development. Prehistoric society in Britain had been undergoing a deep-seated process of change from the later 2nd millennium BC onwards, with new forms of metalwork in particular pointing to strengthening contacts with and influences from the Continent. It was down these already established avenues that Celtic culture was to reach the British Isles.

By around 700 BC, tribes from the region north of the Caucasus had pushed westward into central Europe, moving into the lands occupied by the Late Bronze Age Urnfield culture, a people who probably spoke an early form of Celtic language and whose social organisation displayed many of the features which were later to characterise Celtic civilisation. With them they brought two major developments: the skill of horsemanship; and the new technology of ferrous metallurgy. The Iron Age had arrived in central Europe. Both new skills were eagerly taken up by the Urnfielders and from them developed a new iron-using culture. This, the first major phase of Celtic development, is known as Hallstatt from the village in the Salzkammergut region of Austria where excavation of a cemetery produced artefacts that are typical of the earliest Celtic culture. They were a wealthy people, their prosperity derived from control of and trade in salt and iron, but farming was still the mainstay of their existence. Contact with Mediterranean civilisation through trade routes reaching north from the Greek trading colony of Massilia (Marseilles) at the mouth of the Rhône further stimulated Hallstatt development. By the 6th century BC the main centre of their culture had shifted westwards into the upper Rhine/Burgundy region at the head of the Rhône valley trading network. In the early 5th century BC there emerged in the region of the central Rhône and Marne valley a new phase in Celtic cultural development, named La Tène after a site on Lake Neuchâtel in Switzerland where the distinctive new metalwork and decorative forms were first identified in quantity. In the flowering of La Tène culture, the Celts reached their prehistoric zenith.

These developments did not simply pass Britain by, for, as we have already seen, regular contact between parts of these islands and the Continent had been well established by the later Bronze Age. From the earliest period of Celtic expansion into western Europe, the new styles of metalwork which distinguished the Hallstatt culture were already finding their way into Britain. Trade was probably the most significant means by which the distinctive new Celtic metalwork forms arrived, but it is probable that immigrants of Hallstatt background had begun to move into coastal districts, at least of England and Wales, by quite early in the 7th century BC. Their arrival is marked in particular by the introduction of new styles of sword, which were swiftly incorporated into the repertoire of local smiths. This willingness to absorb new ideas and styles continued, and from the middle of the 1st millennium BC British craftsmen were producing wide ranges of metalwork inspired by later Hallstatt and La Tène styles. But it was not a case of simply slavish imitation of the original, for the ideas which were so enthusiastically taken up in Britain were to travel down different avenues of development, producing a quite distinctive insular Celtic culture that both outlived and culturally surpassed the Celtic cultures of mainland Europe.

But being Celtic is more than simply a question of material culture. The adoption of Hallstatt and La Tène metalwork and artistic styles by the Late Bronze Age peoples of Britain did not alone turn them into Celts, and it is quite apparent that the social structure and, probably, language of the older cultures were already very close to that of the

European Celts. Indeed, it has been argued that Indo-European language, of which Celtic is one branch, had been introduced into Britain in the Bronze Age, and had already achieved dominance by about 1500 BC. After all, do not the contacts between parts of eastern Scotland and the Low Countries which are evident from soon after 2500 BC point towards continuity of kinship links with original European homelands? Of course, we can never prove that the people who introduced beakers into Scotland spoke an Indo-European language, but the establishment of such a language in Britain would very much have facilitated the maintenance of contacts with Europe and speeded up the absorption of later settlers – or simply ideas – into the mainstream British Bronze Age cultures.

Iron Age Society

When dealing with the social organisation of Iron Age Celtic society in Scotland, it is possible for the first time to do more than simply conjecture on the basis of evidence from burials, or to build up elaborate hypotheses founded on often questionable assumptions about the kind of society reflected in chambered tomb or stone circle construction. Several sources of information are available to us, including for the first time written descriptions and accounts. Of course, we are dealing with a prehistoric culture, that is one which is pre-literate and has no recorded history of its own. It was, however, to come into contact with the literate cultures of Greece and Rome, and records of those contacts, including observations on the society of the 'barbarian' Celts, were set down by classical writers. Such records should not be seen as impartial or factual accounts by unbiased scientific observers, for they are loaded with their writers' assumptions and prejudices. Indeed, they often present an idealised view, where the 'simple' barbarian becomes the expression for the writers' concept of perfection and purity, free from the various political and social ills which plagued their own societies. Such currents run strongly in the writings of P. Cornelius Tacitus, whose *Germania*, at face value a study of the character, customs and geography of the German tribes, contrasts the supposed primitive virtues of the Germans with the degeneracy of the contemporary Rome of the late 1st century AD. We can see this idealisation, too, in the wonderful rhetoric and lofty ideals of the speeches which classical writers put into the mouths of the Celtic chieftains who led the resistance to the conquering armies of Rome, a device much favoured by Tacitus. Alongside such literary devices, however, is an abundance of descriptive and anecdotal material. Considerable caution has to be exercised when drawing on this, for the material is generalised, simplified and compressed. In reality, much is simply stage-setting for detailed accounts of Roman military campaigns, and carries more than a whiff of stock 'off-the-shelf' descriptions of barbarians. Nevertheless, there is real gold amongst the dross, and certain classical authorities, such as Julius Caesar in his account of his campaigns in Gaul, represent first-hand descriptions and form the nearest we are going to get to contemporary accounts of Celtic Iron Age society.

A second major body of documentary material has come down to us through the writings of later Celtic clerics, principally in Irish sources. In their surviving form, there is little that is earlier than the 12th century AD, but linguistic analysis suggests that the originals may be many centuries older. The greatest of these accounts, for example, is the so-called Ulster Cycle at the centre of which is the epic poem known as the *Tain Bo Cuailgne* which focuses on the Ulster hero Cuchulain. It has come down to us in a 12th-century document, but shows every sign of 8th-century composition, and certain of its sections may be as old as the 6th century AD. Even then, there can be little doubt that it has a much longer history as an oral account, for the society which it purports to describe is essentially pagan and finds close parallels in the descriptions of late La Tène culture in Britain and Gaul as recorded by Caesar. Various Christian glosses have been inserted in the narratives, and the monks of 8th- or even 6th-century Ireland quite clearly did not understand all the allusions and symbolism of their pagan ancestors. Nevertheless, the accuracy of oral transmission in other cultures around the world suggests that the pre-Christian society which underlies the later sanitizing of the monastic scribes is essentially faithful to the original. Of course, that original should probably be seen as the Ireland of the early 1st millennium AD and, even allowing for the relative isolation of Ireland in this period, it is unlikely that its culture had not developed from that of the later 1st millennium BC.

Taken together, always bearing in mind the built-in biases and limitations of the sources, the classical and later Celtic accounts provide us with a sound core of information from which it is possible to draw out a generalised image of Iron Age society. We must exercise caution when applying that image to Scotland, for the archaeological record indicates, as we should expect, that there was a much greater depth and range to the structure of society. What, then, are the main features which can be recognised?

All the sources indicate that the basis of Celtic society by the end of the 1st millennium BC was tribal. We can assign general territories to the Iron Age tribes in Scotland on the basis of information drawn from the map of Britain produced by the Alexandrian geographer, Ptolemy, and in a few cases can identify fortified sites which may represent their major tribal centres. It is impossible to say how meaningful membership of a tribe was to people in the mid-1st millennium BC, and our sources tend to suggest that the pattern of tribes was constantly changing and evolving. Tribal territories may have depended on the success or otherwise in battle of ruling elites from particular centres, with expansion of the tribe being achieved through conquest of neighbouring territories and the absorption of the indigenous population into the ranks of the victors. It is probable, too, that the significance of the tribe as a meaningful unit varied from region to region. For example, the relatively open country of the east and south of Scotland, where the bulk of the good land and, accordingly, population was located, may have seen the formation of tribal kingdoms with both territorial integrity and a degree of political unity. In the north and west, however, the topography was against such cohesion, and there it is possible that the tribe represented nothing more than a loose alliance of individual petty chieftains and communities. Even in territories where the tribe had a meaningful reality, later sources (mainly Irish) indicate that it was the localised patterns of kin-based relationships which had most day-to-day relevance.

Rule over the tribe lay in the hands of a king or chieftain who was drawn from the ranks of a wider aristocratic elite, supported by his own kin group. His role seems to have been as much symbolic as functional, with his principal duty being as war-leader. In a society as turbulent and warlike as that of the early Celts, the importance of that role should not be understated. Below him was a class of warrior aristocrats, whose exercise of power at a local level may have been more meaningful to most people than the concept of a remote kingly figure. Caesar equated them with the *equites*, the old

Roman noble class. Overlapping with this social group was a separate class (the *druides*, or learned men, in Caesar's account) which embraced all the other privileged members of society: the priestly or druidic class; bards and musicians; lawyers and doctors; and the smiths and craftsmen in bronze. Beneath them was the great mass of ordinary freemen (the *plebes* in Roman sources), who provided tribute payments to the king and whom the Irish sources describe as binding themselves in the service of the nobles in return for gifts, usually of cattle. Finally came a servile class, whose labour supported the agricultural economy on which the whole of this social pyramid was founded. This hierarchical structure occurs both in Caesar's descriptions of Gallic society in the 1st century BC, and in the Irish sources of the later 1st millennium AD, suggesting that in its broad detail it should also reflect the Scottish position. Are traces of such a structure, then, visible in the archaeology?

Hillforts and Settlements

The emergence of inter-tribal warfare, raiding and cattle-reiving, all endemic characteristics of Celtic society, probably lie behind the appearance of defensive fortifications as significant features of the social landscape for the first time. Although elements of defence can be traced as far back as the Neolithic, as in the siting and enclosure of the settlement at Loch Olabhat in North Uist, it is in the 7th and 6th centuries BC that a decisive shift towards provision of fortifications on a major scale becomes apparent, as a movement which appears to have commenced as early as the 8th century BC gained momentum. The most significant of these sites, the hillforts, are concentrated primarily in the south and east of the country. Despite their scale and prominence in the landscape, they remain amongst the most poorly understood and least explored of all the classes of monument of the late prehistoric. Until comparatively recently, a chronology based on the type of defences employed was used to provide relative dating for the major hillforts of southern and eastern Scotland, but the more detailed survey of several important sites in those regions has shown that the progression from one form of rampart to another over time is a fallacy. Indeed, methods of building which were utilised early in the constructional sequence, such as the employment of timber-lacing to provide structural integrity, have been shown to have had a lifespan which stretched towards the end of the 1st millennium AD. Rather than a succession of forms, therefore, what we seem to have is a variety of techniques which may have passed in and out of favour, or have been utilised at different times in different circumstances.

Three main types of rampart defence have been identified in Scotland: timber-laced; stone-faced; and rubble and turf dump. Timber-lacing appears to have been one of the earliest of the forms developed and was to be employed for over a millennium in fortification construction. Radiocarbon dates from Finavon in Angus indicate that occupation of the timber-laced fort there commenced before 700 BC. Dating based on La Tène style metalwork at Castle Law near Abernethy in Perthshire indicates construction in the

Figure 11: The White Caterthun, Angus, hillfort

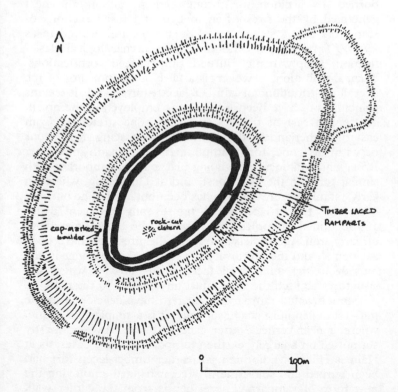

late 1st millennium BC, and the style was still being utilised in the Pictish period down to the 9th century AD, as at Burghead in Moray or Dun Skeig in Kintyre. Essentially, it is a technique for stabilising both stone walls and earth-built ramparts through the insertion of timber beams laid flat at vertical and horizontal intervals through the material of the wall-core. It had been argued that it passed out of favour largely due to difficulties of maintenance, for if the timbers rotted their replacement would require the dismantling of the defences, but evidence from some sites, such as Finavon, would indicate that their timber-laced phase spanned several centuries.

In most cases it is possible to ascertain if a fort had timber-laced defences only through excavation, as at Castle Law in Perthshire where the voids left by the rotted timbers could be seen in the stonework. It is thus difficult to establish how widespread the technique was. Where the fort has been burned, by accident or through enemy action, the heat generated by the fires often melted and fused sections of stonework into a slaggy mass. Such sites are referred to as *vitrified forts*. They are not strictly an archaeological classification, simply being burned timber-laced fortifications. Their distribution, however, is a fairly good indicator of the overall distribution of timber-laced forts, and it seems principally to have been a technique employed in the north, centre and east of the country in a zone stretching from eastern Sutherland to the Forth. Timber-lacing does occur outwith this zone, for example at Dun Lagaidh in Wester Ross, where radiocarbon dating places it contemporary with similar forts on the east coast, and at Dun Skeig, where an early 1st millennium AD date has been obtained. The burning of so many timber-laced forts - figures range between 78 and 105 identified examples - underscores the general instability of early Iron Age society. Some of the fires may have been accidental, and the proximity of some of the buildings in the interior to the inner wall face, as at Finavon where the structures abutted the wall, must have added to the risk.

Stone-fronted ramparts appear to have developed in the mid-1st millennium BC. Essentially, it is a simpler technique, where a near-vertical outer face is backed by and partly supported on a largely earthen rampart. In some cases, as at Kaimes Hill in Midlothian, an earlier timber-laced fort had been burned and subsequently reconstructed employing the new form of rampart. There, debris from the earlier wall, including vitrified rubble and charred beams, were re-used in the core of its replacement. Rubble and turf ramparts are the simplest form, comprising simply dumps of banked up material either scraped up from the ground on either side or excavated from deep quarry ditches on the outer face. Traditionally, they were believed to have been the most recent of the forms developed, and at several sites did supersede earlier timber-laced or stone-fronted defences. At Kaimes Hill, for example, the secondary stone-fronted ramparts were augmented by rubble and turf lines which considerably increased the fort's internal area. At Barmekin of Echt in Aberdeenshire, however, the three lines of bank and ditch were replaced by a pair of stone walls, and at Barra Hill in the same county a pair of ramparts with ditches were superseded by a smaller stone-walled enclosure, while at the Brown Caterthun in Angus a large two-phased *multivallate* (multiple walled) enclosure may have been succeeded by the small stone-walled fort that forms the innermost element of the defences.

Hillforts are generally seen as the top level in the hierarchy of settlement sites of Iron Age date, but there is considerable controversy over their function and the level of population based within them. Much of this is symptomatic of the limited amount of modern excavation of Scottish hillforts, with few fort interiors having been explored to a significant extent. Some archaeologists have gone so far as to suggest that the forts stood largely empty and served only as places of refuge for the population of the surrounding district in times of danger, but this extreme view is supported by neither the evidence on the ground nor by comparison with similar (better explored) sites in England. While there may have been some element of such a function, and low density of settlement within the ramparts would leave ample room for a refugee influx, most sites show clear signs of permanent occupation. At Eildon Hill North in Roxburghshire, for example, the interior is pock-marked by the circular depressions which mark the position of some 300 timber-built houses, indicating a population in the low thousands. Similarly, the outer enclosure at Tap o' Noth in Aberdeenshire contains upwards of 140 platforms cut back into the face of the hill, each probably marking a house site.

Such large concentrations of population suggest that the major hillforts held some specialist role in the social organisation of a wide territory. Very few are on a scale that comes anywhere near the large forts of southern England, where some, such as Maiden Castle in Dorset, have been identified as tribal 'capitals', but a similar role can be suggested in a number of Scottish cases. Eildon Hill North, for example, covered some 16 ha at one stage in its development and has no local rival that approaches anything like that scale. There seems little doubt that it was the principal settlement in the territory of the *Selgovae*, a tribe who appear to have occupied a region centred on the Tweed basin. Traprain Law in East Lothian appears to have fulfilled a similar function in the land of the *Votadini*, and it certainly continued to act in such a capacity down into the early historic period. Its relationship to other large sites in the Lothian plain, such as the fort on Arthur's Seat in Edinburgh, is unknown, but the multiplicity of large settlements in this region probably reflects the relative density of settlement in this fertile zone. The very large site at Tap o' Noth, extending up to 21 ha, should probably be seen as the chief centre of the *Vacomagi*, or possibly the *Taexali*, and like Traprain Law it enjoyed a role as a major centre of power into the early historic period. Similar potential 'capitals' have been identified for the *Damnonii* at either Walls Hill in Renfrewshire or Carman in Dumbartonshire, and for the *Novantae* at Burnswark in Dumfriesshire and the Moyle in Kirkcudbrightshire.

Ptolemy's map lists some 17 important tribal groupings within the region which became Scotland, some, especially those in the south and east of the country, apparently occupying extensive territories. It is impossible to prove just how much the concept of belonging to such a large and dispersed social group was to the individual 'tribesman', but the distribution of hillforts of intermediate and small scale within these supposed tribal territories points to a greater fragmentation of power than our early sources would indicate. For example, would a farmer living in his homestead in the Manor valley in Peeblesshire see himself more as a dependent of the local power based in the fort on Cademuir Hill at the north end of his valley, than as a Selgovae and subject of a tribal chieftain based on the more remote fortress at Eildon Hill North? Local power centres on a level down from the major tribal centres can be suggested certainly in the territory of the Selgovae and Votadini, with examples such as Cademuir Hill in Peeblesshire or Hownam Law in Roxburghshire, and possibly also for the Damnonii of Strathclyde and the Venicones of Fife and, possibly, Tayside. Below these in turn is a further stratum of yet smaller forts, possibly occupied by only a handful of households, but fulfilling the same central functions for their immediate hinterlands as the larger forts and tribal centres. We have, of course, no way of ever establishing the nature of the relationship between these grades of site, but it can be suggested that they form a hierarchy of power extending down from a tribal chief or king, through his principal local leaders, to a still substantial local aristocracy in the kind of social pyramid described in classical and Irish sources.

What functions the hillforts fulfilled apart from as the principal local centres of population remains a subject of great controversy. This is not simply a problem in Scotland, but bedevils hillfort studies throughout Britain. A number of possible roles, however, can be suggested. One major function may have been as the central foci for production of high-quality metalwork, especially the prestige items in demand among the warrior-aristocracy. Evidence for this can be seen at Traprain Law, where high status bronze-work was being produced earlier in the 1st millennium BC. The large quantities of bronze found in the vicinity of Duddingston Loch in Edinburgh, points to another such production centre associated with the site on Arthur's Seat. Certainly, hillforts held this function of manufacturing centre for prestige goods in the early historic period, as the moulds for casting fine brooches, harness mounts and the like from locations as widespread as the Moat of Mark in Kirkcudbrightshire and Craig Phadraig at Inverness indicate. In addition to metalwork, we should perhaps identify the forts as the bases for most quality craftsmen. There may, too, have been a role in the control of trade. This played a major part in the development of the large fort at Hengistbury Head in Dorset, and can again be attested at several early historic sites around Scotland, including the Moat of Mark, Dumbarton Rock on the Clyde, Dunadd in Argyll, and Craig Phadraig. Interrelated with a role as trade centre may be a function as control point for local agricultural surpluses, either in the form of tribute or levies, or simply as a communal, defended central store for the produce of the exposed communities which lay within its hinterland. Even with more widespread and detailed excavation, such a hypothesis would be hard to prove.

Straddling the Anglo-Scottish border and concentrated

chiefly within the hilly districts of the Cheviots, Southern Uplands and Northumberland is a class of site referred to as *palisaded homesteads* or *settlements*. These are defended sites, where protection is afforded by an enclosing palisade of tightly spaced timbers set upright in a narrow trench. The smaller sites, which are generally homesteads (i.e. containing up to about three houses and probably representing the home of a single extended family), usually have only a single palisade, but at some larger examples, mainly classed as settlements (i.e. containing more than three houses and probably representing the communal home of several families) there are two circuits, usually 1.5m to 3m apart. In both cases there is only a single entrance, in single palisade forms simply a gap marked by larger terminal posts, probably to carry the weight of hinged gates, and in some double palisaded sites formed by linking the two circuits with short stretches of timber walling to form a kind of entrance passage, as can be seen at Braidwood in Midlothian. While it is difficult to determine the level of occupation without excavation, the huts within the palisades often leave ephemeral traces on the surface in the form of sunken rings which mark the position of the timber uprights, as at Greenbrough in Roxburghshire, Glenachan Rig and Parkgatestone Hill in Peeblesshire, or Braidwood in Midlothian.

Palisaded sites appear early in the development of defended settlements. Excavation has revealed that they have a chronology that roughly parallels that of hillforts, their relationship to which remains unknown. At several sites, however, a palisaded phase appears to have represented the first stage in a progression from unfortified or lightly defended to fully developed hillfort. At Hownam Rings in Roxburghshire, for example, a palisaded enclosure gave way to a stone circuit, which was itself in turn replaced by a multivallate rubble and turf fort, before finally reverting to an undefended settlement in a process that probably spanned the period from the middle of the 1st millennium BC down to the 2nd century AD, with occupation continuing into the early historic period.

While hillforts and palisaded settlements clearly have a defensive function, contemporary with them is an extensive range of types of site where enclosures are of relatively slight construction, probably designed more for containment of stock, or entirely absent. Where excavated, the scale of the houses identified still points to high status occupants, perhaps equivalent to a substantial farming class at the upper end of the freemen or lower levels of the aristocracy. Excavated sites such as Greencraig and Scotstarvit in Fife, or West Plean in Stirlingshire appear typical of homesteads enclosed by light circuits of bank and ditch. At Greencraig, a single hut circle some 10m in diameter stood within a rectangular enclosure roughly 20m by 18.5m. The hut circle was formed by a low turf and stone bank from which rose upright timbers which supported the outer ends of the sloping rafters of the conical roof, while a second ring of posts internally carried the roof structure. The Scotstarvit house was more substantial, measuring some 18m in diameter within an embanked enclosure some 29m across. At New Kinord in Aberdeenshire can be seen an unenclosed settlement of stone-walled houses, enclosures and trackways, roughly dated to the later 1st millennium BC. This is no mere squalid cluster of humble dwellings, the largest of the hut

**Figure 12: New Kinord, Aberdeenshire, settlement
(after Sir Alexander Ogstoun, 1911).**

1–3 Possible house sites; 4–5 Stock enclosures ?; 6 Souterrain; 7 Droveway ?;
8 Track; 9 Boulder lines marking field boundaries

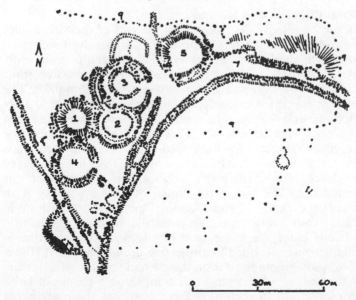

circles, a sunken-floored structure with massive stone walls, being some 19m in diameter, pointing to a similar order of status as the house at Scotstarvit. Further to the north-west, at Romancamp Gate near Fochabers in Moray, recent excavation has revealed a similarly undefended settlement of late 1st millennium BC date. Here the houses, with diameters of between 8.5 and 11.5m, are of currently unique form, their position marked by rings of large pits which contained massive timber posts.

This range of sites from hillfort down to unenclosed hut circle may hold good in general terms for most of eastern and southern Scotland, but in the north and west settlement follows a different pattern which speaks of greater social fragmentation. Here, though Ptolemy still lists several tribal groupings on his map, it is probable that the nature of the topography – with tracts of fertile land separated by extensive zones of often mountainous upland – favoured the development of power on a local level rather than the growth of petty kingdoms as elsewhere in the country. In the mainland it is a region where though hillforts occur they are scarce and spread very thinly, and where the power and prestige of local rulers is expressed through other forms of defensive settlement.

Roundhouses and Brochs

In the Northern Isles from about the end of the 8th century BC there emerged a new form of high status dwelling which seems to mark the development of a wealthy local elite. Referred to as roundhouses, these were of massive stone construction, with walls eventually up to some 5m thick. The earliest excavated example, at Quanterness in Orkney, dates from around 700 BC and continued in use down to at least the early 2nd century BC. These were structures of some sophistication, and the excavated site at Bu near Stromness in Orkney, first constructed around 600 BC, displayed evidence for progressive elaboration throughout its functioning life, with a thickening of its walls giving it an eventual diameter of some 20m. Its interior measured 9m in diameter and was centred on a massive semi-circular hearth, while around the inner face of the wall was a series of compartments formed by projecting upright slabs. At Howe, also near Stromness, a roundhouse had succeeded an earlier settlement of 8th-century date comprising a cluster of small houses within an enclosure. Here, however, the roundhouse stood within a walled and ditched enclosure, and had an upper storey reached via two staircases in the thickness of the wall, adding to the impression of status reflected in the building. Similar development has been identified in the northern mainland. At Crosskirk in Caithness, a massive roundhouse stood, as at Howe, within a walled enclosure, possibly containing ancillary buildings. The appearance of massively constructed roundhouses, but of less substantial form than the Orcadian examples and of a different structural style, is also evident further south in Sutherland. Here, the stone roundhouse on its stone-faced platform at Lairg, with a related example at Kilphedir, may represent a local response to the same social conditions as stimulated the evolution of the Orcadian forms. Quite clearly, the scale of these buildings, and their monumental appearance – at Lairg quite literally head and shoulders above the rest – points to an intention on the part of their occupants to stress their separation from the rest of the population. Surely they are an unequivocal statement of power and prestige, reflecting superior social status.

The impression that the roundhouses represent the efforts of a social elite to express their status through the architecture of their dwellings is underscored by the structures which appear to have evolved from them in the 2nd and 3rd centuries BC, the *brochs*. Brochs are a class of monument unique to Scotland, taking the form of a circular tower of dry-stone construction, its external diameter narrowing as the wall rises and with the upper part at least of the wall hollow. Externally they are featureless except for a single entrance through the thickness of the wall at its base. The original height of the brochs is a matter of continuing academic debate. The best preserved broch, at Mousa in Shetland, rises to 13m, and this was taken as representative of a norm for all brochs, but research has shown that its small diameter and massively thick wall-base would have allowed greater height than was possible at larger, thinner-walled examples. Mousa, therefore, appears to represent a uniquely tall example, with few other sites aspiring to similar heights. How the brochs were roofed is likewise a matter of debate, but since the upper levels survive complete at no site it is an argument unlikely ever to be resolved. Two main possibilities, however, offer themselves. In the first, a single roof covering the whole of the internal space, carried at a level just below the wall-head, is proposed. As the brochs are entirely windowless, this would have made the interiors dark and probably very smoky. An alternative, especially where the internal space of the broch has a large diameter, is that there were roofed timber galleries ranged round the inner face of the wall, their floors supported on stone ledges or *scarcements*, leaving the central area unroofed as a kind of light-well and flue.

Brochs have an extensive distribution. Of the almost 500 examples identified in Scotland, the vast majority lie in Orkney, Shetland, the Western Isles (especially Skye), Caithness, Sutherland, Ross and western Inverness-shire. There are outliers to this main area scattered along the coast of western Galloway and in the district between the Tay and the Tweed, but these are known to represent a late development. There is a remarkable uniformity of design throughout their whole area of distribution, pointing at the very least to a high level of communication allowing the spread of ideas, or possibly, as has been suggested, the activities of itinerant master-builders who sold their expertise to wealthy households who wished to express their power

Figure 13: Dun Carloway, Lewis, broch

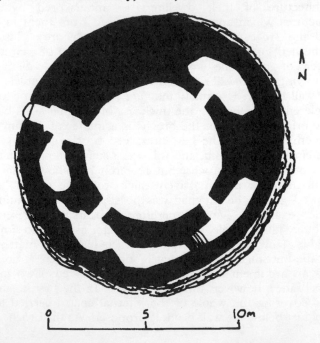

and status through possession of such a prestigious residence.

With such widespread distribution, controversy has arisen over the question of where the broch concept originated. Argument has favoured two main alternatives based on the general distribution of two distinctive features in broch design. In the Western Isles, the brochs are generally of what are referred to as *ground-galleried* form, that is where there is either a continuous gallery/passage, or a combination of galleries and small chambers in the thickness of the wall at ground level, as at Dun Mor Vaul on Tiree. In the Northern Isles and northern mainland most brochs are *solid-based*, that is the lowest level of the wall is broken only by the entrance passage and possibly two or three small cell-like chambers, as at Mousa. Before the discovery of the massive roundhouse form in Orkney, the absence of any obvious precursor to the fully-fledged brochs there was used by some archaeologists to argue that it was imported as an already developed structural form. In the Hebrides, on the other hand, the presence of a class of small forts and duns with galleried walls seemed to point to an obvious source from which the complex broch towers evolved. In particular, a class of galleried dun with a stretch of high, hollow wall forming a curving barrier across the necks of natural headlands, typified by Dun Ardtreck on Skye and labelled *semi-brochs*, was seen as an important step in the development of the circular form. Evidence for the dating of 'semi-broch' sites is scarce, but what is available seems incapable of supporting arguments that they form an early stage in the development of the classic broch tower. Furthermore, there is considerable doubt as to whether the 'semi-broch' form could have achieved any great height, as the short stretch of free-standing wall which forms their main element lacks the structural stability of the circle which allowed the brochs to rise as towers.

At present, the evidence suggests that two independent traditions which later fused in the broch may be represented. In both the north and the west there appears to have been a tendency towards the use of height in architecture as a means of expressing social status. In Orkney, the massive roundhouses probably represent a first move towards the construction of prestige residences. The site at Howe, dated to c.300 BC, may mark an intermediate stage where an upper storey has been added. From this point it is but a short step to the fully developed broch form, and the occupants of Howe may have provided a receptive market to craftsmen bringing new techniques from the Hebrides which were grafted onto the local tradition. Certainly, at Howe the complex roundhouse was superseded roughly a century later by a massive broch.

In the Western Isles and western parts of the mainland the broch towers usually stand in isolation. In the northern mainland, and especially in the Northern Isles, however, the broch is usually placed within an elaborate complex of outer defences, possibly representing a development of the enclosures identified at Howe and Crosskirk. These clearly have a defensive role, to be seen with great effect at Midhowe on Rousay in Orkney where the promontory on which the broch stands is straddled by a massive stone-built rampart fronted by a deep, rock-cut ditch, or at Gurness where the broch is at the core of three concentric rings of wall and ditch. Defence, however, may have been a secondary consideration, for there is also unmistakably a bold declaration of status and prestige once again being made. At Gurness, for example, the causeway across the outer ditch and the gates through the concentric ramparts are all aligned on each other and on the doorway into the broch at their heart. Low buildings are clustered around the foot of the broch within the ramparts, and on either side of the entrance-way, again focusing attention on the towering structure at the centre. It is difficult not to see the structures clustered around the broch's walls as the homes of the social dependants of the tower's occupants, perhaps reflecting the inter-relationship between a war-leader and his followers. Clearly, there is a marked social distinction, reflected in the architecture, between those with the command of sufficient resources to undertake the building of such a massive statement of their power, and those whose homes were dominated by it. There can surely be no greater symbolism of how the broch-builders viewed their place in the social hierarchy than the placing of their towers at the heart of the settlement complex.

Duns

A parallel development to that of the brochs appears to be represented by the rather nebulous group of structures labelled collectively as *duns*. The name, which derives from the Gaelic *dun* (pronounced 'doon'), meaning a fortified place, is applied specifically to a wide range of small, generally circular or oval stone-walled forts with an internal area up to about 375 square metres. The distribution of these sites is concentrated primarily in Argyll, and more thinly throughout the west, where they overlap with areas of broch distribution, and in the south-west of Scotland. In general with much of Scottish archaeology they are an under-examined class of monument, but it is clear that they represent a remarkably long-lived tradition which remained popular into the later Middle Ages in some areas.

The walls of the duns appear most commonly to be constructed of a rubble core between two 'skins' of coursed stone. A variety of techniques were employed to stabilise this rubble fill, including the use of a pronounced external batter on the wall-face, and an internal revetment within the wall-core. Evidence for timber-lacing is demonstrated by occurrences of vitrification at some sites, such as Dun Skeig in Kintyre or Langwell in Sutherland, dated at the latter to

Figure 14: Dun Skeig, Argyllshire, hillfort and dun

1 Timber-laced wall (heavily vitrified)

2 Secondary dun using vitrified material in wall

3 Remains of outer defences

N →

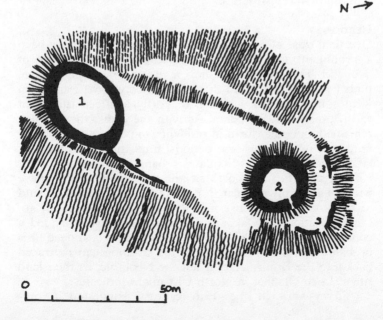

0   50m

87

construction in the 3rd century BC and destruction in the 1st century AD. In some instances galleries were used, possibly to permit building to greater height, or to provide added stability on uneven ground, as at Kildonan in Kintyre or Castlehaven in Galloway. This use of galleries stresses the relationship between brochs and duns discussed above.

The internal arrangements of duns remains uncertain ground, for excavation has generally failed to provide conclusive evidence for structures. In some small examples, such as that at Sunadale in Kintyre which measures only 6m by 4.5m, it is probable that the whole of the internal space was roofed, producing a structure akin to the massive roundhouses of the far north. In effect, these would have been fortified houses for an individual family. At larger sites, such as Castlehill Wood near Stirling, no clear evidence for internal structures was found, but galleries ranged round the inner face of the wall, or free-standing structures within the central area are both possible. There is less equivocal evidence from Ardifuar near Kilmartin in Argyll. There the dun wall is remarkably well preserved, and a scarcement survives running around the upper level. On the broch analogy, this can be interpreted as the supporting ledge for the roof of a single-storey internal range, or for the first floor of a multi-storey structure.

Crannogs
One final class of defended homestead appears to have been a prominent feature of the landscape in many parts of Scotland. This was the crannog, a class of monument where timber roundhouses with diameters of between 12 and 20m were constructed on artificial or partly artificial islands of earth, timber and boulders. As with the duns, the crannog remained a popular form of residence in parts of the country until well into the historic periods, until the government of later 16th-century Scotland banned their further construction. For the most part, the crannog appears to have become generally popular in the late 1st millennium BC, and to have continued in use into the early 1st millennium AD, but excavations at Oakbank in Loch Tay have provided a construction date in the mid-1st millennium BC. Indeed, it is probable that the antecedents of the crannog can be traced back into the Bronze Age, if not the Neolithic, as the island site at Loch Olabhat in North Uist might indicate.

Survey-work in the 19th century suggested a predominantly south-west Scottish distribution for this class of monument, but this bias seems largely to have been a product both of the localised fields of study of pioneers of crannog excavation – such as Robert Munro in Ayrshire – and the prominence of crannogs as features in a landscape where draining of lochs and marshes for agriculture was a continuing process. Early excavations, moreover, were limited only to those sites which stood either in drained ground, or which survived as stony islands on the margins of lochs. In the latter case, only those portions of the site above the level of the waters could be examined. The excavation in 1953 of a crannog at Milton Loch in Kirkcudbrightshire, a site visible only at times of severe drought, marked a milestone in crannog research. Here, it proved possible to explore at least part of the substructure of the platform, where large timbers survived in the water-logged conditions. C-14 dates from the timber piles driven into the loch-bed provided a date of construction in the 4th century BC, while finds from the platform indicated continuing occupation into the 2nd century AD.

Crannogs had long been recognised in other parts of the country, such as at Loch of Kinord in Aberdeenshire and Loch of Kinordy in Angus, or Loch Tearnait in Morvern, but detailed research in the last twenty years has dramatically increased both the geographical range of these monuments and the numbers recognised. The major Highland lochs, for example, particularly Loch Tay, Loch Awe and Loch Treig, have been shown to be fringed with crannogs, most of which are submerged. This discovery has major implications for the understanding of Iron Age population levels and land-use in upland districts, for they are concentrated in areas which had, until then, surprisingly low levels of recognisable settlement sites. The impression of a largely unpopulated central Highland massif must largely be reassessed.

Ritual and Burial
In contrast to the plethora of ritual and burial sites in earlier periods, comparatively little of the Iron Age has been identified with certainty. From around the late 8th century BC and continuing perhaps as late as the 7th or 8th centuries AD, the coastal site at Sculptor's Cave near Covesea in Moray functioned as an important ritual centre. Excavation here in the late 1920s produced large quantities of human bone, including the crania and cervical vertebrae, apparently

severed by a sharp blade, of several children. Head-hunting was a documented characteristic of Celtic society. Towards the rear of the cave were found many items of high quality decorative metalwork dating from the late Bronze Age onwards, all of which had been apparently thrown into a pool of standing water. This appears to parallel the ritual deposition of metalwork and sacrificial victims of similar date known from elsewhere in Britain and Europe, including the classic site of La Tène itself, where the mass of early ironwork had been thrown as votive offerings into the lake shallows, or the famous 'Lindow Man' found in a peat bog in Cheshire. Grouped near the cave entrance were disarticulated lower jaws from the child skulls, together with a series of stakeholes in the cave-floor deposits, interpreted as marking the support struts of wooden-framed racking. This has led to the suggestion that the heads were displayed on stakes until the flesh had rotted and the jaws fallen off, whereupon the crania were placed for display on the racks. This ritual deposit of votive material is attested elsewhere in Scotland. At Deskford in Banffshire, the 19th-century find-spot of the famous 'carnyx' or bronze trumpet-mouth fashioned in the shape of a boar's head, recent excavations have shown that it, along with other items, had been placed in what had been an area of pools and marsh in the Iron Age. The late Bronze Age deposit of tools and weapons, and fragments of a bronze cauldron, found in Duddingston Loch in Edinburgh, may also represent this tradition.

More formal foci for ritual activity, such as the 'temples' identified in south-eastern England, and the sanctuaries described by classical writers on the Continent, are rare. At Ballachulish in Argyllshire a crudely carved wooden figurine of a naked woman was found within the remains of a little wickerwork hut. The figure is of a style which can be attributed on the Continent to the 1st century BC or earlier, but it would also fit descriptions of pagan cult imagery preserved in early Christian writings of the earlier 1st millennium AD. What also appears to have been an Iron Age ritual site was excavated adjacent to the Neolithic long barrow at Dalladies in Kincardineshire. There, a complex of pits, postholes and ditches stretched over an area some 400m by 30m on the gravel terrace above the North Esk. Artefact evidence for domestic activity was lacking, although there were traces of what could have been two huts – shrines, cult-houses? – but the ditches showed signs of having filled rapidly with dark soil which contained large quantities of charcoal and calcined bone. Amongst the finds were several horse and cattle skulls. The evidence in general points towards a ritual function, but a funerary role was also implied by evidence for both cremation and the disposal of the cremated remains on the site.

As in earlier periods, there appears to have been no single form of funerary tradition practised throughout Scotland in the Iron Age. Cremation is attested at Dalladies, and at Glenluce in Wigtownshire, dated by the inclusion of 2nd century AD Roman Samian pottery with the burials, but inhumation in cists appears to have a wide distribution. These could be short cists, presumably representing continuity of rite from the Bronze Age, to much larger forms, such as that from Lochend at Dunbar which contained the remains of 21 inhumations. Also in Lothian, a series of cemeteries comprising burials within oval or round pits, occasionally stone-lined and flagged, have been identified at Dryburn Bridge, Broxmouth and Winton House, apparently representing a local tradition which spanned the period from the mid-1st millennium BC to the 1st century AD. Extending into the early 1st millennium is a second cist tradition with a distribution restricted largely to the region between the Tyne and the Forth, comprising mainly cists with walls formed by coursed stonework. At North Belton Farm near Dunbar, for example, a slab-covered cist of this form was found to contain two flexed inhumations lying side by side. The four long cist burials which represent the final phase in the long functional lifetime of the ritual and burial complex at Cairnpapple Hill appear to be pre-Christian, but the use of long cist interments was to continue well into the Christian era. The general rarity of burial sites to which a securely Iron Age date can be assigned, however, suggests that the elaborate cist burials encountered in Lothian and Berwickshire, and related forms elsewhere, may mark the burial places of the wealthy elite in society. Indeed, the scarcity of Iron Age burials in contrast to the abundance of funerary monuments of earlier periods has been taken to indicate that the approach to death and burial in the later 1st millennium BC might, for most individuals, have been a rather perfunctory disposal of the remains, possibly involving elaborate ritual but unmarked by a formal tomb.

Art and Metalwork

Finds of high-quality metalwork in iron, bronze and gold, or gold alloy, point again to a wealthy warrior-aristocracy who functioned as major patrons of craftsmen. Much of this material, however, post-dates the arrival of the Romans in southern Britain, indeed, little pre-dates the first Roman incursions into Scotland in 78 AD. Amongst the earliest of the finds is a bronze pony cap of 2nd-century BC date found at Torrs near Kirkcudbright in conjunction with what have been identified as two drinking horns. The cap is largely decorated with repousse (raised decoration hammered through from the reverse side) and appears to be of a style produced in the English east Midlands. It had been patched in antiquity, and is now thought to have reached Galloway as an heirloom. Other late 1st-millennium BC finds include a hoard of gold alloy items from Shaw Hill in Peeblesshire. This comprised three penannular twisted torcs (flexible necklets of cable-twisted wires), a torc-terminal, and upwards of forty electrum coins from the Paris region, but only the terminal and two of the coins survive. The terminal has clear parallels in eastern England, such as the torc from Snettisham in Norfolk, and is datable to the early 1st century BC. Fine sword scabbards from the Tweed at Carham, and from Bargany House in Ayrshire, are also of 1st-century BC date, the latter possibly representing an import from Ulster or a copy modelled on Irish examples by a local smith. Taken together, these finds amply illustrate the Celtic warrior's love of display, lavishing his wealth not only on personal adornment and finely finished weaponry, but also on his mount or the trappings of his chariot-horses.

Economy

There is no question that the hierarchical structure described in the foregoing sections was supported by anything other than an agricultural economy, but the basis of that economy, whether arable or pastoral, remains an area of debate. Some fifty years ago, it had been recognised that the development of Iron Age Celtic society in south-eastern Britain had seen the intensification of agriculture and a marked increase in cereal production. The prominence of ears of wheat in the symbolism used on Celtic gold coins of the late 1st century BC, such as those produced by the *Catuvellauni*, leave little doubt as to what kings like Cunobelin saw as the foundation of their people's power and wealth. Generalised arguments which sought to apply the same situation to northern England and Scotland, however, were challenged some forty years ago, as there were clearly recognisable regional differences in the archaeological evidence. In particular, there was little trace of the recognisable patterns of small 'Celtic' fields in northern regions, nor was there much evidence for the kinds of storage pits for cereals which had been identified in southern settlements. Excavations at Stanwick in Yorkshire, recognised as the tribal 'capital' of the *Brigantes*, a major tribe whose territories sprawled from Yorkshire, across the Pennines and northwards to the Cheviots, further stressed the differences in agricultural economy, for large areas of the earthwork enclosures around the site appeared to be corrals for cattle and horses. This, together with reliance on classical sources such as the history of Cassius Dio, written in the mid-3rd century AD, who made the comment that the tribes of north-eastern Scotland, while capable of fielding a substantial army, neither lived in permanent settlements nor supported themselves through cultivation, but pursued a pastoral lifestyle, led to arguments that the economy in the north was based on pastoralism and supported a society which included a nomadic element.

This picture seemed to fit the evidence as it stood in the 1950s, where limited research in upland areas of the country had as yet failed to identify remains which would point to alternative images. There were a few individual sites which appeared to be associated with extensive field systems, but in general the landscape presented an open aspect in which Stuart Piggott envisaged a society of 'Celtic cow-boys and shepherds, footloose and unpredictable, moving with their animals over rough pasture and moorland'. This would imply a high degree of social fragmentation, and while it might fit the more dispersed circumstances of settlement in the north and west, it is more difficult to envisage in the more intensively settled zones of the south and east. Pastoralism is, however, certainly well attested in historical sources in both classical and Irish sources, and in the latter cattle are indeed reckoned as the indicator of noble wealth rather than the grown produce. As the *Tain Bo Cuailgne* clearly demonstrates, however, in the Ireland of the 1st millennium AD, while the herdsmen might live a semi-nomadic existence following their charges, the owners of the cattle lived a settled life in their homesteads. In parts of the Southern Uplands there is physical evidence which might support the idea of free-ranging herds moving in a relatively open landscape of grasslands, but in association with fixed settlements rather than as part of some semi-nomadic system. At some forts, such as Woden Law in Roxburghshire, outlying earthworks – referred to as *cross-dykes* – cut across ridge-tops and the necks of promontories, effectively controlling rapid movement across open ground. Similar features occur in Yorkshire, associated with the great complex around Stanwick, in Wales, and in the south of England, where they appear to have functioned both as land divisions and defensive barriers designed to impede a form of warfare and raiding that depended on chariotry. In southern Scotland a defensive role is favoured over that of territorial division, but it is possible that the cross-dykes in the Cheviots were designed to isolate the grazing land of neighbouring communities, or even to separate pasture from arable, as seems to be the case at Arbory Hill in Clydesdale.

The extreme view of a fragmented pastoral society predominating in northern Britain has been challenged in recent years, having been shown to be as over-generalised as the image of a cereal-based economy which it replaced. Indeed, research has pointed rather towards a broad range of approaches to agriculture which depended on local climatic and topographical character. Where conditions favoured it, there was a move towards a mixed farming base, certainly with more intensive arable agriculture if it could be supported, but always with an element of both pastoral and arable. Again, even following the rapid climatic deterioration of the Middle Bronze Age, mixed agriculture seems to have been the basis of the farming economy.

More intensive aerial photographic reconnaissance in the Southern Uplands and in Perthshire in recent years has served to change our impression of land-use in these areas over the last two millennia, with extensive areas of cultivation associated with settlement – of later prehistoric as well as medieval date – being recognised. On the ground, traces of field systems and cairnfields had long been recognised in some upland zones, especially in the northern Highlands. Where the peat had been stripped back, either through moorland fires or erosion, some groups of cairns were noted as lying in close association with long 'rickles' of stone and possibly with hut circles. The rickles could be seen to bound areas of stone-free ground, the obvious inference being that here were cleared agricultural plots, probably cultivated using spades or hoes rather than ploughs. Extensive areas of plough cultivation, however, are attested in northern Scotland in the Bronze Age, as is indicated by the evidence from Lairg, while the long fields recognised at Tulloch Wood in Moray point to tilling rather than spade cultivation. It is unclear, however, both from these sites and from the earlier excavations at Kilphedir, as to what extent there was continuity of agricultural practices in the north from the later Bronze Age: at Lairg there appears to have been a shift towards stock-rearing, while at Tulloch Wood the nature of land-use in the Iron Age is ambiguous. Again, however, there is a probability that a mixed farming approach was adopted, it having been pointed out that there is a tendency for later prehistoric settlements to cluster along the break-point between lowland arable and upland pasture. This can be seen clearly, for example, at Glen Brittle in Skye, where hut circles lie along the line followed by the head dyke of the pre-Improvement township which divided the rough grazing on the lower slopes of the Cuillins from the better pasture and cultivated land below. The un-excavated site at Stanshiel Rig in Dumfriesshire, however, points to the difficulties of generalising from such a narrow sample of evidence as is currently available. There, clearance cairns are clearly associated with both small plots defined by low banks and with hut circles, but there are also long axial banks which imply larger field divisions similar to the Tulloch Wood Bronze Age examples, but suggested without excavation at Stanshiel to indicate Roman influence, and trackways and some enclosures which might represent droveways and corrals for cattle. There is little doubt that the different features represent a sequence of differing approaches to land-use, but the chronology and order of the sequence is impossible to determine without excavation.

Later Iron Age Folk Movements and the Impact of the Romans

The increasing levels of contact between Britain and the European mainland in the later 1st millennium BC may have forced the pace of cultural and social development, but the active intervention of the culturally more advanced and politically sophisticated power of imperial Rome was to radically and irreversibly realign the pattern of change. The arrival of the Romans, however, was simply the last in a series of movements which had brought about far-reaching developments in regions far removed from their political and cultural epicentres. A combination of political and economic circumstances in the north of Gaul in the last couple of centuries BC had resulted in the movement across the Channel of substantial numbers of Belgic migrants, who settled in the south-east of England. The *Belgae* were a Celtic people, but their late La Tène culture was of the highest order, producing without doubt some of the finest metalwork yet to appear in these islands. They introduced, too, new techniques in the production of pottery, bringing wheel-thrown ceramic technology. In terms of social organisation also they were more highly developed than their new neighbours, displaying a tendency towards urbanisation in their major settlements and moving towards a fully developed institution of kingship in their government.

The repercussions of the Belgic invasions may have been felt throughout Britain. It has been suggested that what does in fact appear to have been a substantial folk movement may have resulted in significant population displacement within the British Isles, with elements of the earlier Celtic peoples being driven out of their former territories. There are some hints of folk movement in the tribal names recorded in Ptolemy's map of the early 2nd century AD. For example, tribes sharing the name *Cornovii* occur both in the Shropshire-Cheshire area of England and in Caithness, and there seems likely to be some inter-relationship between the *Dumnonii* of Cornwall and the *Damnonii* of southern Strathclyde. Pottery and artefact material from sites in the Hebrides, such as from the pre-broch period at Dun Mor Vaul in Tiree, or from Clettraval in North Uist, has been taken as evidence for northwards migration from the Wessex district of southern England in the earlier Iron Age, but this is a contentious issue as much of the material evidence has a broad chronological range. Migration from the Somerset-Wessex area into the Irish Sea and Atlantic west of Scotland in the 1st century BC, moreover, has been linked by some to the development of broch architecture, but recent research is pushing the dates of broch development back towards the 2nd and 3rd centuries BC and points firmly towards evolution from long-established local building traditions. In the south and east of Scotland there are also possible indications of change brought about by the arrival of immigrants, possibly displaced by the Belgic invasions of the later 1st millennium BC, or slightly later by the Roman invasion and occupation of Britain begun by the Emperor Claudius. Here, the development of multivallate defences around settlement sites may stem from the introduction of new technology by migrant peoples, but without a wider range of dating evidence from excavated sites, an open verdict must be delivered in this case also.

Population displacement may again have resulted from the Claudian invasion of south-eastern England in 43 AD, but as there is little indication for any significant impact on the Scottish cultural horizon until the later 70s it is probable that it was the extension of Roman military activity into the north of England which triggered any movement. At present, the only clear evidence for the arrival of new elements among the native population of Scotland is in the sphere of sophisticated metalwork, and it is possible that what – if any – migration occurred was limited to displaced aristocracy with their followers. Such refugee war-bands of nobles and their supporters are attested in later Celtic contexts, with British warriors displaced from their homelands in northern England by Anglian settlement in the 7th century AD active in northern Ireland as mercenaries. Displacement of aristocracies, however, may also have seen the craftsmen whom they patronised following their erstwhile patrons into exile. It is perhaps significant that the two main sources of influence detectable in the exotic new metalwork forms which appear in Scotland by the later 1st century AD are the *Iceni* of East Anglia, whose kingdom was suppressed by the Romans in 60 AD following the revolt of Queen Boudicca, and the Brigantes in northern England, whose kingdom was likewise occupied by the Roman military in the early 70s.

For the most part, the new metalwork forms comprise high-quality decorative items and pieces of horse and military harness. The collection of fine bronzework found in a hoard at Balmaclellan in Kirkcudbrightshire, for example, which included a magnificent polished hand-mirror, included pieces decorated with compass-drawn motifs infilled with engraved basket-work of a clearly Brigantian style datable to the later 1st century AD. Related in style is a magnificent bronze collar from Stichill near Kelso, and a bronze scabbard from Mortonhall in Edinburgh. Perhaps the finest piece of Brigantian influenced work, however, is the Deskford Carnyx. This, the boar's head-shaped mouth of a bronze trumpet, once fitted with a movable wooden tongue and with eyes of brightly-coloured enamel, is of a type of instrument common in the Celtic world. One scene on the Gundestrup Cauldron from northern Denmark depicts a group of trumpeters blowing such instruments, and shows that the heads were mounted on long trumpet-tubes. The blowing of such instruments is attested in classical sources, where they are described as part of the Celts' pre-battle psychological terror-tactics aimed at disconcerting the enemy. The Deskford example is believed to be the product of a Brigantian refugee craftsman and is datable to after *c.*70 AD. Icenian influence is clearly discernable in a hoard of bronze horse-harness mounts from Middlebie in Dumfriesshire. Suggestions that these were produced locally for an exiled Icenian warrior, however, are largely discounted in favour of the finer pieces being genuine imports manufactured in East Anglia, while those items with more restricted and stereotyped decoration are of local manufacture influenced by the original Icenian work.

While the arrival of the Romans within what is now Scotland can be charted quite clearly on the ground in the form of their distinctive military works, the significance of that arrival on the native societies is more difficult to determine. *Multivallate* forts, it has already been suggested, may have appeared in advance of the Roman invasion, possibly as an innovation brought by refugees from the south or more probably simply as a symptom of general developments in military technology. The appearance of defences around previously undefended settlements, or elaboration of existing ones – as at Hownam Rings in Roxburghshire – can perhaps be attributed to anticipation of the Roman threat. One phenomenon which is in urgent need of research is that of the unfinished hillfort. Several of these are known from Scotland, ranging from Cademuir Hill in Peeblesshire to Cnoc an Duin in Easter Ross, but the majority are concentrated in the north-east proper, which may have been the main theatre of military operations under Gnaeus Julius Agricola in the 80s AD. At Dun Mor in Perthshire, overlooking the site of the 1st-century Roman fort at Fendoch at the junction of Glen Almond and the Sma' Glen, the fort, which is situated at an elevation of 465m, seems to have advanced little further than the piling of stones for use in the ramparts, while at Little Conval in Banffshire, some 550m above sea-level, the ramparts are represented simply by marker trenches and low spreads of stone. At Dunnideer in Aberdeenshire, work seems to have commenced on the refurbishment of an earlier vitrified fort, but was abandoned before more than some short stretches of rampart and marker trenches had been completed. Further examples where little more than marker trenches for the line of the projected ramparts were completed occur at Hill o' Christ's Kirk across the valley from Dunnideer; at Durn Hill near Portsoy in Banffshire; and at Knockargetty Wood in Cromar in western Aberdeenshire. It is tempting to see such sites as the results of a scramble for protection as the Roman advance approached, but which were either overtaken by events or abandoned in progress as the Romans withdrew from the country beyond the Forth in about 90 AD.

The abandonment of Roman attempts at total conquest of Scotland after the 1st century AD saw the emergence of distinct zones over which the Romans exercised a greater or lesser degree of influence. In the Southern Uplands in particular, where Roman military control was periodically rigorously reasserted with the northward movement of the frontier to the Forth-Clyde line, or where supervision was exercised from outpost forts in advance of the main frontier on the line of Hadrian's Wall, the impact was clearly greatest. Understandably, an occupying military power was unlikely to tolerate either the existence of substantial defences around important native settlements, nor continuance of the regime of cattle-raiding and inter-tribal warfare which had spawned the hillforts. Both factors would have rendered the policing of the sensitive frontier zone difficult, while the latter would have reduced the potential for tax exploitation by the Roman authorities. The efforts of the Romans to make a real profit from their military domination of southern Scotland should not be overlooked or underestimated. After all, it was partly through the over-zealousness of Roman tax-collectors that the northern frontier suffered its first major crisis at the end of the 2nd century AD.

The tightness of the Roman's supervisory grip over the Southern Upland zone may best be seen in the evidence for the sighting of defences at several sites. At Hownam Rings, for example, the heavily-defended settlement of the later 1st century AD was succeeded by an unenclosed group of circular, stone-walled houses. At Edin's Hall in Berwickshire, circular stone-walled houses partly overlie the defences of an earlier fort, while both here and at Torwoodlee near Galashiels brochs which had been built within or partly overlying earlier fort defences in the early 2nd century AD were apparently slighted by the Romans as they readvanced towards the Forth in the 140s AD. The stone-built houses of the type which superseded the fortified settlement at Hownam Rings appear to be part of a general trend from building in timber to a stone tradition which occurred throughout the south-east of Scotland and northern England. For the most part, Celtic settlement within the Cheviot area in the Roman period is characterised by small sub-circular stone-walled enclosures which contain stone-built houses opening off a sunken yard, as at Cockburn's Law in Berwickshire, but in the western Borders a different tradition developed. Here, rather than a stone tradition, settlement forms are dominated by small earthen embanked enclosures which contained circular wooden houses. The classic excavation of this class was at Boonies near Langholm in Eskdale, where an enclosure of only some 0.07 ha contained originally just one timber house at the rear of the enclosure. This had been rebuilt on seven successive occasions, the final rebuilding also seeing the expansion of settlement to five houses.

Further north, in the country beyond the Forth, the Roman presence may have led to the development of another form of structure whose origins appear to lie earlier in the Iron Age. These are *souterrains* or earth-houses, semi- or wholly subterranean stone-lined passages associated with substantial farmsteads. They have an extensive distribution extending from Tayside to Shetland and display strongly regional characteristics in their scale and planning. Amongst the largest and most sophisticated are those in Angus and eastern Perthshire, such as the excavated examples at Ardestie and Carlungie between Dundee and Arbroath, the now destroyed site at Newmill north of Perth, and the unexcavated site at Pitcur between Dundee and Coupar Angus. These, in contrast to the sites from Orkney, typified by those at Grain and Rennibister, would have been clearly visible from above ground and were obviously not intended as concealed refuges. Current opinion favours the view that they are large 'cellars' for the bulk storage of agricultural produce, probably grain. Alternative interpretations, some of which require serious consideration, have been advanced, including a ritual function as 'sensory deprivation chambers' where initiates partook of hallucinogenic drugs!

The dating and development of the souterrains is

problematic, once again largely as a consequence of the limited number of excavated examples and the early date at which most excavations were conducted. Recent fieldwork in north-east Fife, coupled with detailed aerial survey of the Carse of Gowrie on the opposite side of the Tay estuary, has thrown much new light on the development of the form. A series of elongated banana-shaped cropmarks associated with settlement sites have been identified, and excavation of one at North Straiton near Leuchars confirmed the suspicion that these were an early form of souterrain. In the North Straiton example, the trench was a mere 60cm deep, 1m wide and 10m long, closer in scale to the simple Shetland form, and was associated with a large ring-groove house (where the circular groove marks the site of the house walls). Pottery from the house indicated a date in the last couple of centuries BC. The site at Newmill, excavated in advance of road improvements on the A9, indicated construction and use in the earlier 1st century AD, i.e. before the Roman incursions, and represents a developed form with the passage here being some 20m long and 4m wide at its far end, its deep cut revetted by dry-stone walling. At Ardestie and Carlungie occupation and use extended into the 2nd century, but it appears that in all excavated examples they had gone out of use by the early 3rd century. Excavations at Hawkhill, Easter Kinnear near Kilmany in north-east Fife have unearthed what may represent the successor to the linear passage form of souterrain, circular cellars located directly below the timber house rather than curving around its exterior as in the earlier forms. C-14 dating from the site suggested construction in the 6th or 7th century AD, securely within the historical Pictish period.

The major development of the souterrain form in Fife and Tayside in the late 1st millennium BC, and certainly in the 1st and 2nd centuries BC, has been linked to expansion of cereal production. This is and was grain-producing country, and there is the potential that large agricultural surpluses could have been stored in these substantial cellars. The sites with which they are associated, moreover, appear to be high-status farmsteads, possibly the residence of a local chieftain: the circular house associated with the Newmill souterrain was 17.6m in diameter, indicating an establishment on a par with the Scotstarvit and Greencraigs homesteads in Fife. The scale of some of the souterrains – if they are indeed cellars – indicates that storage was on a scale that would have vastly exceeded possible domestic consumption. Unless these were communal grain stores under the supervision of the local chieftain, it seems probable that surpluses were sold on or taken as tribute. The discovery of Roman artefacts, mainly glass and pottery, or ornamental metalwork, indicates the probable destination of the grain, and it is perhaps not entirely coincidental that the main development of the souterrains appears to coincide with the Antonine readvance into Scotland in the mid-2nd century AD and the re-establishment of the old line of garrisoned forts from Camelon near Falkirk via Strathallan and Strathearn to the Tay. Clearly, our traditional interpretation of the confrontational nature of Roman and native relations requires reassessment, particularly for the zones beyond the immediate area of political domination and military occupation.

Figure 15: Ardestie, Angus, souterrain

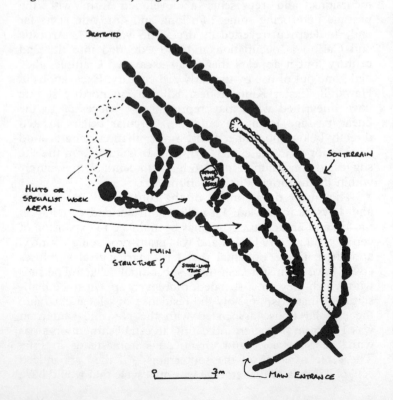

Attitudes towards the relationship of Roman and native in northern Britain have been changing in academic circles in recent years. The discovery of quantities of high-quality Roman artefacts on native settlement sites of later 1st-and 2nd-century date has been subject to various interpretations in the past, with salvage from abandoned Roman military establishments a favoured explanation. The quantity and quality of the items involved, however, favour the alternative view that these are traded goods, probably obtained in exchange for agricultural produce or the exotic merchandise for which the northern territories were famed – skins, hunting dogs, etc. The fine Roman material from the crannog at Hyndford in Lanarkshire, where native items indicate high-status occupants, might point towards deliberate cultivation of the local leaders of native society as part of traditional policies of Romanisation. Tacitus, at his most scathing, talks of the 'captivity' of the Britons in the civil province established in southern Britain, where, won over by the trappings of Roman civilisation, they have given up their liberty and subjected themselves willingly to Rome.

Submission to Rome rather than the consequences of opposition appears to have been the favoured option of some of the tribes of southern Scotland. In contrast with the high density of Roman military posts in the territory of the Selgovae in the central Southern Uplands, the coastal plain stretching from Lothian into Northumberland occupied by the Votadini, and the territories west of Clydesdale occupied by the Damnonii are almost devoid of Roman sites. Here, it has been suggested, the native rulers entered some kind of client relationship with Rome, similar to that of King Cogidubnus of the *Atrebates*, or Queen Cartimandua of the Brigantes, where the Romans gained a stable frontier and the native powers gained the economic benefits of access to Roman markets. But the dangers of basing such interpretations on the absence of firm archaeological or documentary evidence has recently been tellingly demonstrated with regard to Fife. Like Votadinian territory, the land of the *Venicones* in Fife is devoid of Roman military sites with the exception of a line of marching camps cutting down through the north-east end of the peninsula. Instead, the Romans established a strongly-defended line along the western periphery of Fife, from the Stirling Gap to the Tay at Perth. Here, it has been suggested, was a deep buffer zone to protect a client state from the anti-Roman tribes beyond.

It was an interpretation which the absence of Roman sites in the area seemed to support. Recent pollen analysis research, however, has indicated that there was a sharp reduction in agriculture in at least north Fife and an equal increase in the level of tree pollens both during and after the Roman period. This is, of course, open to several interpretations, but a sharp decline in agriculture is certainly at odds with what would appear to be its expansion in the supposedly more hostile territory beyond the Tay. Perhaps in Fife we are in fact seeing the consequences of resistance to Rome, devastation and depopulation? Were there no Roman forts in Fife for the simple reason that the native population had been systematically decimated? The fact that genocide was the solution contemplated in the early 3rd century by the emperor, Septimius Severus, to the threat posed to the stability of the northern frontier by the Maeatae shows that such an approach to an ungovernable area was not beyond the Romans.

Clearly, we should not underestimate the reach of Roman power and their flexibility of response to the native societies of Scotland. Even beyond the effective reach of their land armies, their powerful fleets could terrorise and punish raiders based in remote regions. The ebb and flow of the Roman military presence in southern Scotland has tended to mask the relative stability of the north for much of the 2nd and 3rd centuries, evidence, perhaps for the reality of the pax Romana. It is perhaps no coincidence that in the Northern and Western Isles during this same period brochs fade out of use, to be replaced by less clearly defensive settlement forms. Perhaps again the economics of co-operation with Rome offered better prospects than the uncertainties of conflict? A new prosperity certainly seems to have been the reward for peace with Rome for large parts of central, eastern and southern Scotland, and the stability which the Roman military authorities imposed seems to have led towards greater political development amongst the Celtic tribes in these areas, favouring the formation of the great supra-tribal confederations which had emerged by the end of the 2nd century. Political cohesion was probably Rome's greatest legacy to the peoples who fused together to form the first historically attested kingdoms within Scotland, but with them we move into the realms of history and beyond the scope of this book.

5

INTO HISTORY

WHERE DOES the boundary between the Prehistoric and Historic periods fall? Like so many other of the chronological dividing lines in our past, it is a question to which easy answers are given, although there is in fact no truly sharp division which has a relevance for the whole of Scotland. It also lacks any relevance in strictly cultural terms, for the beginning of recorded history is something abstract, something which had no physical impact on society at large. It is, in fact, a symptom of change in society rather than a cause, and at that a symptom which by its very obvious self-advertisement tends to distract attention from the underlying cross-currents of continuity and change.

Conventional arguments begin the historical period in Scotland with the arrival of the Romans. For the first time, events and places are recorded and described with a level of detail which allows us to add living flesh, almost literally, to the bare bones of the previously voiceless cultures of the remoter past. These are living voices, giving expression to the humanity of these ancient peoples, allowing us to see, hear and experience the emotions, aspirations and inner thoughts of individuals in whom we can recognise ourselves. This is something which archaeology can never hope to achieve for the prehistoric, which will always remain mute no matter how much imaginative interpretation and social reconstruction we indulge in. This does not mean that the study of prehistory is inferior to that of the historic, nor should it be used as a lever in the pointless, but seemingly unending, academic debate over which of history or archaeology is the superior discipline. Both have different levels of story to express, providing a means of access to different aspects of our past and so furnishing us with a more detailed picture of the whole. Unfortunately, however, there is an automatic tendency to regard the 'beginning of history' as a radical new departure in human development, in effect cutting the historic period off from its prehistoric roots. What we must not lose sight of is the fact that what our earliest historical sources are describing to us is the same world that quite literally moments before was the prehistoric.

It is only a new departure in the sense that we now have one more form of evidence to be used in our interpretations of the past, providing us with a window onto the non-physical mechanisms for change. History allows us to see our ancestors as the movers of change, actively moulding their destiny rather than as often passive victims responding to circumstances beyond their control. It allows us to see the causes of change, rather than just the symptoms reflected in new features of the material culture.

There is a danger when faced with the brave new world of the historic period of becoming caught up in the flow of change recorded in the narrative and to lose touch with the continuities from the unrecorded past which are evident in its fabric. For example, we should not lose sight of the fact that the Celtic tribes named by the Alexandrian geographer Ptolemy, writing between 140 and 150 AD, are the descendants of the previously un-named inhabitants of the Scottish landscape, builders and occupiers of the prehistoric monuments which litter the countryside, and probable lineal descendants for the most part of the earliest agricultural colonists of this country; the recording of their name in the photographic flash of an historical snapshot is all that divides the historical Votadini or Guotodin of the Lothian plain from the prehistoric inhabitants of Traprain Law. They did not become the Votadini at the instant when Ptolemy entered their name on his map, but must have been known by that name for an unguessable period beforehand. In reality, the recording of their name changed nothing materially, other than to provide us with a label by which to differentiate them from their neighbours and their eventual successors, and a noun from which clues about their spoken language can be extracted. Four thousand years of cultural development did not reach its climax in the simple recording of a name.

In many ways, the beginning of recorded history is a phenomenon which both illuminates and blinds. Provided with names of places and individuals, we can follow the fortunes of kings, heroes and holy men, trace their movement around the country, see where, how and when they died. Events detectable in the archaeological record, such as the burning of a major stronghold, or the founding of a monastery, give us convenient pegs on which to hang our chronologies. But even at its best, our early documentary sources offer just a series of isolated, disjointed flashes of light in a sea of darkness. It is only by looking away from these brief bursts of information, which draw our attention like moths drawn to a candle-flame, that we can see the bigger picture which remains in the background, and that is a picture of continuity of the patterns of life established in the yet more ancient past.

While it is always dangerous to argue and reconstruct backwards from documentary evidence, it is of course possible to identify many features of our historic past which can be reasonably presented as of much more ancient – prehistoric – ancestry. The manner in which our more recent ancestors viewed and worked the land, how they measured and divided it, and the labels which they applied to it, all can be shown to have origins in at least the Iron Age, if not earlier. It must be recognised that the pattern of agricultural life which predominated in most of Scotland until the later 18th century, and which in parts of the Highlands and Islands survived into the middle of the 20th, were established by the later prehistoric. In terms of landownership, our historical documentation – chronicles, poetry, charters – allow us to trace successive changes in possession of particular portions of land, as families have risen to prominence or failed, or where wholly new waves of colonists have moved in to assert dominance, but until the later Middle Ages the blocks into which the land was divided passed from hand to hand as an unbroken whole. Quite simply, ruling elites were being supplanted, but their properties were passing intact to their successors. Although the evidence becomes increasingly fragmentary the further back in time we move, it remains clear that many of the landed estates which we can identify in the early Middle Ages have their origins in much earlier periods. In some areas of the country, such as Galloway, it is possible to see where various estates passed in the 7th century into the hands of an incoming colonial elite of *Angles* of Northumbrian origin, while others remained in the possession of the native Celtic aristocracy, descendants of the Iron Age *Novantae* of south-western Scotland. Some idea of local patterns of power in the undocumented centuries before *c*.600 AD in this region can be built backwards from such fragments, and it is not stretching the evidence too thinly to suggest that the territorial units which can be identified in this early historic period represent a pattern of land division which had been established in the early centuries AD, if not earlier still.

Similar patterns of succession in property can be argued for in many parts of Scotland. In the Border Counties, the stone-walled houses and farm enclosures which make their appearance in the 2nd century AD remain as the model of wealthier farming communities into the 6th and 7th centuries AD, and can be seen as the residences of the re-emergent warrior aristocracy of the documented petty kingdoms of the Southern Uplands, which were ultimately absorbed into the expanding kingdom of the Northumbrian Angles. Here, many of the native Celtic lords were also simply absorbed into the power structure of their new overlords, or where the natives – descended from the Selgovan and Votadinian nobility – were displaced, their entire estate was bestowed on a member of the Northumbrian ruling elite, as occurred at Doon Hill near Dunbar in East Lothian. In this way, patterns of power already well established in the immediate post-Roman period were fossilised and brought down intact to later generations. North of the Forth, in the heart of the early medieval Scottish kingdom, it is possible to argue for a similar degree of continuity. Here, the Pictish kingdoms which flourished from the 6th to 9th centuries AD can be shown without question to be directly descended from the late Iron Age Celtic tribes of north-east Scotland. Within them, the patterns of land-use and landed power identifiable in the later documentation can be seen as manifestations of a continuity, in at least general terms, from the later Prehistoric.

It is, of course, possible also to see great levels of continuity and survival fossilised in the modern landscape in the place-name record. Place-name scholars have succeeded in showing how names have been laid down in layers, like rock strata, as successive linguistic groups moved into the country. By stripping away those which can be shown to be of recent ancestry, it is possible to recover evidence for the manner in which our ancestors viewed the landscape and labelled it to suit their own needs. The vast bulk of the place-names on the modern map are of Gaelic or English origin, and can be assigned with confidence to the historic period and the beginnings of Scottic migration from Ireland, and the establishment of Anglo-Saxon colonies in southern and eastern Britain. Below them, however, can be identified strata of different origin, chiefly deriving from so-called *p*-Celtic languages (that is those represented nowadays by

Breton and Welsh and formerly spoken throughout mainland Britain by its Celtic inhabitants), as opposed to *q*-Celtic (Irish and Scots Gaelic). On strict historical grounds, the elimination of the Celtic kingdoms of the Southern Uplands in the later 6th and 7th centuries AD can be seen as marking the end of any significant name-forming in *p*-Celtic in those areas, as the new political masters were speakers of the Germanic Anglian tongue. Even allowing for the survival of elements of a native nobility, and of a substantial *p*-Celtic-speaking peasantry, the place-name record shows that Anglian swiftly established itself as the dominant spoken and name-forming language. Elsewhere in Scotland, in the vast sweep of land from the British kingdom of Strathclyde through Pictland in the north and north-east into Sutherland, it was *q*-Celtic Gaelic that supplanted the indigenous *p*-Celtic tongue, and it can be expected that the supplanting of one Celtic language by another, closely related version, has produced some blurring of the picture, but here too it is possible to sift out older strata from the layers of younger names.

In these *p*-Celtic place-names we are hearing the spoken language of the historic successors of our late Prehistoric ancestors. The date of the coining of many of these names, however, must remain open to question as there is no possibility of ever determining how long one had been in currency before it was first recorded on parchment. Certain of the name forms identifiable allow us to distinguish between two main dialect groups within the *p*-Celtic areas in Scotland, with a Pictish area focused largely in the north-east and a so-called Cumbric zone in the region south of the Forth-Clyde line, and from this it is possible to make general observations as to dating. For example names containing the generic *Pit-* (as in Pitreavie, Pitcaple, Pitbladdo) are seen as deriving from *pett*, meaning a portion or share (of land), and have a distribution limited almost exclusively to the heartland of the historical Pictish kingdoms. This is seen as evidence for the main currency of the term in the period from the later 5th century AD when the Picts were emerging as a distinct cultural group. In the Cumbric zone, a similar role is played by names containing the generic *cair-*, meaning a defended settlement (as in Caerlaverock, Carfrae, Caerlanrig). Studies of such place-names generally suggest currency and coinage of the name forms in the post-Roman period, once the dialects within the main *p*-Celtic group within Scotland had begun to diverge. It has to be asked, however, to what extent the form of the name in its first recorded version should be seen as representing a freshly coined example rather than a re-expression of an older name in the then current, fashionable dialect form.

Celtic place-names of greater antiquity do also survive in early documentary sources. Ptolemy's mid-2nd century AD map, for example, takes us one step further back. His map sets out 1st-century circumstances, largely detailing Roman military sites which had been abandoned around 90 AD when the Emperor Domitian withdrew troops from Britain to fight in campaigns on the Danube frontier, and records several place-names alongside those of the major tribal groups. In many cases these are native names applied to Roman forts, e.g. *Blatobulgium*, interpreted as meaning 'flour-sack' and identified with the fort at Birrens, which was a major supply centre with three large granaries. Some, such as *Rerigonium*, meaning 'very royal (place)', and represented now by Loch Ryan and Stranraer, however, may represent the transference of a Celtic name from a nearby native site to the new Roman establishment. Alongside these place-names which may be of late 1st-century AD origin are still older examples which might possibly stem from the earliest period of dominance of the Celtic language in Scotland. These are, for the most part, river-names. Research into them has shown that even in areas where Celtic languages were eliminated very early in the historic period – as in east and south-east England, for example – while most Celtic names had disappeared as English took over as the most common spoken language, the mainly Celtic names for the major rivers were absorbed into the toponymy of the new dominant language. Ptolemy's *Devona*, probably to be identified with the temporary camp at Kintore, represents the transference of the neighbouring river-name to the military site. This, now the Aberdeenshire Don, derives from the Celtic noun for a god or divinity. With such names, we are entering the landscape of mid-1st-millennium BC Scotland. But the line of descent does not end there.

Recorded amongst the river-names, and stretching still further back into prehistory, however, are a group which appear to derive from pre-Celtic forms, but which still belong to the Indo-European linguistic group from which Celtic ultimately developed. These are scattered widely throughout Scotland, ranging from the Blackadder and

Whiteadder rivers in Berwickshire, to the Farrar and Naver in Inverness-shire and Sutherland. Indo-European origins can be advanced with confidence for most of these names, allowing us to move the place-name record back into the pre-Celtic Bronze Age. Such names form part of a common linguistic group which can be traced on the map throughout much of northern, central and western Europe, which has led to the highly plausible suggestion that they belong to a language – labelled 'old European' – which was current around 1500 BC, i.e. before any of the Indo-European dialects, including those which evolved into the various branches of Celtic speech, had begun their divergent development into independent languages. In these river-names, then, we are reaching back into the Bronze Age, and that is currently as far as place-name research allows us to travel, but there are also names for which no satisfactory Indo-European derivation can be advanced, such as Spey, Tweed or Ettrick, or the names of some of the Hebrides. For these, a yet older origin has been proposed, which places them as part of a pre-Indo-European language. In them it is possible that we are hearing whispers from the Neolithic.

Map 2: Gazetteer Sub-divisions of Scotland (excl Shetland)

Key to numbered areas:-

1 Aberdeen and Banffshire; 2 Angus and the Mearns; 3 Argyll; 4 Arran; 5 Ayr, Renfrewshire and Bute; 6 Borders; 7 Caithness; 8 Central Scotland; 9 Dumfries and Galloway; 10 Fife; 11 Inverness and Nairn; 12 Lanark; 13 Lothian; 14 Moray; 15 Orkney; 16 Perth and Kinross; 17 Ross and Cromarty; 18 Shetland; 19 Sutherland; 20 Western Isles

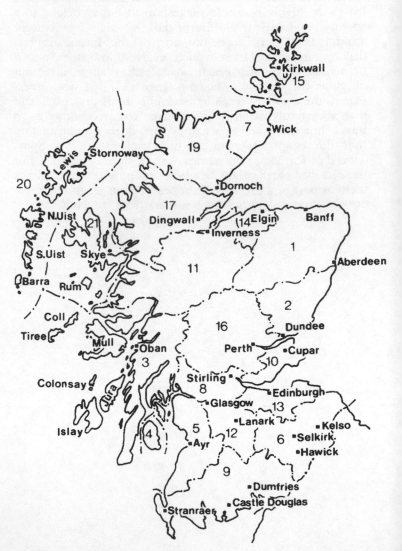

6

GAZETTEER OF MONUMENTS

The sites listed in this gazetteer represent a wide, but clearly far from exhaustive, selection of the main types of pre-historic monument to be encountered in this archaeologically rich country. It is advisable for anyone intending to visit the sites listed below to use Ordnance Survey maps, the relevant number of which is given after the general details of location for each site. By far the best maps are the 1:125,000 Pathfinder Series, but most sites are marked on the 1:50,000 Landranger Series. The gazetteer is divided into a series of geographical units as listed on the map for ease of reference, but arranged alphabetically rather than with any kind of ordered geographical progress around the country in mind. The sites within each section are also listed in alphabetic order, which does not reflect any chronological or archaeological order of relevance.

It is essential to bear in mind that many of the sites listed below are on private ground and inclusion in this book should not be taken as a guarantee of any public right of access. Where a site is in the guardianship of the Secretary of State for Scotland and under Historic Scotland supervision, it is so noted in the lists. Access to many such sites is unrestricted, but several are subject to standard Historic Scotland opening times, regulations and admission fees. In most other cases, permission to visit the site should be sought from the nearest farm, house, forestry or estate office before setting out across country.

Map 3: Aberdeenshire and Banff with Angus and the Mearns

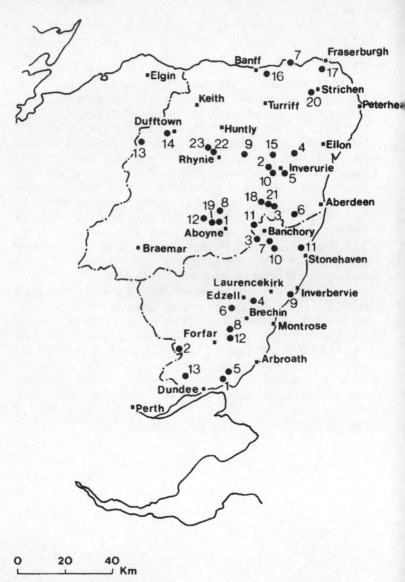

0   20   40 Km

114

ABERDEENSHIRE AND BANFFSHIRE

1. **Balnagowan,** *Long Cairn (NJ 490005) and Field System (NJ 494007), 3km NW of Aboyne, by farm track to Muir Cottage and Airlie farm running W from B9094 Aboyne/ Tarland road just S of Mill of Gellan. At Muir Cottage cross rough grazing to W. The cairn lies on the saddle between Balnagowan Hill and Craig Dhu, amidst the field system which covers most of the E face of Craig Dhu.* **OS sheet 37.**

The cairn, dating from the 4th or 3rd millennia BC, is a magnificently impressive structure of irregular grey boulders. Apparently unchambered, the cairn measures 53.3m along its ESE–WNW main axis by 18.3m wide, rising to a maximum of 1.8m. There is a broad, shallow forecourt at the E within projecting 'horns' which extend 3m beyond the body of the cairn. A hollow in the back of the spine of the cairn at the point where it narrows 12m from the E end indicates that construction may have been in two phases – cairn body and horns.

Around the cairn is an extensive system of field clearance cairns, probably dating from the 1st millennium BC. The cairns measure between 6m and 12m in diameter, and traces of field banks can be followed amongst them. Covering some 145 ha, much of the system is now masked by forestry, but the scale of the operation is obvious.

2. **Balquhain,** *Recumbent Stone Circle (NJ 735240), in agricultural land 0.75km NE of Mains of Balquhain farm, off the unclassified road to Chapel of Garioch from the A96 (T) at Drimmies.* **OS sheet 38.**

A fine recumbent stone circle occupying a levelled position on sloping ground, with clear views to the SE over the Urie valley. The flankers of the recumbent, and several of the uprights of the circle, carry groups of cupmarks. The most noteworthy feature of the site is the tall, outlying pillar-stone of white quartz.

3. **Barmkin of Echt,** *Fort (NJ 725070), 2km NW of Echt, by farm road to Upper Mains and Hillside farms running W from the B977 0.75km N of the village, and across moorland to the hilltop.* **OS sheet 38.**

The rounded summit of Barmekin Hill is encircled by five concentric lines of defence, representing at least two main phases of construction. The three outermost rings are formed by earthen ramparts which are pierced by five entrances and enclose an area c.150m in diameter. At each entrance the ramparts turn slightly inwards towards the gate and the entrance passages are faced with walling. Some 3m within the third rampart is a tumbled stone wall, broken by only two entrances and enclosing an area 137m in diameter. The innermost ring is composed of the tumbled remains of a massive stone wall, broken by two entrances aligned on those in the fourth line. The central enclosure measures 112m in diameter.

4. Barra Hill, *Fort (NJ 803257), 1.25km SSW of Old Meldrum, by track from the B9170 Inverurie to Old Meldrum road opposite Barra Castle some 1.5km SW of Old Meldrum.* **OS sheet 38.**

The ramparts of Barra Hill form a distinctive skyline feature at the north end of the long ridge of high ground on the east side of the valley of the Urie. Three lines of defence, representing at least two phases of development, are clearly visible. The innermost circuit is a heavily ruined stone wall which encloses an area some 120m by 97m, broken by a single entrance on the E side. Outwith this are two ramparts with ditches, both broken by three entrances. Although the site has not been excavated it is suggested that the innermost wall represents a secondary phase.

5. Broomend of Crichie, Henge, *(NJ 779196), 2km S of the centre of Inverurie in open land immediately S of modern housing estate at Port Elphinstone.*

The henge is the most important survival from a major late Neolithic ceremonial complex. It is defined by a low external bank enclosing an area 30m in diameter, broken by entrances at N and S. Within this is a wide ditch, crossed by narrow causeways leading from the gaps in the bank to the central platform. Towards the N end of the platform are two remaining standing stones from a circle of six uprights. The third stone at the centre of the circle is a Class I Pictish symbol stone, moved to this site in the 19th century when the Aberdeen-Inverness railway was built. Excavations in 1855 revealed cremation burials at the base of each stone. In the centre of the platform was a 1.9m-deep shaft-grave with a cist at its bottom.

About 50m N of the henge was a stone circle, 45.7m in

diameter, composed of three concentric rings around a central cairn. This has been destroyed by quarrying. Between it and the henge, and continuing beyond it for a further 400m to the S, ran an avenue of stones. This was originally some 18.3m wide and contained at least 36 stones in each row, but only three now remain.

6. Cullerlie, *Stone Circle (NJ 785 042), 1.25km S of Roadside of Garlogie on the unclassified road from the B9125 to Drum. Signposted Historic Scotland.* **OS sheet 38.**

Excavation in 1934 indicated that the circle was constructed in the 2nd millennium BC. It consists of eight boulders graded in height to the N and enclosing an internal space 10.8m in diameter. Within this are eight small kerb cairns, the largest – in the centre – measuring only 3.4m in diameter. Excavation revealed that the site had been levelled before the erection of the stones and the cairn kerbs. Following this a fire of willow branches had been burned over the entire site. Subsequently cremated bone was placed within seven of the kerbs, which were then infilled. In the eighth cairn, that immediately W of the central setting, human remains and charcoal were found in a fire pit sealed by a large capstone.

7. Cullykhan *(Castle Point), Troup, Promontory Fort (NJ 838661), signposted N of the B9031 Macduff to Rosehearty road, 1km W of Pennan. Follow the rough track to the car park above the beach. Footpath to fort.* **OS sheet 29.**

The cliff-girt headlands of the Banff coast have long attracted occupants in search of easily defended homes. Castle Point at Troup is one of the more spectacular of such sites and excavation has shown that its long summit platform connected to the mainland by only a narrow arrete has been the location of fortified settlements from the early 1st millennium BC until the 18th century AD.

The primary defences lay at the landward end of the promontory and comprised at least one line of timber palisade. This was superseded in about the 4th century BC by a vertical wall of stone and timber with an impressive gateway set back between in-turning sections of walling. Stylistically, the fort displays strong affinities with north German examples, a connection emphasised by the discovery of artefacts of German origin in the area behind the rampart. Here, too, there was considerable evidence for metalworking on the site. The sequence of prehistoric defences was completed probably in the later 1st century BC by the construction further to the east of a timber-laced rampart. This had been destroyed by a major conflagration. In the Pictish period two flat-bottomed ditches were cut across the middle of the promontory, while in the 13th century the site was re-occupied as the location of the castle of the Troup family. It was finally re-fortified in the 18th century as an artillery defence called Fort Fiddes.

8. Culsh, *Souterrain (NJ 504054), 2.5km NE of Tarland on the B9119. Signposted Historic Scotland.* **OS sheet 37.**

This superbly preserved site still extends for 14.3m into the hillside in a curving passage which widens from the entrance into a bulbous end 1.8m wide by 1.8m high. Its dry-stone walling rises from a base course of massive blocks, above which it is corbelled slightly inwards then ceiled with a roof of flat slabs. It probably formed a storehouse for an unexcavated Iron Age settlement immediately adjacent to it.

9. Dunnideer, *Fort (NJ 613281), 1.5km W of Insch, by footpath from the unclassified road from Insch to Dunnideer.* **OS sheet 37.**

The prominent conical mass of the Hill of Dunnideer is now crowned by the rubbly remains of a 13th-century castle, whose outer works make use of the older hillfort on the site. Two phases at least are represented in the prehistoric remains. The earlier phase is represented by the vitrified ruins of a timber-laced rampart which encircles the summit, enclosing a space measuring 67m by 27m, and the more slightly-built rampart within which it stands which survives only on the N, E and W. A hollow at the W end marks the site of rock-cut cistern. The outer defences, 60m below the summit on the steeper slopes, comprise traces of three circuits of unfinished rampart for the most part simply marker trenches, but more substantial on either side of the E and W gates. Five hut platforms are scooped into the N face of the hill and two into the S, both groups lying *c.*45m below the summit. These pre-date the unfinished defences, which respect the edge of one of the S huts.

10. Easter Aquhorthies, *Recumbent Stone Circle (NJ 732207), 3km W of Inverurie, Historic Scotland signposted from A96(T) Inverurie by-pass.* **OS sheet 38.**

Rink Farm, general view across confluence of Tweed and Ettrick to mesolithic flint-scatter site

Nether Largie south – neolithic passage grave

Embo, chambered cairn – S chamber and central cist

Capo long barrow – view looking E along mound

Cnoc Freiceadain, long cairn (N)

Nether Largie, stone rows

The Deil's Stanes, stone circle

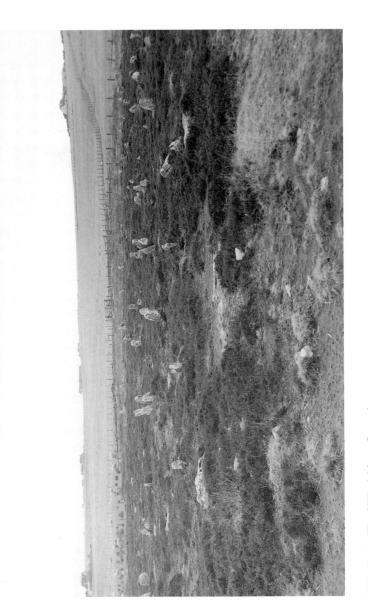

Mid Clyth (The Hill o' Many Stanes), stone rows

Nether Largie mid cairn, secondary cist burial

Nether Largie north, bronze age cairn

Nether Largie south, neolithic passage grave with secondary bronze age cist in foreground

Strontoiller, standing stone and kerb cairn

Tealing souterrain, cup-and -ring marked stones

Cullykhan, Castle Point, Troup, promontory fort

The Chesters, hillfort, west end of defences

The Eildon Hills, the 'Oppidum' of the Selgovae crowns the right-hand summit (Eildon Hill North)

Dun Dornaguil, broch

Carn Liath, broch

Dun mac Sniachain, Benderloch, fort and dun

Superbly positioned on a hill-side site which offers wide views in all directions except N, this impressive recumbent stone circle consists of the recumbent and its flankers, nine erect stones of the ring, and two massive blocks which define an area in front of the recumbent. The 'circle' is in fact almost perfectly circular and measures 19.5m in diameter, with the stones graded in height from the 2.25m tall flankers to the 1.7m high stones directly opposite the recumbent. The stones are enclosed within a low bank. The slightly raised interior, and references to a cist in 1934, indicate that the centre of the circle was later occupied by a ring cairn.

11. Glassel, *Stone Circle (NO 648996), some 6km NW of Banchory. Turn S off the A980 Banchory to Torphins road 3km E of Torphins on the unclassifed road to Brathens. Opposite the gates of Glassel House, some 0.5km down this road on the left side, is a ride through the forestry. Follow this for about 100m, then turn left onto a small path for a further 100m.* **OS sheets 37/38.**

On a level platform above the drop into the valley of the Canny Burn stands an oval setting of stones, measuring 5.5m by 2.8m. There are five stones, the tallest at the SW, and ranging in height from 0.84m to 0.99m. The site had been disturbed in the mid-19th century, and re-excavation in 1904 produced only a small flint flake and fragments of charcoal. The sandstone block at the northern end of the setting may have been a cist cover. The grading of the stones by height and the SW emphasis indicates some link with the recumbent stone circle tradition, and it is probable that it represents a stage in the transition from the recumbent form to the small four-poster settings, such as Templestones near Forres.

12. Knockargetty Hill, *Fort (NJ 455030), in open woodland on the S ridge of the Hill of Corrachree 2.5km WSW of Tarland.* **OS sheet 37.**

This is an excellent example of an unfinished fort. It comprises an oval enclosure defined in part by a slight terrace and in part by a shallow marker trench, with the only substantial construction undertaken at the entrances to the E and W. Measuring some 240m by 117m within its single defensive circuit, it would have formed one of the larger forts in the region, probably representing the principal power-centre of the Cromar district.

13. Lagmore Wester, *Clava Cairn (NJ 176358), turn S off the A95 Aberlour to Grantown road 300m W of Bridge of Avon. Park by the roadside after some 100m, then climb steeply uphill through the fields on the W side of the road to the cairn.* **OS sheet 28.**

Sited on a platform at the nose of the headland which separates the Avon and Spey at their confluence near Ballindalloch, the cairn commands splendid views across the valley to the N. Four stones remain of the enclosing circle, the tallest at 2.3m being on the W. The cairn, which is grass-grown, measures 12m in diameter and rises to 1.2m within the kerb of massive blocks. The entrance is on the S between two stones which project from the kerb to form a 'porch', and open into a passage which is still partly lintelled. The passage appears to have turned a dog-leg part way along its length, and opened into a now collapsed central chamber measuring 3.3m in diameter.

Lagmore Wester is the best preserved of a group of Clava-type tombs in the Inveravon area. A second cairn at Lagmore lies in the field immediately to the E of the junction with the A95. It is quite ruinous, but one of the fallen stones of its enclosing circle is peppered liberally with cup-marks. A third cairn lies at Marionburgh (NJ 183364), some 1.4km towards Aberlour on the A95. It stands among trees on the S side of the E drive of Ballindalloch Castle, and comprises a circle some 23.9m in diameter of which only five stones remain. The tallest, 2.74m in height, stands at the SW. The circle encloses a denuded ring cairn roughly 14m in diameter with a central space 5m in diameter.

14. Little Conval, *Fort (NJ 295393), 2.5km W of Dufftown. Park on the B9009 Dufftown to Tomintoul road 100m S of the junction with the minor road to Kirktown of Mortlach and take the track which climbs by the plantation on the W side of the road. At the head of the track follow the footpath to the Glach-en-ronack, the bealach between Meikle and Little Conval, and strike steeply uphill northwards from there.* **OS sheet 28.**

The rounded cone of Little Conval is the final major eminence on the high ridge of land which separates Glen Rinnes from Strathspey, and commands magnificent views in all directions. The structures which ring its summit represent the remains of an unfinished fort, one of several in the country along the S side of the Moray Firth. Four lines of defence were planned, apparently as a single exercise, but the work was abandoned before the project was even half-finished. The innermost circuit, which encloses an area some 120m by 210m, comprises mainly a band of stones spread to some 3m in width, but in the N–NE sector represented only by a slight marker trench. The second circuit, which is not exactly concentric with the inner line, is represented only by a marker trench, but the third line, which follows an eccentric course, is formed in part by a 2m-thick wall faced with very large stone slabs. This line veers away from the second line on the E side, ending in a group of irregular-shaped enclosures of uncertain date and function. A fourth line, some 100m or so long, covers the approaches up the gentler slopes from the N.

15. Loanhead of Daviot, *Recumbent Stone Circle (NJ 747288), 7km NNW of Inverurie at Daviot village, signposted Historic Scotland from the B9001 Inverurie-Rothienorman or A920 Oldmeldrum-Huntly roads.* **OS sheet 38.**

One of the finest surviving monuments of its class, Loanhead lies just off the crest of the wooded hill to the N of the village, occupying a gently-sloping platform which commands open views to the E and S. The circle measures 20.5m in diameter and consists of eight standing stones, flankers and a massive recumbent. Each of the standing stones was placed on a small cairn which covered pits containing charcoal and pot sherds. The centre of the circle is occupied by a ring cairn enclosed within a prominent kerb. Beneath the ring cairn were traces of burning which, in the central area, contained pot sherds, charcoal, cremated human bone, and flint flakes. It is suggested that a timber-built mortuary house pre-dating the cairn stood in the centre of the circle.

Immediately to the SE of the circle are two stretches of low, rubble bank, forming equal-lengthed arcs on opposite sides of a circular area. Excavation in 1935 revealed that these defined a cremation cemetery of Bronze Age date. In the centre was the partial cremation of an adult male contained within a shallow scoop. Several more cremations, eleven contained in urns, lay to the NE and S of the central burial.

16. Longman Hill, *Long Barrow (NJ 737620), 4km SE of Macduff, in farmland on the crest of Longman Hill 500m W* *of the A98(T) Macduff-Fraserburgh road.* **OS sheet 29.**

Occupying a prominent skyline position, the 70m long earthen mound's three-humped profile reveals the component elements of its construction: a round mound at the SSW; a heel-shaped mound at the NNE; a central oval mound. The barrow probably covers the remains of a timber (or stone) mortuary structure built in the early 4th millennium BC. Urns recovered from the flanks of the cairn in the 1880s suggest that secondary burials were inserted into the barrow in the 2nd millennium BC.

17. Memsie, *Round Cairn (NJ 976620), 0.5km SE of Memsie on the B9032 Memsie-Rathen road, signposted Historic Scotland.* **OS sheet 30.**

A massive cairn of bare stones, 24m in diameter and 4.4m high. The sole survivor of a cemetery of three cairns placed along the low ridge which extends to the SE of Memsie, it is typical of the later Bronze Age cairn-building tradition in the NE of Scotland.

18. Midmar Kirk, *Recumbent Stone Circle (NJ 699064), in the churchyard, off the unclassified road signposted 'Midmar Kirk' N from the B9119 Aberdeen-Tarland road 3.5km W of Echt.* **OS sheet 38.**

Although the stones in the circle have seem re-arranged and the area laid out as part of the modern burial ground, this recumbent stone circle is still an impressive monument of its class. The circle, which is 17.3m in diameter, is dominated by the 4.5m long recumbent between its 2.5m tall fang-like flankers. A central ring-cairn was removed during the landscaping of the cemetery in 1914.

19. New Kinord, *Settlement and Field System (NJ 449001), 8km W of Aboyne on the edge of the Muir of Dinnet National Nature Reserve. Enter from the B9119 1.4km N of Dinnet. The settlement lies on rough ground to the N of the track running W from the car-park, entered via field gate 75m along track.* **OS sheet 37.**

Best seen in late winter when the bracken has died back, the remains here represent one of the best preserved farm complexes of the late 1st millennium BC in NE Scotland. Planned in the early part of this century, the remains comprise a series of massive circular stone foundations disposed along the N side of a curving field-bank and trackway. These have been interpreted as the stone footings of probably three timber-built round houses measuring 17m, 18m and 19m in diameter respectively, the central of which has a souterrain opening from its N side, two large enclosures – probably stock pens – sunken tracks, droveways and small fields defined by discontinuous lines of boulders.

20. Strichen, *Recumbent Stone Circle (NJ 936544), 1km SW of Strichen. Turn W off the A981 Strichen to New Deer road 1.3km S of Strichen on the farm road to Strichen Mains. After 250m fork right. Parking may be difficult, but continue on foot past the cottage and uphill to the false crest below the rounded summit of the hill.* **OS sheet 30.**

This circle has had a chequered history, but excavation and restoration in 1979–83 has successfully rescued an ill-starred site. When visited by Johnson and Boswell in 1773, all that then survived in position were the recumbent and flankers and one of the uprights of the circle, but even these were swept aside in the 1790s in the name of agricultural improvement. The tenant farmer, however, was forced to reconstruct the circle by his landlord, but he rc-erected it on a slightly different site which resulted in the recumbent lying on the N side. This reconstruction remained in place until 1965 when it was bulldozed, but the stones have been re-established in their original positions following excavation.

Strichen is typical of stone circles of this class in Buchan, where the uprights sit on a slight bank. The bank forms a 'flattened' circle, compressed on its N–S axis, and measures 12.1m by 11m. Excavation revealed that the enclosing bank had been liberally scattered with flakes of white quartzite which had been smashed on site, presumably for their reflective qualities.

21. Sunhoney, *Recumbent Stone Circle (NJ 715056), in trees on agricultural land 250m WNW of Sunhoney farm, off the B9119 Aberdeen-Tarland road 2km W of Echt.* **OS sheet 38.**

A very fine example of its class, measuring 25.4m in diameter, and consisting of a fallen recumbent, its flankers and nine other uprights. The upper surface of the recumbent bears 31 cupmarks. A ring cairn, excavated in 1864, occupies the central area, and each of the stones of the enclosing circle stood originally on small cairns.

22. Tap o' Noth, *Fort (NJ 484293), 2.5km NW of Rhynie,* *reached by steep path from Brae of Scurdargue at head of track from the A941 Rhynie-Dufftown road c.2km W of Rhynie.*

The flat-topped cone of Tap o' Noth is one of the most prominent landmarks of W Aberdeenshire. The hillfort which crowns it consists of at least two phases of building. The earlier is probably represented by a stone-built rampart which encloses an area of 21 ha on the lower slopes of the summit cone. Within this are 145 platforms, some possibly hut platforms but most probably representing quarry scoops from which rampart material was excavated. At this elevation (563m OD), such settlement must predate the climatic deterioration of the 1st millennium BC.

The second phase is represented by the vitrified remains of a massive formerly timber-laced stone rampart which encircles the summit. This encloses a rectangular area 105m by 40m and, when excavated in 1894, stood originally 6–8m wide at the base and rising still to 3.5m in height. There is a rock-cut cistern at the S end. Recent dating of material from the rampart has indicated a date of vitrification between the early 1st century BC and the 1st century AD.

23. Wormy Hillock, *Henge (NJ 449307), in forestry 6km NW of Rhynie. Take the unclassified road to Mytice W off the A97 Rhynie-Huntly road 4km S of Huntly. At road end follow track for 2.5km through forest to junction with another track just W of bridge over Ealaiche Burn; henge lies 50m up burn.* **OS sheet 37.**

This remote site consists of a low bank enclosing an area 16.5m in diameter, on the inner side of which is a broad shallow ditch encircling a 6m diameter central platform reached via a single entrance and causeway from the SE. Although now lying in a depopulated area, the land round about bore one of the major centres of early settlement in the NE.

ANGUS AND MEARNS

(see map on p.114)

1. Ardestie, *Souterrain (NO 412382), Historic Scotland signposted in agricultural land immediately N of the A92 Dundee-Arbroath road, just W of the junction with the B962 Monifieth-Monikie road.* **OS sheet 54.**

Although damaged through modern agricultural action this is one of the best preserved monuments of its class, with both the remains of its passage and surface structures left open and consolidated after its excavation in 1949–50. The passage lacks its bulbous N end and is entirely roofless, surviving as a 23m-long dry-stone lined trench. The side walls rise from a base course of massive boulders and are corbelled inwards at the top to narrow the space for roofing. A stone-lined drain runs down the middle of the formerly paved floor. The main entrance to the souterrain is via a narrow sloping passage from the W, possibly descending from a courtyard, while a subsidiary entrance is provided in the N wall. This is reached from a small 'structure' of which only wall-footings remain, itself opening into the first of a sequence of three linked circular structures, traditionally described as the footings of huts, which run parallel to the curve of the souterrain. Recent re-interpretation suggests that rather than being separate huts, these four structures were defined areas associated with particular industrial or domestic activities within a much larger timber roundhouse, similar to that excavated at Newmill to the N of Perth.

2. Barns of Airlie, *Souterrain (NO 305515), on the crest of the ridge at the W end of the second field to the W of Barns of Airlie farm, 250m NNW of Kirkton of Airlie off the unclassified road between the A926 at Airlie and Bridgend of Lintrathen.* **OS sheet 53.**

This is the only survivor of at least seven souterrains found in the vicinity of Barns, five on the farm itself. It is the most complete of such monuments still open, consisting of a stone-lined passage 20.4m long, 2m wide and lintelled at a height of 1.8m. It is roofed with slabs, one of which has been removed to permit access. The underside of one of the slabs bears a series of cup-marks and serpentine grooves. The entrance probably survives infilled at the E end of the passage, but has not been excavated. There are no traces of any of the surface structures usually associated with such sites.

3. **Bucharn**, *Round Cairn (NO 659929), 5km SW of Banchory. Some 1.5km W of Strachan on the B976, turn N onto an unclassified road. After 600m, park and follow the farm track uphill through the steading and skirt the fields to the cairn.* **OS sheet 45.**

A massive mound of bare stone sits on the edge of a terrace commanding extensive views over the river valley and hill country to the S and W. The cairn measures 27m in diameter by 4.5m high. It appears to sit on a stony platform, but this is probably a feature produced by ploughing around the mound and the accumulation of field-clearance debris.nt promontory between Loch Ceann

4. **Capo**, *Long Barrow (NO 633664), in Inglismaldie Forest to the W of the unclassified road to Edzell Air Base between the A90 (T) and B966, 1.75km W of North Water Bridge.* **OS sheet 45.**

Capo is one of the finest surviving examples in Scotland of a Neolithic burial practice which utilised earthen long barrows as opposed to stone-built cairns. It stands on the gravel terrace on the E bank of the North Esk, and is constructed from turfs and scraped up soil. It measures 80m in length by 28m wide at the E end, rising to 2.5m in height. It does not appear to have been disturbed in the past. Excavation of a similar site a short distance to the N at Dalladies, destroyed in the course of gravel extraction, suggests that the barrow is constructed over the remains of a timber-built mortuary structure.

5. **Carlungie**, *Souterrain (NO 511359), Historic Scotland site, signposted from the A92 Dundee-Arbroath road 2km E of the boundary of the City of Dundee.* **OS sheet 54.**

The remains of one of the largest and most complex of the excavated souterrains in this area, Carlungie consists of a long, sharply curving passage, 42.6m in length, with a secondary semi-subterranean chamber which served as a workshop opening from it. The main entrance was from the N at the E end of the passage, where an entrance sloped down from a paved courtyard, but three subsidiary entrances provided additional access at points along its length. The entire passage is roofless and in some places the side walls have been reduced to their lowest course. During excavation in 1950–1 eight paved areas were found clustered around its E end. These were interpreted as the floor areas of small huts but, as has been suggested at nearby Ardestie, may rather represent zones of paving associated with particular domestic and industrial activities within a larger timber roundhouse.

6. The Caterthuns *(Brown and White), Hillforts (NO 555668 and NO 548661), Historic Scotland sites, signposted on the unclassified road from Little Brechin to Bridgend, approximately 7km NW of Brechin. Signposted footpaths to both sites from the car-park at the summit of the road.*

This pair of sites forms one of the most visually striking groups of its kind in Scotland. The Brown Caterthun, the more complex of the two, is perhaps best appreciated from air photographs, its outlines being rather obscured by the dense heather which cloaks its hilltop site. It is a unique monument in Scotland, its only close analogies being simpler hilltop sites in S Aberdeenshire. Even without excavation it appears that there are at least three phases of construction represented in the visible remains. At its centre, lying slightly off the crown of the hill, is a small enclosure defined by a ruinous stone wall. This measures 91.4m by 60.9m and is broken by a single entrance in the N side. Between 18m and 54m below this inner enclosure runs a substantial rampart, possibly marking the line of a stone wall which has spread to as much as 7.5m wide. Immediately outwith this circuit are two slighter ramparts separated by a substantial ditch. All three ramparts and the ditch are broken by nine aligned entrances, suggesting a single construction phase which enclosed an area of some 2 ha. Further down the slopes are two further circuits of rampart, the outer faced by a quarry ditch, which enclose a total internal area measuring 330m by 310m. The inner rampart has a sharp dog-leg in its E side, probably the product of misalignment in the course of construction. These two outer circuits are pierced by eight entrances which in most cases do not align on those of the inner ramparts, implying a separate phase of construction.

The White Caterthun lies 0.75km to the SW. One of the most magnificent Prehistoric ruins in Britain, it is a complex comprising two if not three phases of construction. Roughly oval in plan, a monumental timber-laced rampart enclosed an area measuring internally 152m by 67m. This innermost line of defence was originally between 9m and 12m thick and was broken by a single entrance at the SE. A short distance outwith this enclosure was a second timber-laced rampart measuring only 6m thick. The combined tumble from these two massive walls has spread for over 30m down the hillside. The only original feature visible in the interior is the rock-cut cistern at the W end. Outwith the timber-laced defences is a low rampart with external quarry ditch, and between 30m and 69m below this are the remains of two further lines, neither of which appear to have been completed. On the slopes to the E, outwith the lowest ring of defences, are the footings of several circular houses. Lying on the slope between the timber-laced ramparts and the outer defences at the W end of the fort is a large boulder bearing at least seventy cup-marks on its upper face.

7. Eslie the Greater, *Recumbent Stone Circle (NO 717915), 4km SE of Banchory. Turn S onto unclassified road to Tilquhillie off B974 immediately E of Bridge of Feugh. Fork right after 250m and left after approximately 2km at Blackness farm. Turn right at the next junction and the circle is clearly visible in agricultural land on right.* **OS sheet 38.**

The circle occupies a levelled position on sloping ground below a saddle at the W end of the ridge of Mulloch Hill, and commands excellent views to the N and W. Five uprights remain of the eight standing stones, plus the recumbent and flankers. The 'circle' is in fact an ellipse 26.5m by 23.2m, and encloses a later ring cairn 18m in diameter with central space 6.3m in diameter.

8. Finavon Hill, *Hillfort (NO 507557), on the N side of the unclassified road from Aberlemno to Finavon, 1.5km W of Aberlemno.* **OS sheet 54.**

This fort forms a prominent feature on the skyline viewed from the N from the A90 (T). It is roughly rectangular, measuring 153m by 30–38m within a massive timber-laced rampart, heavily vitrified in its upper parts. Excavation in 1933–5 showed the rampart to survive to 6m thick and to stand 3.6m high internally and 4.8m externally. There is a deep rock-cut cistern towards the E, and the large depression at the W may mark the site of a second cistern/well. The excavations showed that the otherwise featureless interior had timber buildings ranged against the ramparts. A plank recovered from the floor of one of these buildings in a second programme of excavation in 1966 produced a Carbon-14 date of 665 ± 70 BC.

9. Gourdon, *Long Cairn (NO 818706), 3km S of Inverbervie on the A92, turn W up farm road to Nether Benholm, then N along the back road from Benholm Mill and continue uphill for some 1.2km. The cairn is on the summit of the hill, roughly 90m SE of the track.* **OS sheet 45.**

Although it has suffered some disturbance in the past, the long turf-covered mound is a well preserved example of its class. The long axis of the cairn is oriented ENE–WSW, and the mound measures some 46m long by 14m wide at the E end. Both ends are rounded, the E being the higher at some 1.7m.

10. Nine Stanes, *Recumbent Stone Circle (NO 723912), 6km SW of Crathes. Turn W off the A 957 Crathes-Stonehaven road at Blairydryne along the unclassified road to Mulloch and Strachan; after 3km park at Forestry Commission picnic place on N side of road and take forestry track through trees to the stone circle.* **OS sheet 38.**

Currently encircled by trees, the circle occupies a broad shelf on the gently sloping SW flank of Mulloch Hill and formerly enjoyed fine views to the S and W. It is a 'flattened' circle measuring 18m by 14.6m, with the recumbent and its flankers, one of which has fallen, lying on the straighter side. Six other stones remain upright. The centre is occupied by the denuded remains of a ring cairn, disturbed by excavation in the 19th century.

11. Raedykes, *Ring Cairns (NO 832096), on the crest and E slopes of Campstone Hill, 300m NW of West Raedykes farm, 6km NW of Stonehaven.* **OS sheet 45.**

This important cemetery site comprises the substantial remains of four cairns. The SE is a ring-cairn, its outer kerb 9.4m in diameter and enclosing a central setting of stones 3.9m in diameter within a heavily robbed ring of cairn material. This now rises to a maximum of 40cm in height. The cairn is enclosed within the remains of a stone circle measuring 17m in diameter. Only nine standing stones survive from a probable original total of twenty.

The second cairn lies 20m to the WNW. It has been an oval structure, 8.5m by 7.7m bounded by a kerb of small boulders. There is no visible evidence for a central setting in the robbed out hollow in its midst, which suggests that this may be the plundered remains of a Bronze Age burial. It also has no enclosing stone circle.

The third cairn lies a further 15m to the WNW. Similar in form to the previous site, it measures 7.9m in diameter and has evidence surviving only on its W side for a defining kerb. The central part of the cairn has also been heavily robbed, leaving no evidence for a cist or inner setting. Again, there is no enclosing stone circle.

The final cairn, the most complete of the group, lies 80m NW of the first cairn described. It is a fine ring-cairn measuring 10.2m in diameter and rising to 60cm in height. It stands in the centre of a stone circle 13.9m in diameter, of which five stones remain standing from a possible total of thirteen. The outer kerb of the cairn is very elaborate, showing signs of grading in height towards the SW, and there are several pillar stones in its circumference which rise higher than their neighbours.

12. Turin Hill, *Hillfort (NO 514535), between the B9113 Forfar-Montrose road and the B9134 Forfar-Aberlemno road. The fort occupies the highest point of the ridge, 1.5km N of the road-end of the track to West Mains of Turin farm off the B9113, from where the shortest but steepest ascent to the site can be made.* **OS sheet 54.**

The rocky scarps of the hill's S edge greatly add to the natural strength of the fort's prominent site. The fortifications, which are strung out along its ridge, clearly belong to several phases of building and are highly complex. The earliest appears to be a double-ramparted oval enclosure 270m by 120m which was possibly never completed. A smaller, stone-walled (possibly timber-laced) fort was subsequently built within this. It measures 152m by 39m and bears close similarities to the nearby fort at Finavon Hill. This second fort was in turn superseded by a stone-walled dun 27.4m in diameter within walls 3.6m thick, which partly overlies its N defences. Two more ruinous duns lie 45m to the E and W of this better preserved example, indicating that this was a site of considerable importance into the early historic period.

13. West Mains of Auchterhouse, *Round Cairn (NO 315377), on the summit of West Mains Hill, 1.5km W of Auchterhouse.* **OS sheet 53.**

The substantial remains of this Bronze Age burial mound stand on the brow of West Mains Hill, surmounted by a modern pillar and trig point. The cairn measures 21m in diameter and rises to 2.5m in height. Excavation in 1897 revealed a double cist which contained a partial cremation with a rivetted bronze dagger and a horn sheath mount. The cist was encircled by a roughly built stone wall, and both it and the wall had been covered by a small mound of turfs contained within a stone kerb. Over this was heaped the main cairn mound of stone contained within a second kerb.

Map 4: Argyll and Arran (with inset detail of Kilmartin Valley)

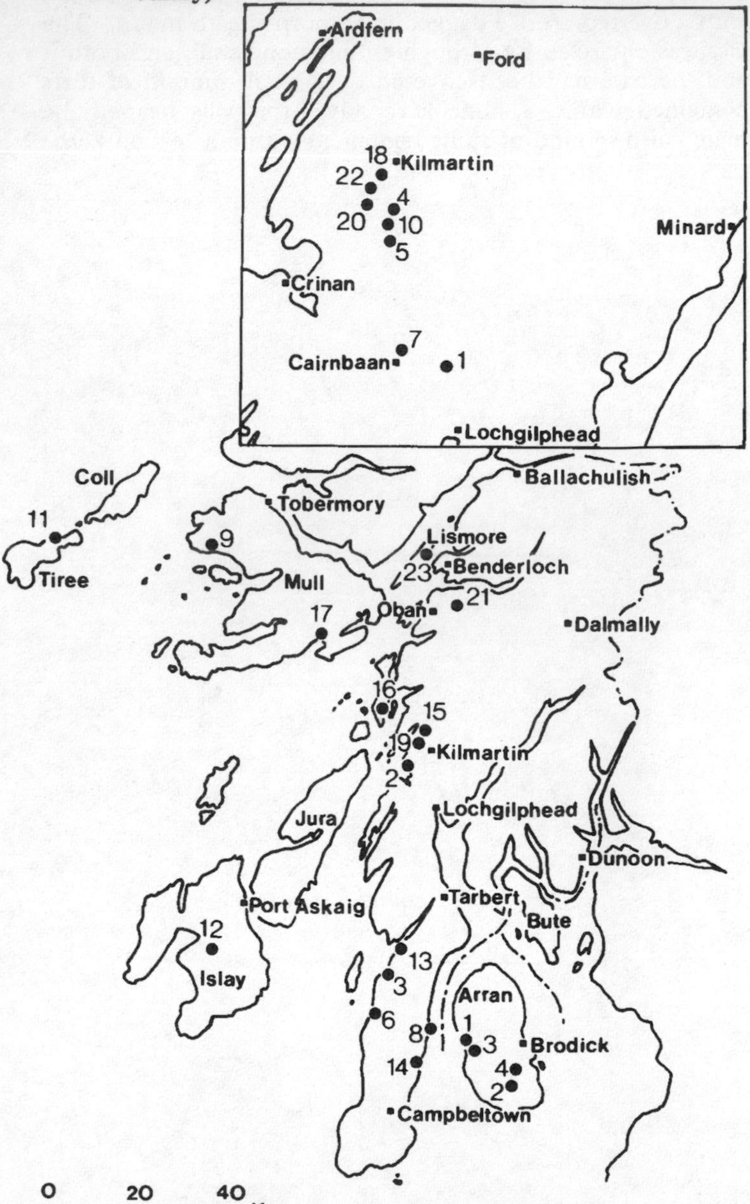

Ardfern

Ford

18 Kilmartin
22
4
20 10
5

Minard

Crinan

7
Cairnbaan 1

Lochgilphead

Ballachulish

Coll

Tobermory

11
Tiree

9

Lismore
23 Benderloch
21

Mull

Oban

Dalmally

17

16
15

19
2 Kilmartin

Jura

Lochgilphead

Dunoon

Port Askaig

Tarbert
Bute

12
Islay

13
3

6
8 1
14

Arran
3 Brodick
4
2

Campbeltown

0   20   40
Km

ARGYLL

1. Achnabreck, *Cup-and-Ring marked Rock (NR 855906),
take the unsignposted road to Achnabreck farm, E from the
A816 Lochgilphead-Oban road 1.75km NNW of
Lochgilphead. At the Historic Scotland designated car-park,
follow signposted path behind farm to the first group in an
enclosure adjacent to the forestry plantation. The second group
lies 140m E in the forestry along a marked path.* **OS sheet
55.**

Carved into the surface of two expanses of bared rock are
amongst the largest areas of cup-and-ring markings in
Britain. The first enclosure contains two groups of carving.
The first has over 50 cup-and-ring marks (one cup-mark has
nine concentric rings carved around it) and a profusion of
plain cup-marks carvings, several being linked by grooves.
The second group lies 30m NW, and contains one of the
largest cup-and-ring carvings yet recorded, comprising a
central cup and seven concentric rings almost 1m in
diameter. Further carvings towards the upper limit of the
rock are more difficult to see, especially if the lighting
conditions are not quite right. The carvings here include not
only cup-and-ring marks but a series of double and triple
spiral motifs. The second enclosure contains a further series
of cup-and-ring marks, several of which have radial 'spokes'
linking the cup and concentric grooves.

2. Ardifuar, *Dun (NR 789969), 3.5km WSW of
Slockavullin, by track and moorland path from Slockavullin.*
OS sheet 55.

Situated 0.5km from the sea in a valley overlooking a
sheltered anchorage on the N side of Loch Crinan are the
substantial remains of a large stone-built fortification.
Measuring 19.8m in diameter within walls some 3m thick
and surviving up to 3m high, it possesses a number of
features more usually associated with brochs, a class of
monument with a significantly smaller diameter. Within the
thickness of the wall at ground level are mural cells and a
staircase leading to the upper levels, the upper section of the
walls containing a gallery. On the inner face of the wall,
1.5m above ground level, is a scarcement ledge which
probably carried the roof or an internal floor of buildings
ranges around the sides of the central space. A low platform
bordered with an irregular kerb runs round most of the inner

face, possibly marking the position of the timber structures. Excavations in 1934 revealed evidence for at least two major phases of occupation, the first dating from the second quarter of the 1st millennium BC and the second probably relating to a reoccupation in the early Middle Ages.

3. Ballochroy, *Cist Burial and Standing Stones (NR 730523), in agricultural land 150m E of the A83 Campbeltown-Lochgilphead road 5.5km SSW of Clachan.* **OS sheet 62.**

An alignment of three upright stone slabs running NE and SW and an exposed cist constructed of massive slabs are the remains of a substantial monument which originally comprised the standing-stones and a large stone cairn of probably Bronze Age date. The cairn, which stood at the SE end of the alignment, has been almost entirely robbed away.

4. Baluachraig, *Cup-and-Ring marked Rock (NR 831969), in a fenced enclosure immediately to the W of the A816 Lochgilphead-Oban road approximately 2km S of Kilmartin. Historic Scotland.* **OS sheet 55.**

The exposed rock-face within the railings is pock-marked with upwards of 130 plain cups and 32 cup-and-ring markings. Unlike the site at Achnabreck, none of the cup-and-ring markings here have more than two concentric rings.

5. Ballymeanoch, *Henge and Standing Stones (NR 833962), in private ground but clearly visible from the A816 Lochgilphead-Oban road 400m S of the Historic Scotland car-park at Dunchraigaig.* **OS sheet 55.**

The remains of a substantial ritual complex of later Neolithic date stand on the gravel terraces on the E side of the Kilmartin Burn at the S end of the archaeologically rich Kilmartin Valley. The standing stones form two alignments, almost parallel to each other, with four stones in the E alignment and two in the W. Near to the two-stone setting is a fallen stone pierced by a hole. The two middle members of the four-stone alignment are decorated with cup-and-ring markings. Recent excavations around the fallen stone produced cremated bone from the stone's socket. The henge, which has been almost ploughed out, is just visible 150m to the SSW of the stone settings.

6. Beacharra *(Leac-an-Fhamhair), Standing Stone (NR*

692433) and Cairn (NR 692434), on an elevated position in agricultural land adjacent to the farm track to Beacharr, E from the A83 Lochgilphead-Campbeltown road 2.75km S of Tayinloan. **OS sheet 62.**

The impressive standing stone, clearly visible from below at the N end of an outcrop from the main hill mass to the E, is the largest in Kintyre, measuring almost 5m in height. To the E lie the remains of a chambered cairn excavated originally in 1892 and re-excavated in 1959. The chamber was some 6m long by 1.5m wide, and the E portal stone and sill of the entrance have survived. The E side of the façade was formed by a straight stretch of dry-stone wall 0.6m high, which turned a right-angle and merged into the body of the cairn. Some fine pottery from the excavation is now in Campbeltown Museum.

7. **Cairnbaan**, *Cup-and-Ring marked Rocks (NR 838910), follow Historic Scotland signposted path from the Cairnbaan Motor Inn on the N side of the B841 Lochgilphead-Crinan road, 250m WNW of its junction with the A816.* **OS sheet 55.**

Two extensive areas of carving lie on exposed rock surfaces some 100m apart. The first outcrop is carved with over 80 plain cup and cup-and-ring markings. The second group contains cups with up to four concentric rings, several abutting onto adjoining rings.

8. **Carradale**, *Fort (NR 815364), 2km S of Carradale village, across grazing and moorland from the unclassified road from Carradale to Port Righ.* **OS sheet 68.**

The vitrified remains of a timber-laced fort occupy the highest central portion of the narrow tidal promontory of Carradale Point. An oval rampart encloses an area 58m by 22.8m, with traces of additional outworks at the N and S ends.

9. **Dun Aisgann**, *Mull, Dun (NM 377452), on a rock knoll overlooking Loch Tuath, across open country 0.6km SSW of the B8073 Calgary-Kilninian road near Burg.* **OS sheet 48.**

Spectacularly positioned and commanding magnificent views S and W over the islands to the W of Mull, this is one of the best-preserved duns on Mull. An irregular outerwork encloses the knoll, which is crowned by the main circular, stone-built fortification. This measures 10.5m in diameter within a wall up to 2.75m thick, which has a pronounced batter in its outer face. The wall still stands 2.75m high in sections. In the W is the entrance passage, with jambs halfway along its length to take a timber door secured by a draw-bar. Traces of a mural gallery are visible in the NE arc of the wall.

10. Dunchraigaig, *Chambered Cairn (NR 833968), signposted Historic Scotland on the W side of the A816 Oban-Lochgilphead road, 2.25km S of Kilmartin.* **OS sheet 55.**

A large cairn constructed of water-worn boulders from the valley floor. It still survives to over 30m in diameter and 2m in height, despite being the target of three excavations, the most recent being in 1929. Two cists are visible.That on the SE is, unusually, constructed of boulders and measures 2.6m by 1m by 1m, and is sealed by a massive capstone measuring 4.2m by 2.5m. It contained the remains of at least ten cremations at one end, an inhumation in the centre, but no grave-goods. The second visible cist, higher in the mound, is clearly not a primary burial. It contained a cremation, a food vessel, and flint flakes. A third cist, not now exposed, lay to the E of the centre,

11. Dun Mor Vaul, *Broch (NM 042492), situated on a rocky mound 300m N of Vaul on Tiree.* **OS sheet 46.**

Excavation in 1962–4 revealed a sequence of construction and occupation spanning the period from the mid-1st century BC to the late 2nd century AD. The broch stands within an irregularly shaped outer enclosure encircled by a massively built wall. The broch measures 9.2m in diameter within a wall 4.5m thick and surviving up to 2.2m high. The entrance to the broch is on the ESE, its passage provided with checks for a timber door secured by a draw-bar, and guarded by a circular cell, 2m in diameter, which opens into the passage from the N. There is an almost continuous gallery at ground level within the wall, entered through three doorways from the central area. The main entrance to the gallery is at the NNW, where it opens also onto the stair leading to the broch's upper levels. Ranged against the inner face of the broch wall were timber buildings, the scarcement ledge 1.4m above ground level having originally carried floor or roof joists. At a later period the upper sections of the walls were lowered and the stone re-used to build an additional lining wall which blocked the two smaller entrances to the gallery. Artefact evidence from the excavation indicated that the broch had experienced phases of occupation and abandonment which extended down into the 9th or 10th centuries AD.

12. Dun Nosebridge, *Islay, Fort (NR 371601), on a prominent outcrop at the SW end of the hilly ridge on the N bank of the River Laggan 3.5km SE of Bridgend. Take the unclassified road from Bridgend to Ballygrant via Ballitarsin and Cluanach. Park at the bridge over the Laggan and follow the track which runs eastwards from the N end of the bridge, then strikes uphill in a north-easterly direction.* **OS sheet 60.**

Without excavation it is impossible to offer a firm date for this site, as it is almost without parallel plan in western Scotland. The summit of the ridge is ringed by the grass-grown remains of a stone wall, which encloses an area some 25m by 15m. A second rampart runs round the E, N and W sides of the inner enclosure at a lower level, leaving only a narrow terrace of level ground between the two circuits. There is no clear evidence for a complete circuit along the craggy S face of the ridge. This outer ring is pierced by a gateway at the NE. Beyond this is a second outwork thrown across the spine of the ridge.

13. Dun Skeig, *Fort and Duns (NR 757571), from the picnic place overlooking Dunskeig Bay, 1.5km NW of Clachan off the A83 Lochgilphead-Campbeltown road, climb steeply over rough ground to the summit of Dun Skeig hill.* **OS sheet 62.**

The conical summit mound of this prominent hill overlooking the mouth of West Loch Tarbert from the S is crowned by a series of fortifications. The earliest phase is probably represented by the slight remains of a stone rampart encircling the entire summit. Subsequently, a dun measuring 26m by 18m internally was built at the S end of the fort. The wall of this dun, of timber-laced construction, is heavily vitrified and has recently produced a date range spanning the period from the late 1st to late 4th centuries AD. A third phase is represented by a second and smaller dun measuring 15m by 13m internally, constructed in part from vitrified material from its predecessor, and with a clearly defined entrance on the NE. The third phase would thus appear to date from the early Middle Ages.

14. Kildonan, *Dun (NR 780277), close to the roadside on the E side of the B842 Campbeltown-Carradale road, 9km N of Campbeltown.* **OS sheet 68.**

This D-shaped dun is one of the best preserved of its class, both its inner and outer wall-skins surviving to over 2m in height. Internally the dun measures 19m by 13m, its shape largely dictated by the restrictions of the rocky outcrop on which it stands. The entrance on the SW has door-checks and a draw-bar slot. There is a small mural chamber in the thickness of the wall on the NE, while at the W a double stair rises in the thickness of the rampart to the wall-head.

Excavations in 1936–8 and 1984 produced evidence for three phases of occupation of the site. The earliest, contemporary with construction of the dun, dates to the 1st or 2nd century AD. The dun was re-occupied in the 9th century and partly rebuilt, and occupied finally again between the late 12th and early 14th centuries.

15. Kintraw, *Cairns and Standing Stone (NM 830050), in a field on the E side of the A816 Oban-Lochgilphead road at the head of Loch Craignish, 7.5km N of Kilmartin.* **OS sheet 55.**

This superbly sited monument has attracted attention recently more for its supposed evidence for use as a Bronze Age observatory than for either its magnificent location or archaeological value. The standing stone re-erected after collapse in 1979 which, at nearly 4m in height, is the most prominent feature of the site, lies between the remains of two cairns. The E cairn measures 14.5m in diameter, but was consolidated in such a way after its excavation in 1959–60 that neither its enclosing kerb nor central cist are now visible. The smaller W cairn was not reconstructed after excavation and survives only as a kerb of irregular boulders with a small central cist.

16. Leccamore, *Luing, Dun (NM 750107). Follow the unclassified road S towards Toberonochy from the ferry pier at Port Mary. Some 4.2km S of Port Mary branch left onto the farm road to Leccamore (where permission to visit the dun should be obtained). The dun occupies the summit of the ridge to the SW of the farm.* **OS sheet 55.**

This well preserved site occupies a naturally strong position on the summit of a narrow ridge. Additional protection was provided by an outer enclosing wall, while on the N side two ditches cut across the spine of the ridge. The dun itself measures some 20m by 13m within a wall some 5m thick, and has two entrances, to the NE and SW, the entrance passage of the latter still rising to nearly 2m in height. The SW entrance passage is provided with drawbar slot, barhole, and checks for a wooden door close to its outer end, one of the massive jamb stones bearing some 15 cup-marks. The wall in the SW sector of the dun is especially fine, showing a pronounced batter. The NE entrance is more ruinous, but may have been the main doorway. There are mural cells on either side of the passage, that on the NW side having a corbelled roof and a flight of steps rising from its W side, presumably leading to the wall-head.

17. Lochbuie, *Mull, Stone Circle (NM 617251). Leave the A849 some 10km SW of Craignure on the unclassified road for Lochbuie. The circle stands in the grounds of Lochbuie House.* **OS sheet 49.**

On the level grasslands to the N of the mansion, lying at the centre of the pocket of fertile land at the head of Loch Buie, is one of the best of the small group of stone circles scattered throughout western Scotland and the Hebrides. Originally comprising nine stones, one has been destroyed and replaced subsequently by a boulder, the circle has three outlying monoliths, the furthest lying some 300m to the NNW.

18. Nether Largie, *Cairns (NR 828979, NR 830983 and NR 831985), Historic Scotland signposted sites W of the A816 Oban-Lochgilphead road, approximately 0.75km SSW of Kilmartin.* **OS sheet 55.**

These three cairns form the central part of the important Neolithic and Bronze Age ritual complex towards the N end of the Kilmartin valley. The S cairn is the earliest of the group. It is a chambered round cairn of Clyde type, originally over 40m in diameter. At the time of its excavation in 1864 a substantial amount of the superstructure had already been robbed, but the central chamber and two secondary cists remained intact. The central chamber, which has its entrance facing N, is roughly rectangular measuring 6m by 1.2m, and is constructed of slabs and sections of drystone walling. The chamber was divided into four compartments by three slabs rising from the floor. The present floor level is much higher than originally and the slabs project only slightly above its level, but stood up to

0.80m above the Neolithic level. Only fragmentary remains of burials were found within the chamber.

Nether Largie Mid is a chamberless round cairn some 30m in diameter. Excavated in 1929, two cists were found within the mound. The N cist was slab-built, the end slabs slotted neatly into grooves in the side panels. This cist was not reinstated after excavation and its position is now marked by concrete posts. The second cist, at the S, does survive, its capstone propped open on metal supports for inspection. Both cists were empty.

Nether Largie North, like the Mid cairn, is a chamberless round cairn some 21m in diameter. However, it covered only a single cist cut into the old ground surface under its centre. Visitors can descend steps into a modern chamber in the heart of the mound to inspect the cist and its superb capstone more or less *in situ*. Excavated in 1930, only one tooth, a piece of ochre and a little charcoal were found within the cist. The cist, however, has the carvings of two Bronze Age flat axeheads on one end panel, while on the underside of the capstone are ten axeheads and forty cup-marks.

19. Ormaig, *Cup-and-Ring marked Rocks (NM 822026), in the valley of the Eas Mor on the E side of upper Loch Craignish, approximately 2.5km S of Kintraw by footpath and track from the A816 Oban-Lochgilphead road.* **OS sheet 55.**

This rather remote group of rock-carvings are well worth the effort of visiting. Six rock outcrops bear cup-and-ring markings, two of them being particularly richly decorated. The lower of these has been weathered in part, but markings on a large section from which the turf was stripped in 1974 are still very clear. As well as the more common plain cup and cup-and-ring carvings, there are several so-called rosette motifs where a central cup-and-ring is surrounded by a ring of smaller cups, themselves encircled by an outer ring. During the stripping of the turf in 1974 a slate disc and a small flint tool were recovered from the site.

20. Ri Cruin, *Cairn (NR 825971), Historic Scotland signposted site W from the A816 Oban-Lochgilphead road approximately 2km SSW of Kilmartin.*

Lying at the S end of the Kilmartin valley complex, Ri Cruin cairn has been heavily plundered for stone in the past and survives now as a low mound of water-worn boulders. As with Nether Largie Mid and North cairns, it was originally a chamberless round cairn, in this case covering three cists. The slab-built cists are carefully constructed, two being grooved and rebated like that found in Nether Largie Mid cairn. The S cist has carvings of axeheads.

21. Strontoiller, *Stone Circle, Standing Stone and Cairn (NM 907289), at the mouth of Glen Lonan 4.5km E of Oban.* **OS sheet 49.**

This interesting group of Bronze Age monuments lies at the N end of the rich archaeological landscape surrounding Loch Nell. The stone circle, one of very few to survive in Argyll, lies to the N of the cairn and standing stone. Measuring 21m in diameter, it is composed of thirty-one water-worn boulders, the largest rising to barely 1m in height. The standing stone, known as Diarmid's Stone and traditionally regarded as the burial place of the nephew of the legendary Finn mac Cumhail, is an impressive pillar 4m in height. Immediately adjacent to it are the remains of a small kerb-cairn excavated in 1967.

22. Temple Wood, *Stone Circle and Standing Stones (NR 826978 and NR 827977), Historic Scotland signposted site to the W of the A816 Oban-Lochgilphead road, 2.25km SSW of Kilmartin.* **OS sheet 55.**

One of the most striking components of the great ritual complex in the Kilmartin valley. The main monument is an almost perfectly circular stone circle, 12m in diameter, which served as the focus for burials over a period of several centuries. Excavated in 1929 and again in 1974–9, it has been restored to its final form with the stones almost enveloped by a cairn of stones. The excavations revealed that a ring of twenty-two stones was the earliest component of the monument. Some of the stones have been removed in the past, their relative positions now marked by concrete blocks. Two of the stones bear carvings. At a later stage smaller upright stones were placed in the gaps between the original circle.

Several burials were made in and immediately around the circle, but it has been impossible to determine the sequence in which they were made. Two of the burials were under cairns, one on the NE and the other on the W of the circle, both covered cists containing inhumations. The W cairn was enclosed by upright stones linked by dry-stone walling. Its slab-sealed cist was paved with flat stones covered by a layer of earth which contained only one surviving tooth from the burial of a 4–6-year-old child. The NE cist was covered by a large slab and was floored with a pebble pavement. Placed on this were a beaker, a flint scraper and three fine barbed and tanged arrowheads. In the centre of the circle is a third cist burial covered by a kerb-bounded cairn of stones. The slab-built cist was set partly into a pit dug into the ground and lacked a lid, suggesting that it had been opened in the past. Only traces of charcoal were found within it.

The 1979 excavations revealed the existence of a second, apparently older stone circle to the N of the main monument. Measuring roughly 10.5m by 10m, it appeared that an original setting of between six and nine timber posts, with a tenth post placed in the centre had been replaced by a ring of at least five stones with one in the centre. The layout is reconstructed using concrete markers.

In the fields across the road to the E, not in Historic Scotland guardianship and not normally accessible to the public, are three groups of standing stones. The central group comprises a pillar – which is decorated with cup-and-ring markings – with four smaller stones around it. There are pairs of stones 36m to the ENE and WSW respectively.

23. Tirefour, *Broch (NM 867429), on the E side of the island of Lismore, 2.5km NE of the ferry pier at Achnacroish.* OS sheet 49.

This well preserved broch has, unfortunately, begun to deteriorate in recent years. It occupies a superb position on a rocky outcrop – from which its building-stone was obtained – near to the shore of the island and enjoys magnificent views over Loch Linnhe. The wall still rises in places to 5m in height and encloses a central area 12m in diameter. Rather than separate small chambers in the base of the wall, there is a continuous passage. Remains of a gallery can be seen higher in the wall, above an unusually wide scarcement ledge. The entrance is in the S where the wall has been most damaged.

ARRAN
(see map on p. 132)

1. Auchagallon, *Cairn (NR 892346), Historic Scotland signposted site off the unclassified road between the B880 and A841 2km N of Tormore.* **OS sheet 69.**

Occupying a fine position on a terrace above the old shore line on the W side of the island, with clear views towards Kintyre. The cairn appears to have been robbed for stone in the past, leaving its kerb of fifteen upright stones standing in isolation. It is believed that what appear to be the remains of the cairn mound, roughly 14.3m in diameter, may in fact be relatively modern field clearance debris.

2. Carn Ban, *Chambered Cairn (NR 991262), Historic Scotland signposted site remotely situated in a clearing amongst forestry on the SW slopes of Tighvein. Access by footpath from the head of the track to Auchareoch N from the A841 0.75km E of Kilmory.* **OS sheet 69.**

This well preserved Clyde tomb, 30m long by 18m wide was excavated in 1902. The crescentic façade at the NE backed a deep forecourt. The chamber opening from this was 4.6m long, divided into four compartments, and roofed with stone slabs.

3. Machrie Moor (Tormore), *Chambered Cairn, Cairns and Stone Circles (individual map references given below), Historic Scotland signposted sites E off the A841 at Tormore.* **OS sheet 69.**

The monuments on Machrie Moor comprise part of a major complex of ritual and burial sites of Neolithic and Bronze Age date, accompanied by extensive areas of Bronze Age settlement and field systems. The chambered cairn at NR 903310, 1km S of the main concentration of sites, is one of the earliest monuments in the group. What survives is the well preserved chamber and crescentic façade of a Clyde tomb stripped of its covering cairn superstructure. Excavations in the chamber in 1901 produced sherds of grooved ware, a stone mace-head and two flint knives.

The main series of sites are reached via the old farm track to Moss Farm from the signposted parking place by the side of the A841 300m N of Tormore. The first monument reached is a ruined round cairn (NR 900326), known as the

Moss Farm Road cairn, in an enclosure on the S side of the track. Some 1km E of this along the track is the first of a series of stone circles, usually labelled No 5 (NR 908323). Known also as 'Fingal's Cauldron Seat', this is a double ring of substantial granite blocks. The inner ring consists of a circle of eight stones 11.6m in diameter, while the outer element consists of fifteen smaller stones and has a diameter of 17.4m. A ruined cist was found in the centre of the inner circle. Circle No 4 lies roughly 100m to the E and comprises four squat granite blocks arranged in an ellipse measuring 6.4m along its long axis. It, too, enclosed a central cist, excavation of which produced an inhumation burial with a food vessel, a bronze awl and three flint flakes. Circle No 3 (NR 910324) lies 75m to its N. Consisting now of only a single upright sandstone monolith over 4m high, the stumps of three others and traces of several more, it appears to have formed a focus for burials. Excavation revealed two cists, one in the centre of the circle which contained an inhumation accompanied by a pot, and one off-centre which contained a crouched inhumation and a number of flint flakes. Circle No 1 lies 250m NE of No 4, to which it bears close similarities, and is the furthest from the road. It is an elliptical setting originally of eleven stones – alternating granite boulders and sandstone slabs – measuring 14.6m by 12.7m. Excavations in 1985 showed that the stones had been preceded by a double circle of timber uprights, itself constructed on a former agricultural landscape divided into 'fields' with lines of stakeholes – interpreted as fence lines – and scarred with plough marks. The cremated remains of an adult male, aged c.25–30, were buried in an inverted urn in the centre of the circle, together with a bone needle and a flint knife.

The most impressive member of the group is circle No 2 (NR 911324), which lies midway between Nos 3 and 1. This measured 13.7m in diameter when complete, but is comprised now of three massive sandstone uprights, the tallest 5.5m high, with the remains of at least five other fallen or broken stones alongside. One of the fallen stones has been roughly chiselled to form a millstone, but the attempt was abandoned unfinished. Excavation revealed two cists in the centre of the circle. One contained four flakes of flint and a decorated food vessel, but the probable inhumation in the second had completely decayed.

4. Monamore, *Chambered Cairn (NS 017288). At the S end of Lamlash on the A841 turn W on the unclassified road known as the Ross road. After 400m park in the Forestry Commission car park and take the track that runs uphill, following the signs for Meallack's Grave.* **OS sheet 69.**

The re-excavation of this Clyde-type cairn in 1961 proved a milestone in Neolithic studies, providing C-14 dates which pushed its construction back to *c.*3950 BC, rendering it currently the oldest such site yet explored. Although heavily plundered for stone, it is nevertheless worthy of a visit as all its major components are clearly visible. The main cairn structure is a trapezoid measuring 13.5m on its main NE to SW axis, by some 10.5m wide at the SW end. The chamber lies behind a shallow forecourt at the SW end and comprises three slab-built compartments. The forecourt is unusually asymmetrical, possibly an indicator of its early date, and is formed from upright slabs, graded roughly by height, separated by stretches of dry-stone walling. The tallest stones are in the centre of the façade, where they form the portal stones to the entrance passage.

Map 5: Ayrshire, Renfrewshire and Bute with Lanarkshire

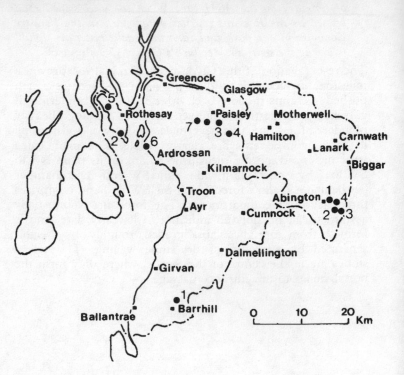

AYRSHIRE, RENFREW AND BUTE

1. **Balmalloch**, *Chambered Cairn (NX 264485), in moorland 3.75km NE of Barrhill.* **OS sheet 76.**

The ruins of this large cairn are remote from the nearest modern road. Plundered extensively for stones in the past, the remains comprise an irregular mound from which protrude portions of two substantial stone-built chambers arranged radially. The S appears to be a cist 2m by 0.75m, its walls built of slabs and corbelled dry-stone walling, roofed with a slab. The E chamber is represented by a massive, roughly square, capping slab, 1.8m square, below which can be traced portions of walling.

2. **Dunagoil**, *Bute, Fort (NS 085530). On the W coast of the island, 1.5km NW of Garroch Head.* **OS sheet 63.**

The fort crowns a narrow volcanic ridge which rises dramatically from the shoreline of Dunagoil Bay in a single 30m sweep. Steep slopes offer considerable natural defence, but this has been augmented by a timber-laced wall. This has been destroyed in a major conflagration and is heavily vitrified. There are reports that two entrances, complete with bar-holes, were identified during clearance of debris from the site. On a smaller outcrop at a lower level to the S of the fort are the remains of a dun excavated in the late 1950s. This was shown to have been occupied intermittently from the late Bronze Age until the mid-13th century AD.

3. **Duncarnock**, *Renfrewshire, Hillfort (NS 500559). Roughly 2.5km W of Newton Mearns. Turn W off the B769 just S of its junction with the unclassified Newton Mearns to Barrhead road, and after 1km fork right for Neilston. Some 100m past the junction turn left to Duncarnock farm, from which permission should be sought to visit the site, which lies on the hilltop 500m to the W.* **OS sheet 64.**

The irregular summit of the hill has been enclosed originally by a single 3m-thick stone wall, with traces of a possible inner enclosure around the higher rocky outcrop at the N end. The main enclosure has measured 192m by 100m, while the smaller summit enclosure is some 24m by 33.5m. There are no traces of internal structures.

4. **Dunwan**, *Renfrewshire, Hillfort (NS 547489). In the hills some 3km SW of Eaglesham overlooking Dunwan Dam from*

the SW. The fort occupies the NE end of the summit ridge of Dunwan Hill, an eminence surrounded on all sides by boggy ground, and is best approached by a circuitous route round the E and S sides of the reservoir from the access track which runs S from the B764 1.5km SW of Eaglesham. **OS sheet 64.**

The fort, which is roughly triangular in plan, has been defended by a single rampart some 3.6m wide. The internal area measures roughly 79m by 49m, within which can be traced the sites of two timber-built roundhouses. There are slight traces of an outer line of defences round the lower slopes of the hill.

5. Glecknabae, *Bute, Chambered Cairn (NS 007683), in farmland 8.5 km WNW of Rothesay off the A844.* **OS sheet 63.**

Excavation of this Clyde cairn found that it was built overlying an earlier Mesolithic midden. Extensively robbed for stone, two radially set chambers survive from a probable original three. Both chambers have entrances partly blocked by slabs inside the portal stones. Pottery recovered from the site showed continuity of burials here into the Beaker period.

6. Portencross, *Fort and Dun (NS 171491), on the ridge of Auld Hill overlooking Portencross, 3.2km WNW of West Kilbride off the B7048.* **OS sheet 63.**

At least two main phases of construction and occupation are reflected in the rather denuded remains of this impressively located stronghold. The earlier period appears to have comprised a timber-laced rampart enclosing an area some 30m by 15m, and probably originally larger and incorporating the higher area of ground along the ridge to the S. Traces of vitrification indicate that this early fort was destroyed by fire. At some later date, the spine of the ridge has been cut by two rock-cut ditches, to the S of which, on the highest point of the ridge, are the remains of a dun.

7. Walls Hill, *Hillfort (NS 411588), the shortest assent to this site is from North Castlewalls farm, via unclassified road and farm-track S of the A737 Johnstone-Beith road.* **OS sheet 64.**

One of the largest forts in S Scotland, this site occupies the almost level summit of the rocky-scarped Walls Hill. The summit area measures 487m by 213m, the remains of the rampart enclosing an area of some 7.3 ha. There are no surface remains of structures within the fort interior, but excavations in the 1950s demonstrated that the hilltop had been occupied in two phases in the early Iron Age. Evidence for circular timber houses was uncovered. It is suggested that this may have been the chief tribal centre of the Damnonii.

LANARKSHIRE
(see map on p.146)

1. **Arbory Hill**, *Hillfort (NS 944238), on the summit of Arbory Hill to the W of Abington. The easiest line of approach is via the footpath which follows the line of the Roman road up the S side of the valley of the Raggengill Burn from the unclassified road from Abington to Cold Chapel. At the head of the path turn NE then W along the wide spurs running down from the summit of Tewsgill Hill. The more energetic may prefer to make a direct assault on the steep SW flanks of Arbory Hill.* **OS sheet 72.**

The summit of this magnificent view-point is crowned by the grass-grown defences of at least two phases of fortification. The earlier phase is represented by twin concentric ramparts constructed from material excavated from external ditches, enclosing an area measuring 80m by 70m internally. Both ramparts are broken by five gateways. At a later date, a circular stone-walled fort was built on the highest point of the central area. This measures 43m in diameter within walls 3m thick, broken by two entrances. Within this secondary fort can be traced the positions of three ring-ditch houses and a hut platform, and further probable structures can be traced in the space between the inner of the earlier ramparts and the stone-walled fort. Some 75m E of the fort a single earthen bank cuts across the shoulder of the hill. This may represent a further line of defence to protect the most easily approached flank, or may simply mark a boundary between the cultivated area immediately E of the fort – traces of cultivation have been noted adjacent to the outer rampart – and grazing for livestock on the ground further to the E.

2. **Corbury Hill and Normangill Rig**, *Unenclosed Platform Settlements (NS 967210 and NS 966215), on opposite sides of the valley of the Midlock Water about 1km NE of Crawford. The Corbury Hill site lies on the S side of the valley mouth, immediately SW and higher up the hillside from the prominent bank eroded into the lower slopes by the Midlock Water. The Normangill Rig site lies partly within the square plantation of trees on the SW flank of Normangill Rig.* **OS sheet 72.**

These two sites are broadly representative of a class of late Bronze Age monument which are distributed widely through the Southern Uplands and have a high concentration of well preserved and accessible remains in Upper Clydesdale. They take the form of a series of scoops dug out from the face of the hill – usually arranged in rows – the excavated material being built up on the downhill side to form a roughly circular platform on which would have stood a circular timber house. There is no evidence that these settlements stood within any form of defensive enclosure. At Corbury Hill five platforms are clearly visible running across the face of the hill. The Normangill Rig sites are more complex. At the E edge of the plantation lie eight platforms which measure between 11m and 21m in diameter, while on a terrace further up the hillside to the NE are up to 14 small cairns. These may represent burial sites, or piles of field dump material. A further 250km to the SE is a second group of platforms.

3. Normangill, *Henge (NS 972221), bisected by the line of the unclassified road from Crawford to the Camps Reservoir, 100m E of the farm-track to Normangill farm.* **OS sheet 72.**

Despite mutilation by the road-builders and the already heavily eroded nature of the site, the general features of a fine Class II henge can still be traced. The bank and internal ditch enclosed a central platform measuring some 60m by 55m. Both entrances are well preserved, as are the causeways which approach from the NNW and SSE.

4. Ritchie Ferry, *Settlement (NS 945215), on the S flank of Castle Hill on the N side of the Clyde 1km NW of Crawford.* **OS sheet 72.**

This interesting group of earthwork remains lie on the lower slopes of the hill above the gravel terrace of the Clyde. The largest element comprises a settlement of some eight timber roundhouses enclosed within a bank of earth and stone. The bank is broken by four entrances – one in each side – which has led to suggestions that defence was not the main consideration. There is no external ditch and the bank appears rather to have been formed from material scraped up from either side. Two types of house site are represented within the enclosure. Five are of the scooped platform style visible slightly further down the valley at Corbury Hill or Normangill Rig, and three are of ring-ditch construction. To the W of the settlement is a so-called 'homestead'. This takes the form of an oval enclosure and associated hut platform within a substantial stone-walled defence.

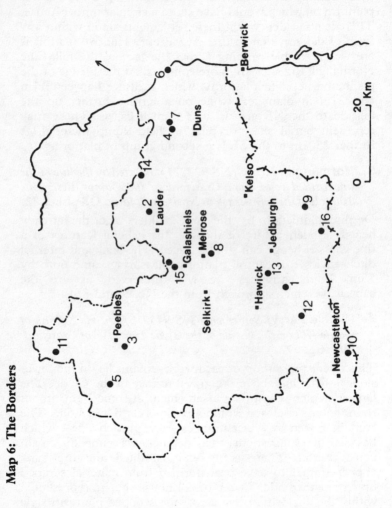

Map 6: The Borders

BORDERS

1. Bonchester Hill, *Hillfort (NT 595117), on the summit of Bonchester Hill 0.75km E of Bonchester Bridge, off the A6088 Hawick-Newcastle road.* **OS sheet 80.**

This is a highly complex site comprising several phases of fortification, the layout of which are difficult to follow on the ground. What is believed to be the earliest phase consists of a grass-covered stone wall which encloses an area 100m by 85m. Two further ramparts may represent successive phases of development. In the N part of the interior are the stone footings of several structures. Excavation produced evidence for occupation in the mid-1st millennium BC, followed by a re-occupation in the 2nd century AD.

2. Borrowstoun Rig, *Stone Circle (NT 557523), on an elevated moorland site 5.25km NE of Lauder.* **OS sheet 73.**

Occupying a position on the high plateau E of the main ridge of Borrowstoun Rig is an egg-shaped setting of 32 stones, ten of which remain upright. The largest of the stones is barely 0.60m in height.

3. Cademuir Hill, *Hillforts (NT 224370 and NT 230375), on the summit and SW spur of the long ridge of Cademuir Hill at the N end of the Manor Valley. Access by footpath and moorland from the unclassified road from Kirkton Manor to Peebles via Kings Muir, 4km SW of Peebles.* **OS sheet 73.**

The main summit of the hill is occupied by the remains of a large fort within a ruinous rampart measuring 210m by 120m, enclosing an area of some 3.25 ha. There are two clear entrances represented by breaks in the stony rampart at the NE and SW (the modern track enters and exits via these). In the interior can be traced the footings of upwards of 30 timber-built houses.

On a lower spur 500m to the SW are the remains of a smaller fort. The main enclosure, defended by a substantial stone wall, measures 70m by 40m. Appended to this are several subsidiary outer enclosures and fortified terraces. On the E side, carefully hidden in an area of dead ground in a dip at the end of the long sweep of level ground down from the main summit, is a substantial *chevaux de frise* defence, comprising staggered lines of jagged earthfast boulders which would have broken any charge towards the fort.

4. Cockburn Law, *Hillfort (NT 675597), on the summit of Cockburn Law 2.25km S of Abbey St Bathans. The quickest ascent is by footpath from the unclassified road between the B6355 Preston-Gifford road and Abbey St Bathans, 2km S of Abbey St Bathans. Follow this SSE to the crest of the broad ridge running SW from the summit of the Law, then turn NE along the ridge to the fort.* **OS sheet 67.**

The large fort on Cockburn Law is overshadowed, figuratively speaking, by the more famous site at Edinshall 1km to the ENE. The enclosure on the summit of the hill measures 110m by 85m within a series of grass-grown ramparts. The innermost line appears to be the earliest, being overlain in part by a series of hut-platforms, but its entrance is clearly aligned with that of the second ring, which suggests that both may have been constructed as one phase, but that only the outer was retained in a secondary redevelopment. There is a third line of defences on the N and W sides, the ramparts turning inwards at the entrance break. At the highest point of the hill are the remains of a large round cairn.

5. Dreva Craig, *Hillfort and Settlement (NT 126353), on the summit of the headland jutting S towards the confluence of the Holms Water with the River Tweed, 1.5km SE of Broughton. Access from the NE from the unclassified road from Broughton to Stobo and Peebles.* **OS sheet 72.**

Two substantial stone-built walls encircle the summit of a rocky outcrop which commands the good agricultural land on the gentler slopes to the S. The walls enclose an area measuring 58m by 43m. On the SW side of the fort is an area of *chevaux de frise*, deliberately set earth-fast jagged boulders which would have broken any enemy charge towards the walls from this direction. On the NW slopes below the hillfort are the extensive remains of a settlement comprising several large stone-walled enclosures, houses and scooped-out yards. More fragmentary remains of a similar site lie to the NE of the fort.

6. Earn's Heugh, *Forts (NT 892691), 3.25km NNW of Coldingham. Take the unclassified road to Coldingham Loch from the A1107 250m W of Coldingham. The forts are on the clifftops 600m NE of Westerside farm at the road-head.* **OS sheet 67.**

Perched on the brink of 150m cliffs, the two adjacent D-shaped enclosures probably represent the remains of two forts, at least 50 per cent of which have been eroded by the sea. The eastern of the two, now measuring roughly 70m by 35m, is bounded to its S by a remaining arc of rampart and ditch, broken by an entrance in the W. An outer pair of ramparts was added to this original enclosure. To its W lies what is now a larger structure, its remaining stretches of rampart on the S and W defining an area roughly 55m in diameter. This was enclosed originally by a single rampart, to which two further lines – which overlie the outer defences of the E fort – were added subsequently.

While the E fort has no visible internal features, the W contains some nine circular stone foundations ranged round the inner face of the innermost rampart. These probably represent a late period in the occupation history of the site, possibly of 2nd to 4th century AD date.

7. Edinshall, *Fort, Broch and Settlement (NT 772603), on the lower NE slopes of Cockburn Law overlooking the valley of the Whiteadder Water. Signposted Historic Scotland site N off the B6355 Preston-Gifford road at its junction with the B6365, 3km W of Preston.* **OS sheet 67.**

A complex site representing several phases of development. The earliest period is represented by the substantial remains of an oval fort 134m by 73m, which is sited awkwardly on shelving ground perched on the lip of steeper slopes falling to the river. The fort was defended by double ramparts and ditches, and there are signs of at least two phases of development in the circuits. The remains of a low bank divides the interior into roughly equal E and W halves. The western half is occupied by the base of a very large broch, its dry-stone walls still standing up to 2m high. Measuring 17m in internal diameter, it is unlikely that the broch rose to any great height. The entrance on the E is checked for a door roughly half way along its length, behind which guard cells opened from either side. There are cells in the 5m thickness of the wall to the N, S and W, that on the S leading to the stair which rose originally to the wall-head.

The E half of the fort is occupied and its defences are partly overlain by a lightly defended settlement dated to the 2nd century AD. The rectangular enclosure around the broch may also date from this phase. The remains of the settlement comprise the footings of a series of roundhouses and attendant yards and enclosures. Probably contemporary with this is a further series of hut-circles and enclosures some 90m to the SE.

8. Eildon Hill North, *Hillfort (NT 555328), occupying the summit of the northern of the trio of hills overlooking Melrose from the S. Access by footpath (signposted 'Eildon Walk') from the B6359 in Melrose, or from the A6091 1.5km E of Melrose.* **OS sheet 73.**

Believed to be the site of the chief centre of the Iron Age tribe known as the Selgovae, this is one of the largest forts in S Scotland. Its remains reveal several phases of occupation, the earliest of which is now represented by a scarcely discernable earthen rampart overlain by some of the later house-sites on the gentler slopes around the summit. The most prominent defences lie further down the hillside on the steeper ground and enclose a roughly circular area 16 ha in extent. In its final phase there may have been three concentric rings of defences, each built on terraces cut back into the face of the hillside. In the interior of the fort are the pit-like depressions which mark the sites of upwards of 300 circular huts, representing the homes of a population of between 1000 and 2000 people. On the W extremity of the summit are the earthwork defences of a Roman signal tower, excavated in the 1950s, connected with the major Roman fort at Newstead 2km to the NE.

9. Hownam Law, *Hillfort (NT 796220), on the summit of Hownam Law, 3.75km SE of Morebattle.* **OS sheet 74.**

Possibly serving as one of the tribal centres of the Selgovae, this large fort covers an area of 8.5 ha. The defences comprise a single rampart some 3m thick with only one obvious entrance at the SW. The interior is pock-marked by the footings of over 155 hut circles.

10. Long Knowe, *Long Cairn (NY 527862). This site lies remote from any public road in the midst of Forestry Commission plantations, but the level of preservation merits viewing. At the S end of Newcastleton turn E across the Liddle Water onto unclassified roads, cross the river and turn first right. After just over 3km fork left for Kershope Bridge/ Roansgreen. Cross the bridge into England and park, then take the forestry track on the N side of the road and follow this upstream for about 1.2km to the bridge which re-crosses into Scotland. Cross this bridge and after about 300m fork left.*

After a further 500m fork right and after 400m the track takes a sharp turn to the left. Turn right at the next forestry track and follow this for 1.1km. The cairn is in a clearing on the left of the track. **OS sheet 79.**

This great mound of stones in the midst of the Newcastleton Forest is perhaps the finest of the long cairns of southern Scotland. Shaped like an elongated pear, it measures some 52m in length by 13.5m across at its widest point. A number of slabs can be seen protruding from the mound, marking the position of cists within the structure. While its remoteness has guaranteed the largely intact survival of the cairn structure, it has been the target for 19th-century antiquarian investigation, the results of which were never published.

11. North Muir *(NT 105503), turn left off the A702 1km N of Dolphinton onto the unclassified road to Garvald and Medwynbank. After a little over 1km turn right for Medwynbank, then follow footpath NE to the cairns.* **OS sheet 72.**

This is one of the best-preserved cairn cemeteries in the region, comprising at least nine round cairns clustered around the 280m contour and running for about 1km along the SE flank of North Muir. The first of the group, Nether Cairn, is one of the better preserved, measuring over 15m in diameter and rising to 3.7m in height. Traces of a 1.8m wide ditch can be detected about 1m beyond the spread base of the cairn. Three less well preserved cairns lie between this and the largest of the group, the Upper Cairn, some 730m to the NE. This is quite overgrown, but still measures over 20m in diameter by 4.2m high. It does not appear to have been surrounded by a ditch, but shows considerable signs of disturbance.

12. Ninestone Rig, *Stone Circle (NY 518973), in forestry at the S end of Ninestone Rig 900m ESE of the Whitropefoot Bridge on the B6399 Newcastleton-Hawick road.* **OS sheet 79.**

This elliptical setting of nine stones – eight earthfast and one fallen – measures 7m by 6.4m. The eight standing stones reach a maximum of 2m in height and all have a pronounced lean towards the centre of the circle. Tradition relates that the stones were the setting for the cauldron in which the wicked Lord Soulis of Liddesdale was boiled to death in molten lead.

13. Rubers Law, *Hillfort (NT 580155), on the summit of the isolated conical mass of Rubers Law 3km SSE of Denholm.* **OS sheet 80.**

The defences which crown this craggy summit represent a complex sequence of several phases of development. The lowest ring comprises a denuded rampart on the slopes below the summit, which encloses an area of about 2.8 ha. Within this are two substantial, ruinous stone walls, both of which incorporate dressed sandstone blocks of Roman style. These, it has been suggested, were obtained from a Roman signal station or monumental tower on the hilltop, and indicate the re-occupation of the site in the early 1st millennium AD.

14. The Mutiny Stones, *Long Cairn (NT 622590), in a remote moorland setting on the SE headland of Byrecleugh Ridge in the Lammermuir Hills, by farm-track and footpath to Killpallet SSW from the unclassified road from Gifford to Longformacus, 7km NW of Longformacus.* **OS sheet 67.**

This ruinous long cairn is still an impressive structure despite having been robbed extensively for stones to build the nearby sheep fank. Aligned ENE and WSW, it measures 80m in length and still rises to 2.5m at its ENE end. Partial excavation in 1871 failed to produce evidence for chamber or burials, while re-excavation in 1924 produced evidence for a short section of walling which may have represented the fragmentary remains of a chamber entering the cairn from the side.

15. Torwoodlee, *Fort and Broch (NS 465384), on the headland at the E end of the NE spur of Mains Hill overlooking the Gala Water 3.5km NW of Galashiels. Access to the site by farm-track from Torwoodlee Mains, N of the A72 Galashiels-Clovenfords road.* **OS sheet 73.**

The severely denuded ramparts of an earlier Iron Age fort are overlain by the remains of a broch of probably late 1st or early 2nd century AD date. Measuring 137m by 106m internally, both ramparts have been plundered for stone in the past, in part probably by the builders of the broch. The broch wall has been reduced to its lowest courses, in no place rising higher than 1m, and is 5.5m thick around a central area 12m in diameter. The entrance passage on the SE has checks for a wooden door and is guarded by a chamber on its S side. A mural stair rose to the wall-head from a chamber in the thickness of the wall at the SW. The findings of excavations in 1950 indicated that the broch had been dismantled deliberately, much of its stone being used to infill its enclosing ditch. Large quantities of Roman pottery and glass were found in the floor levels of the broch.

16. Woden Law, *Hillfort (NT 768125), on the crest of Woden Law overlooking the valley of the Kale Water in the Cheviots. The easiest access to the fort is from the NW, where a footpath climbs from Tow Ford at the junction of the unclassified roads down the valley from Hownam and Pennymuir to Upper Hindhope. At the highest point of the path – which is here following the course of the Roman road known as Dere Street – turn SW and climb the steepening slopes towards the summit.*

Like most of the major forts in this area, Woden Law's complex of defences indicates that several phases of development are represented. The earliest phase appears to have been a single stone rampart enclosing the summit of the hill. Onto the S and E sides of this were added two further lines of rampart and ditch, the steep natural slopes on the N and W requiring no further protection. The innermost of the four visible ramparts appears to belong to a third phase of development in the early 1st millennium AD. Some 12 to 30m outwith the outermost of the fort's ramparts a great earthwork consisting of a double bank with one central and a frontal and rear ditch runs in an arc from the rim of the steeper slopes on the N round to the SW. Further discontinuous lines of ditch and bank lie beyond these. These have been interpreted as the remains of practice siege-works associated with the temporary Roman camps at Pennymuir. On the broad shoulder between Woden Law and Hunthall Hill is a series of five cross-dykes, probably of pre-Roman date, representing outlying defences associated with the Iron Age fort.

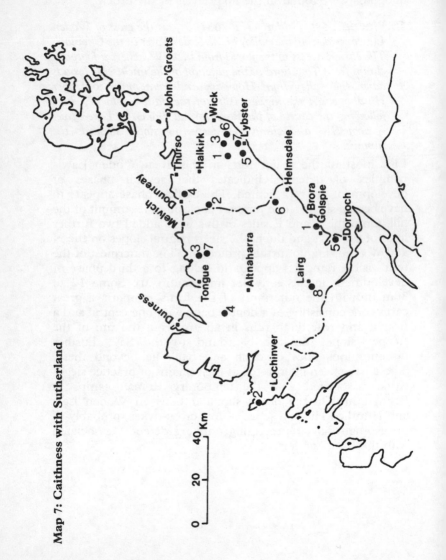

Map 7: Caithness with Sutherland

CAITHNESS

1. Achavanich, *Chambered Cairn and Stone Setting (ND 187417), immediately E of the unclassified road from the A895 at Achavanich to Lybster, at the S end of Loch Stemster.* **OS sheet 12.**

A horseshoe-shaped setting of standing stones, the tallest only 2m high, stands on the crest of a low moorland promontory overlooking Loch Stemster from the S. Thirty-six stones remain from a possible original fifty-four, each set into a low bank of earth and rubble which may be the product of a levelling of the central area. The setting is believed to date from the Bronze Age, and formed a focus for ritual and burial; the remains of what may be a group of cist burials lie just to the NE of the stones.

To the SE of the stones, separated from them by a shallow, boggy depression, are the remains of a heavily robbed chambered cairn of Neolithic date. The cairn has been round, roughly 18m in diameter, and has been erected over a substantial, slab-built chamber. The tall, angular slab rising in the centre of the site formed the back of the chamber.

2. Beinn Freiceadain, *Hillfort and Cairn (ND 059558). Roughly 6.5km WSW of Halkirk. Leave the B870 at Plocan, 3.5km N of Scotscalder Station on the unclassified road to Brawlbin. After some 2.5km fork left for Dorrery. The fort occupies the N of the two summits of the prominent hill to the W of the road.* **OS sheet 12.**

The largest hillfort in northern Scotland, its single rampart encloses an area some 270m by 145m on the summit of the highest piece of ground in the area. The wall, which is about 4m thick, is pierced by a single gateway at the WNW, the passageway of which has been lined with large slabs set on edge. On the summit of the hill near the N end of the enclosure are the ruinous remains of a chambered cairn of unknown type.

3. Camster, *Chambered Cairns (ND 260442 and ND 260440), Historic Scotland signposted monuments in moorland on the W side of the unclassified road from Lybster to Watten.* **OS sheet 12.**

Consolidated after excavation for public viewing, these cairns are two of the finest Neolithic monuments of their kind to be seen in mainland Scotland. The long cairn, which occupies a prominent skyline position to the N of the lower-lying round cairn, is one of the key sites which advanced understanding of the longevity of both use and development of these great funerary monuments. The excavation showed that the NE of the two burial chambers contained within the heart of the 60m-long cairn had originally lain within a small cairn bounded by a 1m-tall dry-stone wall. Its original entrance passage is represented by the inner half of the existing extended approach, and runs N to S on a different axis from that of the long cairn – which is oriented NE to SW. The extension to the passage is oriented on the new alignment, requiring a dog-leg turn to the SE. A second chamber lies at the centre of the long cairn. It is approached along a straight passage, but the excavation suggested that it, too, had been extended and that this chamber may also have originally lain at the heart of a separate round cairn. It is these two separate chambers which give the long cairn its distinctive hump-backed profile. The cairn superstructure, which was carefully restored after excavation, includes a magnificent horned forecourt at the NE, complete with a platform for 'ritual' activity. There is also a smaller horned forecourt at the SW end.

The round cairn lies 200m to the SE. It takes the form of a round mound of bare stones 18m in diameter by 3.6m in height. It, too, has been restored in part, especially in the walling of its small forecourt at the ESE. Access to the centrally located polygonal chamber is along a very low passage (the roof in places in only 75cm high). The chamber itself is massively constructed, rising 3m to its corbelled and lintelled roof.

4. Cnoc Freiceadain, *Chambered Cairns (ND 013654 and ND 012653), on the NE spur of Cnoc Freiceadain 1.5km NNW of Shebster off the unclassified road from Balmore to Achreamie and Shebster.* **OS sheet 12.**

These two cairns form prominent skyline features on the crest of the hill. The N cairn measures some 67m by 16m and is probably the product of several stages of construction. It is possible that an original round cairn at the SW end has been incorporated into a long cairn with prominent horns enclosing a forecourt at its NE end. Upright slabs protruding from the mound of cairn material indicate the presence of several burial chambers.

The second cairn, known as Na Tri Shean, lies 120m S of the first on the true summit of the hill. It appears to be a chambered long cairn with its main axis running NW to SE. The cairn structure measures 75m in length and appears to be the product of the linking of two independent heel-shaped and horned cairns by an intervening mound. It rises to 2m at the NW end and 3m at the SE.

5. Forse, *Wag, Dun and Settlement (ND 204352), 1.6km NNE of Latheron off the A9, in moorland.* OS sheet 11.

Preserved in what is now rough grazing land are the remains of an extensive settlement complex with evidence of occupation spanning the period from the later 1st millennium BC through to the early 1st millennium AD. Excavations in 1939 and 1946 revealed that the earliest settlement may have comprised a cluster of huts, represented by stone wall-footings, or by the circular enclosure which has been described variously as a broch or a dun. This measures 14m in diameter within a wall 1.2m thick, which is widened at the NNE to accommodate the entrance. To one side of the entrance is a guard chamber, while on the other is a flight of stairs leading originally to the wall-head. The dun appears to have been plundered extensively for stone to build a series of long, rectangular pillared houses known locally as 'wags'. One of the wags to the W of the dun is quite well preserved. Measuring 12m long, it contains the remains of two rows of pillar stones within low dry-stone walls, one of which is still connected to the outer wall by a massive lintel. The wags were probably roofed with slabs and turf, although the original excavator proposed rather that they were unroofed cattle corals where the animals were placed each night for protection.

6. Garrywhin, *Chambered Cairn (ND 313411), Historic Scotland signposted site. Access N from A9 at Ulbster and moorland path.* OS sheet 12.

This, the so-called Cairn of Get, is a small passage grave within a cairn which possesses projecting horns at both ends, the whole structure being some 25m long. Both passage and burial chambers are now roofless, and there are signs that the cairn had been substantially robbed in the past. The narrow entrance (0.80m wide) at the SW lies between a pair of portal stones at the centre of the horned façade, and opens onto a 3m-long passage. This leads to a rectangular outer compartment, opening in turn onto a circular inner chamber. Excavations in the 19th century revealed a deep layer of mixed cremated and un-cremated bone in the circular chamber, as well as leaf-shaped arrowheads, flint and several pot sherds. The rectangular chamber contained at least seven inhumations.

7. Mid Clyth, *Stone Rows (ND 295384), Historic Scotland signposted site N off the A9 7km N of Lybster.* **OS sheet 11.**

Known more commonly as 'the Hill o' Many Stanes', this remarkable site lies on S facing slopes and commands fine open aspects to the S. It comprises a series of 22 stone rows which originally contained 250 stones. The rows are aligned roughly N–S, but gradually diverge into a fan-shaped arrangement towards the S. None of the stones – mainly slabs – are large, the tallest being under 1m in height. The function of the monument is unknown.

SUTHERLAND
(see map on p.160)

1. Carn Liath, *Broch (NC 870013). On the S side of the A9 (signposted and car-parking), some 4km ENE of Golspie.* **OS sheet 17.**

The broch, which is clearly visible from the road, lies on a gravel terrace above the old raised beach. The edge of the terrace is lined by a stone wall which encloses structures of several different phases, crammed into the narrow space between it and the broch. The approach to the broch is through a narrow stone-walled passage leading in from the outer wall at the E end of the terrace. This was originally lintelled and was provided with door-checks. The broch entrance proper leads through a second passage provided with door-checks, and slot and socket for a draw-bar, into the central yard. A blocked door on the right led into a chamber. Opposite the entrance passage a door opens onto the staircase to the upper levels, evidence for which can be seen in traces of the scarcement and portions of a gallery near the entrance. The inner wall face is largely obscured by the walling of a house built in the broch interior after the collapse or demolition of the upper portions of the structure.

2. Clachtoll, *Broch (NC 036278). On the shore to the W of the B869 Lochinver-Stoer road, immediately N of Clachtoll. The most direct approach is from the N along the shoreline from Bay of Stoer.* **OS sheet 15.**

Still impressive despite the collapse of part of its wall over the low cliff to its W and the rubble-choked interior, the broch appears as a substantial flat-topped mound crowning a rocky knoll above the slabby foreshore from which its building-stone was won. The broch stands within a substantial outer defence formed by a wall which cuts across the shallow headland, ending at the cliff edge. An entrance pierces the wall and from this a path ran to the broch doorway. This was flanked by various structures crowded into the space between the rampart and the broch, but these are largely obscured by tumbled stone and later buildings. It appears that the inner end of the approach path was covered over in advance of the entrance passage proper. This was fronted by a doorway capped by a massive triangular lintel. The passage beyond this is largely blocked with fallen stone, but door-checks and small openings leading into flanking mural chambers can be seen.

3. **Coille na Borgie**, *Chambered Cairns (NC 715590). Near Rhinavie, roughly 3km S of Bettyhill in Strathnaver. Leave the A836 Bettyhill-Thurso road on the unclassified road to Skelpick. The cairns are visible as an elongated ridge of stone protruding through the heather above the road.* **OS sheet 10.**

The remains of two – not three as sometimes suggested – horned long cairns lie end to end on a terrace above the river. The northern cairn has been cut in two by a later trackway, leading to the mistaken identification as two separate cairns. The cairns, which are oriented N and S, are only 10m apart. The N cairn is 57m long, while the S is 72m. There are horned façades at both ends, the longer horns lying at the N in both cases. From the centre of the N façades of both cairns, passages ran south to the chambers.

4. **Dun Dornaguil**, *Broch (NC 457450). At the roadside 500m S of Altnacaillich farm on the unclassified road from the A838 at Hope to the A836 at Altnaharra.* **OS sheet 9.**

The superb location of this broch above a sharp bend on the Strathmore River, with Ben Hope as its northern backdrop, possibly outweigh its archaeological merits. The broch measures 8.2m in diameter within a wall up to 4.2m thick, but the interior is choked with fallen rubble. The entrance to a chamber can still be traced above the rubble infill, and it is clear from the high surviving portion of walling over the entrance at the NE, some 6.7m high supported on a modern buttress, that the upper levels of the wall have been galleried. Over the blocked entrance is a massive triangular lintel.

5. **Embo**, *Chambered Cairn (NH 817926). In a car-park at the SE end of Embo.* **OS sheet 21.**

The oval cairn, measuring 12.8m by 9m, has been excavated and consolidated. It contained two passage graves and two cists, indicating re-use of a Neolithic tomb in the Bronze Age. The S chamber, an oval built of six upright slabs with dry-stone walling in the spaces between, measures 2.3m by 1.7m and is entered from the S along a short passage. It contained several inhumations and sherds of Beaker pottery. A secondary cist had been inserted into the chamber, containing a single inhumation with a food vessel and sixteen jet beads. The chamber at the N end was heavily ruined, but contained at least one inhumation. Immediately to its S was a second cist. It contained the remains of two infants with a food vessel and portions of a beaker. There had also been at least nine cremations inserted into the cairn. Large quantities of fish and animal bones had been deposited both within the cairn material and in the chambers themselves.

6. Kilphedir, *Broch (NC 994189). On the hillside on the N side of Strath Ullie, overlooking the River Helmsdale 500m ENE of Kilphedir on the A897 Helmsdale-Kinbrace road.* **OS sheet 17.**

Strath Ullie offers a rich archaeological landscape for exploration, containing monuments of all phases from the Neolithic to the Clearances. Kilphedir broch is just one of several spaced along the valley, but its superb position and imposing outer defences make it a good example for visiting. The broch itself is quite ruinous, looking like a rubble mound with scree spilling down the flanks of the knoll which it crowns. The outer defences look at first like heather-covered earthen banks, but are in fact stone-built walls which enclose terraces to E and W of the broch. Outwith these a deep ditch encircles the entire knoll, beyond which is a second circuit of heather-clad stone wall.

To the W of the broch, on the lip of a ravine, are remains of three stone-built hut-circles. One has thicker walls, beneath which is a souterrain. Further hut circles can be seen on the W side of the ravine and further up the burn.

7. Skelpick, *Chambered Cairn (NC 723566). Some 5km SSE of Bettyhill near the Skelpick Burn, off the unclassified road from the A836 Bettyhill-Thurso road to Skelpick.* **OS sheet 10.**

Like the cairns at Coille na Broige, the horned long cairn at Skelpick is aligned N and S. Measuring some 61m in length, its chamber is entered via a 4.6m-long passage running S from the centre of the façade between the N horns. The chamber is divided into three compartments. The N compartment is 2m long by 1.2m wide and 1.3m in height. It opens into the middle compartment through a portal capped by a 3m-long lintel. This chamber measures 3m by 2.4m. A second portal opens into the final chamber, a polygon measuring some 3.6m by 3m, formed from six massive slabs with dry-stone walling in the interstices.

8. The Ord, *Hut Circles and Chambered Cairns (NC 5705).* *On the low rounded hill at the S end of Loch Shin opposite Lairg. Cross the River Shin on the A839 Lairg-Invercassley road. Turn right then second left to the car-park at the start of a signposted trail.* **OS sheet 16.**

The Ord has been a favoured place of settlement from the Neolithic and the recent past, and monuments of all periods are scattered over its crown and slopes. Near the summit of the hill, adjacent to the TV mast, are the remains of a cairn excavated in 1967. Although the chamber, antechamber and most of the passage were infilled following the dig, some of the passage is visible. The cairn is otherwise a roughly circular mound of bare stones some 27m in diameter, with a shallow forecourt. The grass-grown boulder platform which surrounds it is part of the ritual sealing of the tomb at the end of its functioning life. There are fragmentary remains of a second chambered cairn on the summit of the hill, represented now by the surviving slabs of the chamber and entrance passage.

Early settlement on the hill is represented by the 23 or so hut-circles which have been recorded on its slopes, and by the clearance cairns which mark the location of early agriculture. A particularly clear example of a hut-circle can be seen to the S of the summit of the hill, lying immediately to the NE of a prominent Bronze Age kerb-cairn. Towards the SE limit of the open ground is an unusual structure, crossed by a post-medieval enclosure wall and partly cut by a modern field fence. Described in the past as an unusual form of ditched ring-cairn, it looks more like a substantial hut circle with an enclosing ditch and outer bank.

CENTRAL SCOTLAND

1. Castlehill Wood, *Dun (NS 750909), not marked on the OS map, the site lies on the lip of a low crag at the SE spur of the Touch Hills in an area of rough ground designated as an MoD testing site. The easiest access to the site is across moorland on the N side of the unclassified road from St Ninians to Fintry.* **OS sheet 57.**

Excavation at this well preserved site in 1955 indicated that occupation may have commenced in the late 1st millennium BC and extended into the 2nd century AD. The remains comprise a strongly built stone wall 4.9m thick, broken on the E by a single gateway and entrance passage provided with the checks for a timber door. The wall enclosed an oval area 23m by 15m which, despite almost total excavation, revealed no evidence for internal structures, except for an external staircase which rose up the face of the wall some 5m to the N of the entrance. There were also two narrow mural chambers which had been used, probably in a later period, as corn-drying kilns.

2. Coldoch, *Broch (NS 696981), on the N edge of a shelter-belt of trees 250m W of Coldoch House, lying to the S of the B8031 running between the A873 Blairdrummond-Thornhill road and the B822 Thornhill-Kippen road.* **OS sheet 57.**

This is one of the better preserved of the group of brochs lying between the Tay and the Tweed. The remains comprise a ruinous stone wall 5.5m thick and rising in places to 2.4m in height, enclosing a central area 9m in diameter. There are three small chambers in the thickness of the wall-base, and a mural staircase rising originally to the wall-head.

3. Dumyat, *Hillfort (NS 832973), access by footpath from the W from the summit of the unclassified road from Bridge of Allan to Sheriffmuir.* **OS sheet 57.**

The complex defences of this fort represent several phases of development over a period extending from the late 1st millennium BC to the early 1st millennium AD. It crowns the lower SW spur of Dumyat proper, perched above the precipitous slopes of the southern flank of the Ochils. The steepest slopes lie to the E and NE, and the greatest depth of defence has accordingly been massed on the W. The defences of the earliest phase comprise two closely-set stone ramparts which enclose an area measuring 130m by 48m,

Map 8: Central Scotland and Perthshire

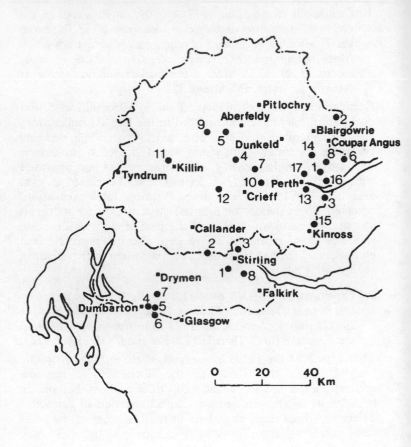

- Pitlochry
- Aberfeldy
- 9
- 5
- 2
- Blairgowrie
- Dunkeld
- 14
- Coupar Angus
- 11
- 4
- 7
- 8
- 6
- Killin
- 17
- 1
- Tyndrum
- 10
- Perth
- 16
- 12
- Crieff
- 13
- 3
- 15
- Callander
- Kinross
- 2
- 3
- Stirling
- Drymen
- 1
- 8
- 7
- Falkirk
- 4
- Dumbarton
- 5
- 6
- Glasgow

0   20   40
Km

entered by a single gateway in the W. Outside the gate are a series of further earthworks which may represent a subsequent phase of development. A second major phase appears to be represented by the ruinous massive stone wall which encircles the summit. This is a dun-like enclosure which measures 27m by 16m within the wall. This inner enclosure is linked to the earlier works by a very ruinous stretch of wall. It has been suggested that the name of the site – transferred in a later period to the main hill behind it – is derived from a role as the principal fortress of the great tribal confederation known as the Maeatae (i.e. Dumyat = 'fort of the Maeatae') who were based in S Central Scotland and who were noted as opponents of the Romans in the early 3rd century AD.

4. Dunbuie Hill, *Dun (NS 421752), on the SW end of the summit of the small conical hill overlooking Loch Bowie at the N end of Dumbuck Hill. Access via the unclassified road running N to Barnhill from the A82 at Milton. The dun lies 500m SW of Barnhill.* **OS sheet 64.**

Excavations in 1895 revealed the remains of a stone wall nearly 4m thick, much of which is still visible, enclosing an area 9m in diameter. The entrance, which is only 0.90m wide, lies on the E side. The brief excavation report mentions two mural chambers lying on either side of the entrance passage, but these are no longer traceable. The excavation was notable chiefly for the descriptions of what proved to be a large number of faked slate weapons recovered, but the genuine material constituted a standard early 1st millennium BC assemblage including bone implements, whetstones, pounders and portions of two rotary querns.

5. Greenland, *Cup-and-Ring Marked Stones (NS 434746), on the N side of Sheephill 300m SW of Greenland farm. Access via track from the E-bound carriageway of the A82 100m W of the Cardross roundabout.* **OS sheet 64.**

Several natural rock outcrops on the summit of the hill SE of the disused quarry-face bear large expanses of incised decoration. The largest area includes 22 cup-and-ring markings, several of the cups having up to nine concentric rings. Some of the rings are pierced by radial grooves running out from the central cups, which extend into curving channels.

6. Sheephill, *Hillfort (NS 434744), location details as for Greenland above. The fort occupies an isolated basalt outcrop overlooking Cardross and the Clyde 150m due S of the cup-and-ring markings.* **OS sheet 64.**

The remains of this vitrified fort were excavated between 1966 and 1970. The defences comprise two circuits of formerly timber-laced ramparts, the inner earlier than the outer line. The outer defences, which lie on a terrace below the summit platform, enclose an area 80m by 50m.

7. Stockie Muir, *Chambered Cairn (NS 479812), the site occupies the crest of a low moorland eminence above the deep valley of the Carnock Burn 3.25km WNW of the car-park at the Queen's View on the A809 Milngavie-Drymen road.* **OS sheet 64.**

The remains of this ruinous Clyde cairn form part of a scattered group dispersed through the rough country N of the Kilpatrick Hills. The cairn measures 18.3m along its main E–W axis, and about 9.1m across at its widest point, but its general outline has been blurred by the tumble of stones from its upper sections. The two large earthfast boulders which protrude from the rubble near the E end may mark the position of the entrance passage or a portion of the façade. About 1m to the W can be seen the remains of the chamber, which measures 3.96m by 0.90m. One of the covering lintels remains in place.

8. Tappoch, *Broch (NS 833849), in the midst of forestry 500m to the W of Torwood village. Access via a path running W from the track which runs SSW from Tappoch to Tor Wood Castle from the unclassified road from Torwood to West Plean.* **OS sheet 65.**

Positioned on the edge of a low cliff to its W, the broch at Tappoch (or Torwood as it is sometimes called), occupies what would have been a strongly defensive site overlooking the fertile agricultural lands around Plean. The interior of the site was cleared in the middle of the 19th century, but is now once again quite overgrown, but no clearance of the outer face of the wall was undertaken. It comprises the well preserved remains of a broch 10m in diameter within a wall 7m thick and surviving up to 2.5m in height. The entrance passage, which has checks for a wooden door and the slots for a draw-bar, has been cleared for its entire length and still retains two of the massive lintels with which it was roofed.

There are no mural chambers, but a staircase providing access to the wall-head rises in the thickness of the wall. The crags to the W required no further defence in that direction, but on the N, S and E are the remains of two very ruinous stone walls.

PERTH AND KINROSS
(see map on p.170)

1. Arnbathie, *Hillfort (N) 170259). Some 3km E of Scone on the summit of Law Hill. Take the unclassified road to Kilspindie from the A94 just over 2km NE of New Scone. After 2km turn left onto the farm-track to Arnbathie. The quickest approach is by a steep scramble up the hillside to the N of the track.* **OS sheet 53.**

The fort, which is oval in plan, is enclosed by a single stone rampart for most of its circuit. To the N, where the approach is easiest, there are two additional outer ramparts. A depression towards the centre of the N half of the fort may mark the position of a rock-cut cistern. Outwith the fort, especially on the gentler slopes to the N, can be traced numerous hut circles.

2. Barry Hill, *Hillfort (NO 263504). Crowning an isolated flat-topped conical outcrop at the E end of the Hill of Alyth, forming a prominent feature on the northern skyline of this part of Strathmore. The quickest access is by a steep scramble from the B954 Alyth-Glenisla road 2km NE of Alyth.* **OS sheet 53.**

Tumbled stone remains of a probable timber-laced rampart – vitrified material has been recovered from the site – enclose an area some 61m by 36m. There are outer ramparts to the S and W to command the break in slope on these sides, that to the W enclosing the rock-cut cistern.

3. Castle Law, *Hillfort (NO 183153). On the NE spur of Castle Law, 1km SW of Abernethy. Access via track from the unclassified road from Abernethy to Strathmiglo.* **OS sheet 58.**

The superbly situated fort on Castle Law forms a conspicuous feature of the hilly skyline of the N side of the Ochils. It is a magnificent site, commanding extensive views over the E end of Strathearn and the upper reaches of the Tay estuary. Excavation in the 1890s revealed the remains of a stone-walled enclosure measuring 41m by 15m. The wall, which was 7.5m thick and still standing up to 2.1m high, was found to contain slots for horizontal timbers to bind the stonework together. On the W side, where gentler slopes join the outcrop to the higher ground beyond, there is an additional rampart, some 5.5m thick. The only discernible internal feature is a rock-cut well.

4.   Clach na Tiompan, *Chambered Tomb (NN 830330). In upper Glenalmond, some 6km W of the A823 Crieff to Aberfeldy road. Access by private track (no vehicles) from Newton Bridge at the head of the Sma' Glen. The cairn stands on the N side of the track roughly 1km beyond Conichan.* **OS sheet 52.**

Although quite ruinous, having been damaged when the road up the glen was pushed through in the 19th century, the cairn is still well worth the visit both for its great scale and its atmospheric location. It is aligned NW and SE, measuring some 57m long by over 11m wide at its broader E end. Excavations in 1954 revealed four burial chambers spaced along its back, which would suggest that it has developed in stages rather than its great length being the product of a single build. The best preserved chamber lies at the E. This comprised a main chamber formed by four upright slabs roofed by a capstone, with two smaller slab-built chambers running towards it from the SW to form a 'passage'. This was entered from the SW from the centre of a slab-built façade, the entrance proper having been carefully infilled with horizontally-laid slabs.

5.   Croft Moraig, *Stone Circle (NN 797472). On the S side of the A827 Aberfeldy-Kenmore road, some 6km WSW of Aberfeldy. The circle stands in a small enclosure adjacent to the entrance to Croftmoraig farm.* **OS sheet 52.**

An interesting sequence of construction phases was revealed by excavation of the site in 1965. In its earliest form, fourteen upright timbers formed a horse-shoe-shaped setting, measuring some 8m by 7m. At the centre of this was a hearth. The timbers were replaced by a setting of eight stones, also horse-shoe-shaped. The outermost element of the monument – two arcs of boulders – and smaller stones lying to the NW and SE of the setting, appear to have formed part of the second phase redevelopment. In the third phase, a circle of nine stones, with a diameter of 12.2m, was erected. This has two outliers on its SE quadrant, forming a porch-like extension, in front of which were two deep grave pits.

6. Dron Hill, *Hillfort (NO 289321). Some 2km NW of Longforgan on the rounded summit above Knapp. Leave the A85 1.5km W of Longforgan on the unclassified road to Knapp and Tullybaccart. After 1.2km take the second road to the right (Dron and Fowlis), climbing steeply into the Braes of the Carse. After 1.4km turn left to Dron farm, where permission to visit the fort, which lies in grazing land on the hilltop 700m to the W, should be sought.* **OS sheet 53.**

Commanding magnificent views S and E over the Carse and Tay estuary, this is one of the finest sites in E Perthshire. The fort is oval in plan, its single stone rampart, spread to about 4.5m in thickness, enclosing an area some 100m by 76m. Crescent-shaped annexes clasp the N and S sides, bounded by the low remains of outer ramparts.

7. Dun Mor, *Hillfort (NN 906304). Some 6km S of Amulree in the Sma' Glen. The fort occupies the summit of the steep-flanked hill which overlooks the junction of the Sma' Glen and lower Glenalmond from the NE. There is no easy access to the site, but the best approach is from the N along the hill ridge on the E side of the Sma' Glen. Parking is available at Newton Bridge, 2km to the NW.* **OS sheet 52.**

Spectacularly sited at some 450m above sea-level, the fort overlooks the site of the Roman fort and signal tower at Fendoch. An enclosure some 35m by 27m is contained within the spread ruins of two stone ramparts, which are pierced by a single entrance at the NW. The remains of the walls are so slight as to suggest that they represent work abandoned unfinished at an early stage.

8. Dunsinnan, *Hillfort (NO 213316). Occupying the conspicuous rocky summit at the W end of the King's Seat-Black Hill ridge on the N side of the Sidlaws. Access by footpath from the unclassified road from Collace to Abernyte, 100m SE of Collace.* **OS sheet 53.**

Shakespearean associations have meant that this very interesting structure has suffered severely at the hands of antiquarian investigations. Quarrying poses a more modern threat and, whilst the fort itself appears to have been saved, the W slopes of the hill are being eaten away, substantially altering the character of the site. It occupies a superb defensive position which commands wide views over the W end of Strathmore. The main element of the defences is a ruinous timber-laced wall enclosing an area some 55m by

30m on the summit of the hill. Three outer lines of defence run down the easier slopes to the N and W; the E face of the hill is quite precipitous in places. Excavations in 1854 revealed what may have been a souterrain in the fort's interior, but there is no visible trace of this today.

9. Fortingall, *Stone Circles (NN 745469). In agricultural land on the S side of the unclassified road from Keltneyburn to Fortingall, 300m E of Fortingall.* **OS sheet 52.**

The wide gravel terrace on the N side of the River Lyon below Fortingall appears to have been the location for an important ritual complex of Early Bronze Age date. Three stone settings, two of which were excavated in 1970, lie to the E of the village. That nearest the road now comprises three visible stones, but originally eight formed a rectangular setting with four large uprights at each corner and smaller boulders in the middle of each side. The second setting now consists of four boulders, but again originally comprised a rectangular setting of eight. Although prehistoric material was found, the presence of Victorian debris beneath one of the fallen stones suggests that the site was deliberately toppled in the comparatively recent past. The third setting comprises a massive central boulder flanked by two tall uprights.

10. Fowlis Wester, *Cairn and Stone Circle (NN 924249). Lying to the S of the track running W to Loch Meallbrodden from the unclassified Fowlis Wester to Bucharity road, 1km N of Fowlis Wester.* **OS sheet 52.**

This interesting ritual complex lies on a gently sloping moorland terrace on the S side of the Moor of Ardoch, and commands a magnificent panorama S over Strathearn towards the Ochils. It comprises a kerb-cairn, a ruined stone circle, and two standing stones (one fallen), forming a line running roughly E to W. Excavation in 1939 revealed a deposit of cremated bone, charcoal and chippings of white quartz on the E side of the remaining standing stone, accompanied by a pit packed with white water-worn pebbles. Of the cairn, only the kerb survives, forming a ring 4.8m in diameter. The 1939 excavations revealed evidence of burning, cremated bone, and carefully positioned deposits of quartz chippings in the centre of the kerb. The cairn stood within a circle of eleven stones, four of which remain, the rest being marked in the excavations by their vacant sockets.

The stone circle to the W appears to have been deliberately slighted, all its stones now being fallen. Measuring 7.5m in diameter, excavation revealed traces of burning and cremated bone in its centre.

11. Glenlochay, *Cup-and-Ring marked rocks (NN 532358). On the valley floor between the unclassified road up the glen and the river, about 4.5km NW of Killin.* **OS sheet 51.**

An elongated outcrop of schist is covered for a distance of some 18m by an extensive scattering of carvings. These include single cups, cups with single rings and some with double concentric circles.

12. Kindrochat, *Chambered Cairn (NN 723230). Adjacent to the line of the old Comrie to St Fillans railway, roughly 4km W of Comrie. Access by farm-track from the A85 to the N, crossing the River Earn. The cairn stands on the S side of the agricultural land.* **OS sheet 52.**

Together with similar cairns at Clathick, Cultoquhey, and Rottenreoch, Kindrochat represents a distinct group of chambered tombs of a developed Clyde style located in upper Strathearn. The cairn, which is now quite ruinous, forms a long, low mound of water-worn boulders and stones aligned E and W, measuring 41m by some 11m wide at its broader end. Excavation in 1929–30 revealed that the cairn structure was retained within a kerb, and that it contained three small, slab-built chambers.

13. Moncreiffe Hill, *Hillfort (NO 136199). On the summit of the rocky scarp of Moncreiffe Hill overlooking the M90 to the N of Bridge of Earn. Access is from the N via farm and forestry track from the unclassified road from Friarton (A912) to Rhynd, 250m E of the entrance to Tarsappie farm.* **OS sheet 58.**

The spectacularly sited remains on the highest point of the undulating ridge of the hill are of two main periods. The earlier comprises a pair of ruinous stone-built walls which enclose an area measuring 170m by 100m. Within this and apparently partly overlying part of the inner of the earlier circuits, there has subsequently been constructed a stone-walled fort, 50m by 36m within a massive wall some 3.5m thick. There are numerous hut-circles visible in the interior of the larger fort.

14. Newbigging, *Cup-and-Ring-marked Stone (NO 155352).*
Turn S off the A93 Perth-Blairgowrie road at Cargill onto the
unclassified road to Gallowhill and Whitefield. After 1.25km
turn right on the farm road to Newbigging. **OS sheet 53.**

This boulder, moved in 1981 from its original position in
agricultural land to its present site by a field gate close to the
farmhouse, is richly decorated with cup-marks and cup-and-
ring markings. The dominant feature is a large cup-mark
surrounded by some five rings broken by a radial 'spoke'.
The carvings are unusual for their class in that they are
enclosed on three sides by straight lines forming a 'frame'.

15. Orwell, *Standing Stones (NO 149043). In agricultural land*
on the N side of the A911 Milnathort to Scotlandwell road,
1.5km W of Wester Balgedie. **OS sheet 58.**

This striking pair of standing stones occupies the crest of a
low mound in the undulating country to the N of Loch
Leven. Excavations in the early 1970s following the fall of
one of the stones (subsequently re-erected) revealed that
they had been the focus for Bronze Age ritual and burial
activity. The E stone was found to have been placed in a
socket within which were two cremations, placed one above
the other and separated by a horizontal slab. The cremations
contained the remains of several individuals.

16. St Madoes, *Stone Setting (NO 197210). In a field at the E*
end of the housing estate towards the E end of the village. **OS**
sheet 53.

A fine linear setting of three stones, aligned NNW–SSE. The
S stone has fallen, but the remaining pair both stand over
1.7m high. The N stone is liberally speckled with cup-marks
in its upper part.

17. Scone Wood, *Stone Circles (NT 133264). Amongst*
housing in Scone, about 50m SW of the junction of Sandy
Road and Stormount Road. **OS sheet 53.**

The remains of two stone circles here stand side by side.
The western is the more complete, and comprises seven
stones in a ring with an overall diameter of 5.4m. Excavation
in 1961 revealed a cremation buried in a flat-rimmed urn
close to the centre of the circle.

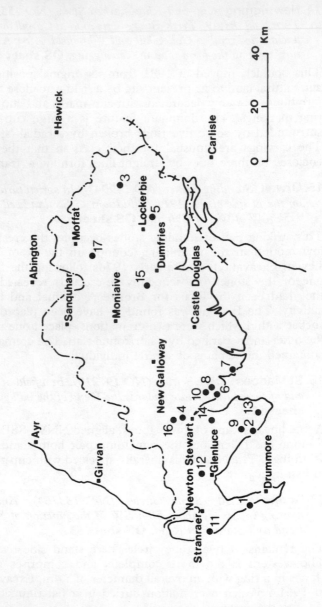

Map 9: Dumfries and Galloway

DUMFRIES AND GALLOWAY

1. **Ardwell Point**, *Broch (NX 067446). Turn W off the A715 some 0.5km S of Sandhead on the unclassified road to Clachanmore and High Ardwell. Follow the rough track from High Ardwell farm to the car-park at Ardwell Bay and follow shoreline round the S headland for some 350m. The broch lies on a rocky spit above the foreshore.* **OS sheet 82.**

This is the best preserved of the small group of brochs found in western Galloway. Like the scattering of similar structures between the Tay and the Tweed in the east, these south-western examples are remote outliers of a tradition concentrated mainly in the Western Isles and far north of Scotland, but should probably be seen as projects commissioned from itinerant broch-builders by local chieftains rather than evidence for colonisation out of the main broch areas.

Although reduced to its lower levels of stonework, Ardwell displays all the main characteristics of broch construction. Internally it measures some 9m in diameter within walls up to 4.6m thick, which contain at least two mural cells. Unusually, there is more than one doorway, a second entrance being provided on the seaward side opposite the landward entrance. On the landward side there is evidence for outer defences in the form of a wall cutting across the ridge on which the broch stands. A natural gully beyond the wall seems to have been enlarged for additional protection, but has been spanned by a built causeway.

2. **Barsalloch Point**, *Fort (NX 347412), Historic Scotland signposted site. The quickest, though steepest, approach involves a scramble up the overgrown slope of the old shoreline on the N side of the A747 Whithorn-Port William road, 1km W of Monreith.* **OS sheet 82.**

A D-shaped area of land, roughly 0.1 ha in extent, has been cut off from the level ground at the head of the former shoreline by a curving ditch. The excavated material from the ditch has been piled on both its outer and inner lips to form two banks. This still considerable barrier measures 10m from crest to crest of the banks and is 3.5m deep. A single entrance can be traced at the NNE of the defences. No structures are visible in the interior.

3. **Boonies**, *Settlement (NY 304900), behind the cottages on*

the N side of the B709 Langholm-Eskdalemuir road, on the
lip of the steep slopes to the River Esk 650km W of Bentpath.
OS sheet 79.

Excavations in 1973–4 at this well preserved example of a
class of monument peculiar to Dumfriesshire revealed the
remains of a settlement dating from the earlier centuries of
the 1st millennium AD. The site comprises an enclosed area
measuring 37m by 30m within a massive, 2m-high earthen
bank. Within the enclosure had stood a succession of timber-
built circular houses, 12 in total representing at least seven
phases of construction.

4. Boreland, *Chambered Cairn (NX 405690), follow the*
unclassified road up the E side of the River Cree from
Minnigaff, heading N for Glentrool. Roughly 1.4km N of
Minnigaff Kirk park take the hill track leading N from the
road, and follow this uphill for some 2km. The cairn is
adjacent to the track. **OS sheet 83.**

This is a good example of a Clyde-style cairn. The cairn is
well preserved, standing nearly 2m in height and extending
some 21m in length by 12m in width near the SE end. At the
SE are the remains of a crescentic forecourt, four uprights of
the façade surviving in position. The boundary kerb of
massive boulders is clearly visible in places, but the passage
and chamber are completely covered.

5. Burnswark Hill, *Fort (NY 185785), overlooking lower*
Annandale 5.6km SE of Lockerbie. **OS sheet 85.**

The 300m-high hill crowned by the fort which gives it its
name is a conspicuous landmark for many miles around on
both sides of the Anglo-Scottish border. Several phases of
development from the 7th century BC onwards were
identified in the course of excavations in 1966. The earliest
defences, represented by a palisade trench at the E end of
the summit, measured 274m by 198m, but in about 600 BC a
new earthen rampart with external timber revetment which
enclosed the entire 7 ha summit was built. This was
subsequently re-faced with stone. There are three entrances
on the SE side, where the slopes are gentlest, and here also is
an outer rampart to provide additional defence on the
weakest flank. The scale of the fort and its defences has led
to suggestions that it was the chief centre of the Iron Age
tribe known as the Novantae.

On the slopes to the NW and SE of the fort are the

remains of camps of 2nd-century AD date or later, that on the SE enclosing an earlier Antonine period fortlet. In advance of the rampart of the SE camp are three earthen platforms which are believed to have been the emplacements for ballistae, large quantities of ballista ammunition having been recovered in the course of excavation of the hillfort interior. In the 19th century this was interpreted as evidence for the siege of the native stronghold by the Romans, but the 1966 excavations indicated that the fort had in fact been abandoned before the 1st century AD. It is now suggested that the Roman earthworks are simply camps where siege tactics were practised.

6. Cairnholy, *Chambered Cairns (NX 517539 and NX 518540), Historic Scotland signposted site, N off the A75 Gatehouse of Fleet to Creetown road, 7km SE of Creetown.* **OS sheet 83.**

These two Clyde style cairns, which are both in Guardianship, form the most prominent elements in an extensive landscape of ritual and funerary sites in the hilly country W of Gatehouse of Fleet. Excavated in 1949, the cairns still command attention as key sites in our understanding of the constructional techniques employed in such monuments. Furthermore, the rich assemblage of artefacts recovered in the excavations forms one of the most significant groups of Neolithic ritual deposits.

Cairnholy I, the more southerly of the two cairns, measures 43m by 10m. The cairn superstructure has been extensively robbed, leaving the eight monoliths of the façade standing proud with the narrow entrance passage and chamber behind. The curved façade formed by the monoliths and linking sections of dry-stone walling backed a shallow forecourt, which had served as a setting for ritual activity. At the end of the functioning life of the cairn, the narrow entrance in the centre of the façade was blocked by a single monolith and the forecourt itself was subsequently infilled. A rich array of pottery, sea shells and a jet beads, placed as ritual deposits amongst the infill material, was recovered in the excavation. It would appear that the chamber, which is a simple rectangle formed by massive slabs, is the earliest element and stood originally in a smaller cairn, the entrance passage and façade being subsequent developments. The 'entrance' to the chamber proper is blocked by a massive single upright, indicating that burials must have been placed in the tomb from above, prior to its final sealing with capstone slab. The chamber had apparently been disturbed in antiquity, sherds of a food vessel and a cup-and-ring marked slab propped against one side suggesting its re-use in the Early Bronze Age. Material associated with the earlier burials was recovered from the passage, including fragments of a jadeite axehead, potsherds and a fine leaf-shaped flint arrowhead.

Cairnholy II is less well preserved and at 21m by 12m is considerably smaller than its neighbour. Positioned some 150m to the N on a small rock outcrop, it has been plundered extensively for stone. Despite that, the chamber survives almost intact, its table-like capstone dominating the site. There is no clear evidence for a façade, but a massive 3m-high portal stone remains on the N side of the entrance passage in the E face, its broken twin lies at an angle to the S. As with Cairnholy I, there is no direct communication between the passage and the chamber, rendering it likely that an originally simple cairn containing a plain rectangular chamber underwent considerable later elaboration. The tomb had been plundered in the past, but sherds of Beaker pottery indicated that it, too, may have been re-used in the Bronze Age.

7. Castle Haven, *Dun (NX 593482), immediately N of the beach at Castle Haven Bay, on the edge of agricultural land to the S of the unclassified road from Borgue to Kirkandrews and Knockbrex, 3.5km W of Borgue.* **OS sheet 83.**

Apparently forming part of a group of remote outliers of a building tradition more commonly found in Argyll and the Western Isles, Castle Haven dun possesses features which set it apart from both other duns in Galloway and from monuments of this type in general. It is a D-shaped structure, measuring roughly 18.3m by 10.7m internally, its straight edge running along the lip of a low cliff above the shore. The walls are galleried and ground level, and there are traces of an upper level of gallery reached by stone steps. The main entrance was in the N, but the wall here – and in several other parts of the enclosure, most notably on the W where the wall was rebuilt from the foundations – has been rebuilt following excavations in 1905, a stone panel in the wall informing the visitor that everything above the painted line (now vanished) is reconstruction. A subsidiary entrance in the S leads down rough steps to the beach. An outer D-shaped enclosure, roughly concentric to the dun, lies to the N and E of the main structure. The whole structure is heavily overgrown. Finds from the excavation indicated several phases of occupation, the earliest dating from the 7th century BC and extending through into the Middle Ages.

8. **Cauldside Burn**, *Cairns, Stone Circles and Cup-and-Ring Marked Stone (NX 529572, NX 529571, NX 529571 and NX 527575). Access to this interesting group of sites is difficult and involves a strenuous walk over rough ground. The monuments lie just to the E of the crest of the broad col between Cairnharrow and Cambret Hill in the hilly country between Gatehouse of Fleet and Creetown. The quickest access is from the N from the summit of Cambret Hill, which can be reached via the access road to the transmitter station located on its summit. The sites are clearly visible some 200m below to the SSE.* **OS sheet 83.**

Despite its remote location, the northern of the two cairns has been almost completely robbed for building stone, leaving only the lowest levels of the mound and a massive slab-built cist sunk into the ground surface. Some 100m or so to the SE stand the substantial remains of a second cairn. This measures 19.2m in diameter and rises to 3m in height. The cairn has been robbed in the past, the depression in the summit opening onto the centrally positioned slab-built cist. Adjacent to both cairns are the remains of stone circles. That of the N cairn has been almost entirely destroyed, but the southern circle, which stands just to the S of its cairn, is better preserved. Measuring 21m in diameter, it comprises 10 irregularly spaced slabby stones surviving from a possible original 20.

The cup-and-ring marked stone lies N of the burn on the lower slopes of Cambret Hill, 365m NNW of the first cairn. A large block carries two figures. The first measures 0.60m in diameter and comprises a central cup within a single ring from which a single groove spirals out in five and a half turns. The second consists of a cup with three concentric rings.

9. **Drumtroddan**, *Cup-and-Ring Marked Stones and Standing Stones (NX 364443 and NX 362447). The standing stones are a prominent skyline feature on the N side of the B7021 Whithorn-Port William road 0.5km E of its junction with the A714 Wigtown-Port William road. The*

cup-and-ring markings are a Historic Scotland maintained site, signposted from the A714 0.9km N of its junction with the B7021, and lie in fenced enclosures in farmland SW of Drumtroddan farm. Park in the farmyard and follow signposting. **OS sheet 83.**

The two exposed areas of greywacke slab on Drumtroddan farm are broadly representative of the scale and form of the numerous expanses of carving of this type found scattered across the rocky countryside of S Wigtownshire. The carvings are now beginning to suffer from the results of weathering and are best viewed in strong oblique sunlight. The more westerly of the two groups is the more varied in content, including simple cups and cups with up to six concentric rings, some linked by radial grooves. The largest exposed figure measures 0.38m in diameter.

The standing stones lie 360m to the SE of the cup-and-ring markings. This was formerly an alignment of three massive uprights, 3m in height, running NE to SW. The two outer stones are still upright and stand 13m apart, the third member of the trio lying prostrate between them.

10. Glenquicken Moor, *Stone Circle (NX 509582), in rough grazing on the S side of the old military road from Anwoth to Creetown, 3.5km E of Creetown.* **OS sheet 83.**

The circle occupies a level piece of ground on Glenquicken Moor, commanding clear views to the N and NW. It consists of 28 low boulders set close together to form a ring 15.2m in diameter. The stones are positioned with their broadest face on the circumference of the circle. The stones appear to be graded in height towards the SW. In the centre of the circle is a single massive pillar of granite 1.8m high.

11. Kemp's Walk, *Promontory Fort (NW 974598), towards the N end of Broadsea Bay on the W side of the Rhins peninsula. Access by farm-track running W from the B738 6km N of Portpatrick.* **OS sheet 82.**

The finest of the numerous promontory forts which fringe the Galloway coast, Kemp's Castle occupies a bold promontory set back from the sea-shore proper. The interior of the fort, which measures some 90m by 50m, is devoid of any surface indications of structures. The perimeter of the promontory appears originally to have been encircled by a rampart, and there is an additional line of defences on all sides except the W. At the N, where the promontory connects with the mainland, a third line of ditch and rampart gives extra protection to the W of the entrance, which lies towards the E end of this side. The third ditch and rampart has not been extended E of the entrance.

12. Mid Gleniron, *Chambered Cairns (NX 186610 and NX 187609), lying in pasture on either side of the farm road to Mid Gleniron farm 3.75km NNW of Glenluce, running E off the unclassified road from Glenluce to New Luce.* **OS sheet 82.**

The cairns, which were excavated between 1963 and 1966, are part of an archaeologically rich landscape in the upland pasture and moorland on the E side of the Luce Valley. The first cairn lies 300m SW of the steading on the N side of the track, and is now a somewhat amorphous mound from which protrude the remains of the chamber. Excavation revealed a complex constructional history, commencing with the southernmost chamber which was contained within a small cairn. Subsequent to this a second chamber was constructed to its N, also contained within a separate cairn structure. In a third phase of development a lateral chamber was inserted in the space between the two cairns and the whole assemblage enclosed within a single cairn provided with a crescentic façade centred on the passage leading to the N chamber. Like several Neolithic chambered tombs in Galloway the chambers had been largely cleared out in the Bronze Age and seven cremations contained in urns had been inserted into its SE side.

The second cairn lies 120m to the SE. It had been severely plundered for stone in the past, exposing what was probably the original chamber in its SE side contained within a small round cairn. A second chamber was added on the SW and both were encompassed within a single trapezoidal cairn with a façade at its S end.

13. Rispain, *Settlement (NX 429399), Historic Scotland site signposted from the A746 Whithorn-Port William road 1km W of Whithorn. Park in designated area in farmyard at Rispain and follow signposted footpath to the site.* **OS sheet 83.**

This site has, in the past, been variously described as a Roman fort or a Medieval homestead moat on account of its regular rectilinear outline. Excavations in 1978–81, however, revealed that occupation commenced in *c.*60 BC and extended into the early 1st millennium AD. Occupying an elevated position on a rocky ridge rising above good agricultural land, an area measuring 68m by 52m has been enclosed within a deep v-shaped ditch, the excavated material from which has been piled to form banks on its inner and outer lips. A now obliterated outer ditch lay on the gentler slopes to the S and E. The single entrance lies on the NE side, access to it being across a causeway of uncut ground. The excavation produced evidence for a timber-built gatehouse structure, and in the NW of the interior remains of a single roundhouse of timber post, plank and ring-ditch construction.

14. Torhouse, *Stone Circle (NX 382565), Historic Scotland signposted site, in fenced enclosure on the S side of the B733 Wigtown-Kirkcowan road 5km WNW of Wigtown.* **OS sheet 83.**

This fine boulder circle occupies what appears to be an artificially levelled platform overlooking the valley of the River Bladnoch. It consists of 19 irregular granite boulders arranged in what is called a flattened circle measuring 21.5m by 20m. The stones are graded in height, the largest lying at the flattened SE sector. Towards the centre of the circle is an alignment of three boulders on a NE to SW axis, thus having a long side facing SE. The central stones are incorporated into the remains of an almost obliterated ring-cairn. There is a single standing stone some 24m S of the stone circle, and on the opposite side of the road, in a field to the E is an alignment of three stones.

15. Twelve Apostles, *Stone Circle (NX 947794), in agricultural land on the N side of the unclassified road running NW from the A76 at Newbridge, roughly 1km N of Lincluden on the NW outskirts of Dumfries.* **OS sheet 84.**

Cut in two by a modern field boundary in a low-lying position close to the N side of the road, it is difficult to appreciate that this is the largest stone circle in mainland Scotland and the fifth largest in Britain. Eleven boulders out of a probable original twelve form a flattened circle with a maximum diameter of 88m. Only five of the stones are still earthfast, the tallest rising to 1.9m in height. What would have been the tallest stone, at 3.2m, lies fallen at the SW sector.

16. White Cairn of Bargrennan, *Chambered Cairn (NX 353784), in forestry 450m W of Glentrool Village, signposted from the adjacent Forestry Commission access road.* **OS sheet 77.**

Excavated in 1949, this is the 'type site' of the so-called Bargrennan style passage graves, a small class of monument unique to western Galloway. The cairn has been heavily robbed, but was originally circular and measured some 13.7m in diameter. In the central area it still stands 1.4m high. The entrance to the burial chamber lies in the S side of the cairn and opens onto an undifferentiated passage and chamber constructed from massive boulders and roofed with slabs. From a fire pit located near the entrance was recovered a mix of cremated bone and oak charcoal, accompanied by a burned flint tool. Both chamber and passage had been robbed in the past, but on an undisturbed area of paving in the passage lay further cremated bone and sherds of Neolithic pottery.

17. Stidriggs, *Long Cairn (NY 041987), at the N end of Broadshaw Rig in the moor-country between Annandale and Nithsdale. Turn W off the A701 (T) 2.5km S of Beattock onto the unclassified road to Tath Hill and Cauldholm. After some 0.75km turn left for Cauldholm. On the W side of the bridge over the Kinnel Water immediately beyond Cauldholm, take the farm track for Stidriggs and continue along the footpath past the house. After about 300m begin to make SW across the shallow valley of the headwaters of the Green Burn and follow the old path for some 1.5km to the cairn.* **OS sheet 78.**

Forestry and rough grazing are the two favoured options for the exploitation of this rather desolate tract of upland, but hut circles, scatterings of field clearance cairns and burial cairns point to more intensive settlement and agriculture in the prehistoric. The long cairn measures some 30m long by 9m across towards the N end and 18m near the S end, where it also rises to some 1.8m

Map 10: Fife with Lothian

FIFE

1. Balbirnie, *Stone Circle (NO 285029), to the W of the N drive of Balbirnie House, off the unclassified road from the A92 to Markinch 1.25km N of the Cadham roundabout in Glenrothes.* **OS sheet 59.**

The circle was excavated and moved to its present site in the 1970s in advance of road improvements on the N side of Glenrothes. The 'circle' of ten stones measures 15m by 14m and encloses a rectangular central setting of stones (now bounding an area of modern paving). Despite considerable disturbance to the interior of the circle, the excavations revealed evidence for at least three phases of burial activity commencing in the Early Bronze Age. Two cists were constructed in pits at diagonally opposed corners of the central rectangular setting, suggesting that its ritual function may have ceased. That at the SE had been plundered in antiquity, but at the NW the burial was undisturbed and comprised the cremated remains of an adult female and child, a complete food vessel and a flint knife. The smaller cist at the SE had a side slab decorated with cup-and-ring markings, replaced by a cast in the reconstruction (the original is in the National Museum in Edinburgh). In a final phase, the entire interior of the circle was filled by a large cairn, possibly incorporating smaller cairns which had covered the individual cists, and at least a further 16 cremations were inserted into the mound.

2. Balfarg, *Henge Monument (NO 281031), in an open area in the middle of a modern housing estate on the N side of Glenrothes, access from the A92 1.5km N of the Cadham roundabout.* **OS sheet 59.**

The henge site at Balfarg is the still visible component of one of the most important Neolithic and Bronze Age ritual and funerary complexes yet excavated in Scotland. The central platform, nearly 60m in diameter, is enclosed by a broad ditch which has been partly re-excavated, except at the SW where a natural gully was utilised. Originally there was a bank round the external lip of the ditch formed by the upcast material from its excavation, but this had been largely obliterated through agricultural action. There was a single entrance through the bank at the W, leading to a narrow causeway across the ditch to the central area.

Excavation of the central area revealed evidence for a

complex sequence of development commencing in around 3000 BC. The earliest evidence suggested the ritual smashing of pots and burning of fires on the platform. This was followed at a later phase by erection of a large circle of 16 massive timber uprights set in pits, while two additional especially large timbers gave added emphasis to the formal approach from the W, forming a 'porch' in advance of the circle. The position of the timbers is marked by a ring of short modern posts. This wooden setting was replaced at a later period by what appears to have been two concentric rings of stones, of which only the two large uprights near the causeway on the W remain. A final phase was represented by the burial of a young adult in a pit at the centre of the henge, the body being accompanied by a remarkable beaker with a handle and a fine flint knife. The original capstone which covered the burial, a massive slab weighing about 2 tonnes, has been reinstated in the centre of the site.

To the NE of the site, adjacent to the old Balfarg steading, excavation of a series of crop-marks revealed evidence for two substantial timber structures dating from the middle of the 4th millennium BC. These have been interpreted as mortuary houses, where the dead were exposed to allow the flesh to rot away before burial of some of the bone remains. The structures were subsequently buried beneath earthen mounds, one surrounded by a ditched enclosure. No remains are currently visible.

3. Dunearn, *Hillfort (NT 211872), on the summit of Dunearn Hill on the E side of the A909 2km WNW of Burntisland.* **OS sheet 66.**

At least two phases of development are visible in the extensive series of defences which crown this prominent height. The earlier is represented by a ruinous rampart enclosing an oval area some 120m by 40m internally, with an additional outer work giving defence in depth to the entrance at the E end. The second phase is marked by the remains of a smaller, circular fort wholly enclosed within the earlier rampart. This measures roughly 36m in diameter within a wall 3.6m thick. Although quite heavily ruined, stretches of facing stones can be traced on both its inner and outer faces.

4. Glassamount, *Stone Setting (244884), in agricultural land on Glassamount farm, 3km WSW of Kirkcaldy. Leave* *the A907 3km W of Kirkcaldy on the unclassified road to Kinghorn. At the crossroads after 1km turn left, and the stones are on rising ground on the N side of the road 400m W of the track to Glassamount.* **OS sheet 66.**

This fine pair of stones stand some 6m apart on an E-W axis. Both rise to about 2m in height and, while the western stone is of irregular profile, the eastern is a four-sided pillar-stone. The site has not been excavated, but analogy with Orwell might indicate that they served as a focus for burial activity.

5. Greenhill, *Cairn (NO 345228), in woodland on the summit of Greenhill, 3km W of Gauldry, to the N of the unclassified Gauldry-Creich road.* **OS sheet 59.**

Measuring some 15m in diameter and still rising to 1.5m in height, this cairn was 'excavated' between 1899 and 1901 in a glorified treasure-hunt. The excavation revealed an unusual structural arrangement, with the central component being an upright slab set on the old ground surface. Immediately to the W of this was a robbed cist, but some 1.75m N of this was a slab-covered pit containing a food vessel and an incense cup. From the eastern quadrant of the cairn came two more food vessels and some cremated remains, together with two disc beads, and to the S of these were 72 beads from a jet necklace. A fourth food vessel with the remains of an interment were located under a stone in the W quadrant, with a similar fifth pot close by. One further complete food vessel and fragments of a seventh were located in the S quadrant.

6. Lundin Links, *Standing Stones (NO 404027), on the S side of Lundin Links golf course. Permission to view the site should be sought at the clubhouse.* **OS sheet 59.**

Three massive stones remain from a setting which originally comprised at least four stones. The SE stone rises to 3.96m and is 1.5m thick at its widest. The S and N stones are both in excess of 5m tall.

7. Norman's Law, *Hillfort (NO 305202), 6.5km E of Newburgh. The easiest access is from the S via the farm tracks serving Ayton and Denmuir farms which run N of the A913 about 2km W of the Parbroath crossroads with the A914.* **OS sheet 59.**

Forming one of the most prominent features of the N Fife

landscape, the strong natural defences of Norman's Law attracted settlement over a long period extending into the 1st millennium AD. The summit and slopes of this conical massif are enclosed within a complex of fortifications whose exact chronological sequence is difficult to disentangle convincingly. What are probably the latest defences are the best preserved. This takes the form of a stone wall enclosing an oval area some 50m by 30m within a wall 3.6m thick. Outwith this is a ruinous stone wall which encircles the entire summit area in an enclosure measuring some 213m by 76m. A second wall, possibly contemporary with the latter and forming an outer annexe, takes in the whole of the hill's SW side. The two enclosed areas together have a maximum extent of 305m by 167m. The stone foundations of numerous circular houses dot the interior and partly overlie the earlier defences.

8. Tuilyies, *Standing Stone (NT 0298865), in a field on the S side of the A985 Rosyth-Kincardine Bridge road 1km WNW of the Cairneyhill roundabout.* **OS sheet 65.**

This impressive monolith, 2.4m in height, is decorated with a rash of cup-marks on its E face. The parallel vertical grooves on the upper part of the stone are the product of natural weathering.

LOTHIAN
(see map on p.190)

1. Braidwood, *Settlement (NT 192596). Leave the A702 800m SW of Silverburn on the farm track to Eastside. After 450m turn S off the track and climb uphill to the summit of the low eminence which overlooks the main road to the S.* **OS sheet 65.**

Excavation revealed that the earliest phase of the settlement at Braidwood was represented by a palisaded enclosure. This had been a single wooden palisade around an area of some 0.5 ha, the shallow bedding trench for the timbers still being a visible surface feature. Concentric to this, and some 14m further out, was a second palisade, the two being joined at the entrance by connecting fences. The timber defences had been superseded by earthen ramparts, but these appear never to have been completed. The outer rampart is almost ploughed away and survives only as an ephemeral bump. In the enclosed area can be traced the ring ditches of up to 12 timber-built round or oval structures.

2. Cairnpapple Hill, *Henge and Cairn (NS 987717), Historic Scotland site on the summit of Cairnpapple Hill, 2km ESE of Torphichen. Signposted from the B792 Torphichen-Bathgate road at the SE end of Torphichen village.* **OS sheet 65.**

This superbly positioned hill-top site holds a key position in the interpretation of ritual and funerary monuments in the later Neolithic and Bronze Ages. Excavations in 1947–8 uncovered a sequence of activity extending into at least the 1st millennium BC. The earliest phase comprised of an arc of seven small pits, six of which held deposits of cremated bone, two of which were accompanied by bone pins. In the centre of the arc were sockets for three standing stones, removed in subsequent developments. The second phase saw the construction of a Class II henge measuring 44m by 38m, whose outer bank, broken by the diametrically positioned entrances and causeways to the central platform, still forms the substantial boundary around the site. Within this was an oval setting of 24 standing stones, measuring 35m by 28m. To the W of the centre of the setting was a grave pit containing an inhumation accompanied by two beakers and wooden objects. A second burial containing a beaker was found adjacent to one of the stones on the E side of the oval setting. The third phase saw the dismantling of the stone setting and construction to the W of the centre of the henge of a large cairn, 15.25m in diameter, covering a cist burial with a beaker and also enclosing the earlier main beaker burial. This has now been replaced by a concrete dome to allow inspection of the burials. The original cairn was bounded by a kerb of massive boulders, believed to have been formed from the standing stones of the Phase Two setting. In a fourth phase, the cairn was considerably enlarged, reaching a diameter of 30m, thus overlying in part the silted-up ditch of the henge. Two cremations, placed under inverted urns, were discovered within this enlargement. A fifth phase, probably dating from the late 1st millennium BC, was represented by four graves on the E side of the old henge enclosure, all empty at the time of excavation, but originally containing fully extended inhumations.

3. Castlelaw, *Hillfort (NT 229 638), Historic Scotland signposted site, W off the A702 Edinburgh-Biggar road, 3km S of the Fairmilehead interchange on the Edinburgh city by-pass. Access by farm track and foot-path.* **OS sheet 66.**

Occupying a rounded knoll towards the S end of the SE ridge of Castlelaw Hill in the Pentlands, this fort commands magnificent views over the valley of the North Esk and the Lothian plain. The three ramparts and ditches – of which the middle circuit is now the most prominent feature on the site – enclose an area measuring 82m by 37m entered through three gateways placed centrally in each side except the N. They speak of a complex constructional history, but two programmes of excavation have failed to provide clear evidence for the building sequence. The 1948 excavations revealed the middle rampart to be largely of earth and clay dump construction, while the E gate was provided with a timber-revetted passage some 3m wide.

On the E side of the fort, built into the inner ditch, is a 20m-long souterrain with a 'bee-hive' chamber opening from the passage midway along its length on the W side. The main passage appears originally to have been roofed largely with timber, no lintel stones having been found in the excavations. A number of objects recovered from the souterrain in the course of excavation – including fragments of a Roman bowl, glass and a bronze buckle – point towards construction in the 2nd century AD.

4. Cockleroy, *Hillfort (NS 989745), 1.5km SSW of Linlithgow. Access by footpath from the car-park on the W side of the unclassified road from Linlithgow to Torphichen via Beecraigs.* **OS sheet 65.**

Cockleroy is the more rugged of the two prominent hills to the SW of Linlithgow. Defended to the N and W by rocky outcrops and crags, its S and E slopes are more grassy and gentle, bearing traces of medieval cultivation. The summit, which commands magnificent views in all directions, is enclosed within the ruinous remains of a massive stone wall, measuring some 125m by 61m, broken in the SE by a single entrance. There is an outer rampart on the NW side only.

5. The Chesters, *Drem, Hillfort (NT 507782), Historic Scotland signposted site 1.5km S of Drem. Access via farm road from the unclassified road S to Camptoun from the B1377, 400m W of Drem.* **OS sheet 66.**

A remarkable array of stone and earth defences protect the summit of the long hillock immediately to the E of the farm steading. More remarkable, however, is that the defences are commanded by the higher ridge immediately to the S, from which missiles could easily be lobbed into the fort's interior. This measures 119m by 49m within two concentric rings of rampart, the outer of which still stands up to 6m high. On the N, there are three outer lines of ditch and rampart, combining to give some 55m of defence, while at the E and W ends there are no less than five additional lines, presumably to provide defence in depth for the fort's two entrances. Foundations of up to 30 circular stone structures can be traced in the interior.

6. Kingside Hill, *Stone Setting (NT 627650). In rough ground to the N of the B6355 Giffard-Cranshaws road, 2km W of the Whiteadder Reservoir.* **OS sheet 67.**

This monument has been described occasionally as a disc cairn, but it is probable that two separate elements are represented by the visible remains. It comprises a ring some 12m in diameter, composed of 30 smallish boulders, none of which are more than 40m high. A larger stone in the centre, nearly 60cm square, rises from a low mound some 3m in diameter.

7. Newbridge, *Huly Hill, Barrow and Standing Stones (NT 123726). Rather lost amongst the motorway junction and*

industrial development at Newbridge, 4km W of Edinburgh.
The cairn is clearly visible from the A89 Newbridge-Broxburn
road. Signposted from Newbridge village. **OS sheet 65.**

The earthen round barrow, retained within a modern dyke,
measures 30m in diameter by 3m in height. The recovery of
a bronze rapier from it in excavations in 1830 point to a
Bronze Age date, but it possibly occupies a ritual site of
greater antiquity. Enclosing the barrow, which lies off-
centre, is a stone circle some 100m in diameter, if the three
stones spaced around the mound are in fact the survivors
from a complete ring. The stones which remain are massive,
the largest at the NW being over 2m in height. Some 320m
to the E across the roundabout is a single massive standing
stone, known as the Lochend Stone, which measures over
3m in height. Its relationship to the barrow and circle at
Huly Hill is unknown.

8. Tormain Hill, *Ratho, Cup-and-Ring Marked Stones (NT*
129696). Leave the B7030 Ratho-Wilkieston road 1km SW
of Ratho. Follow a track S through the woodland shelter belt
from the road for 500m to the hilltop. **OS sheet 65.**

The summit ridge of the hill has a scattering of natural rock
outcrops, at least eight of which have been found to carry
cup-and-ring markings. Only about five sets are currently
visible, the remainder being turfed over. A wide variety of
forms are represented, ranging from single cups to groups of
20, individual cups with single rings to large cups
surrounded by one complete ring and three additional
concentric arcs linking it to four other rings.

9. Traprain Law, *Hillfort (NT 581746), 2km SE of East*
Linton, on the S side of the unclassified road from East Linton
to Haddington via Traprain and Sunnyside. **OS sheet 67.**

Rearing in a whaleback hump over the Lothian Plain,
although only some 100m high Traprain Law is a
conspicuous feature of the landscape between Edinburgh
and Dunbar. Chance finds and discoveries made in the
course of the quarrying which is nibbling away at the hill's
margins, supplemented by the products of excavation, show
that this has been a site of great importance since the later
Neolithic. The main visible remains, however, appear to be
largely of Iron Age and later date, the finest of the finds from
the site – the so-called Traprain Law Hoard, on display in
the National Museum of Scotland – indicating that

occupation continued into the mid-1st millennium AD.

The most prominent of the surviving lines of defence on the hill are believed to represent the final stages in a long sequence of development and probably date to the period between the 3rd and 5th centuries AD. A wall, some 3.6m thick, runs along the N flank of the ridge and encloses a broad terrace on its W, forming a defended area some 12 ha in extent. The outer rampart, which swings lower on the N side to embrace several hut-platforms, had an internal area of some 16 ha. One of the largest forts in Scotland, this is believed to have been the tribal capital of the Votadini, a people who are thought to have enjoyed some kind of client relationship with Rome.

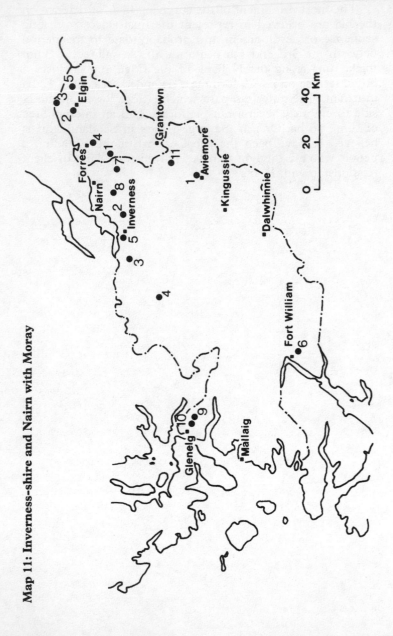

Map 11: Inverness-shire and Nairn with Moray

INVERNESS AND NAIRN

1. Aviemore, *Ring Cairn (NH 896134), Historic Scotland signposted site at the N end of the village.* **OS sheet 36.**

Wrongly signposted as a 'stone circle', this ring-cairn stands in landscaped ground in a modern housing development. The cairn material has been almost entirely removed, leaving the near-complete outer kerb exposed. The kerb, graded in height to the SW, enclosed an area 13.25m in diameter. The inner kerb enclosed an area almost 7.5m in diameter, reducing the ring of cairn superstructure to a narrow band only some 2.8m wide. Four stones remain of the stone circle which enclosed the cairn.

2. Balnuaran of Clava, *Chambered Cairns (NH 757444), Historic Scotland site, signposted from the B9006 Inverness to Croy road 0.5km E of the NTS Visitor Centre at Culloden Battlefield. In a secluded setting amongst trees on the S side of the valley floor of Strathnairn.* **OS sheet 27.**

The four cairns in the Guardianship area form part of a more extensive Neolithic cemetery which runs along the valley bottom. This is the type site which has given its name to an important class of highly distinctive burial monuments known as Clava Cairns. The group comprises a row of two large passage-graves and one ring-cairn, plus one smaller kerb-cairn. The three main monuments form a line running NE to SW along the gravel terrace on the S side of the River Nairn, and are constructed from water-worn boulders and pebbles recovered from the terrace. The NE cairn – known as Balnuaran of Clava – is a passage-grave in a round cairn standing within an enclosing circle of stones. The cairn is bounded by a kerb of massive boulders some 17m in diameter, the largest placed nearest the entrance in the SW, the smallest behind the chamber to the NE. A platform of cairn material extends beyond the kerb. The passage, which is now roofless, is constructed from granite boulders and sandstone slabs, as is the lower section of the 4m-diameter central chamber. The granite boulder to the N of the entrance in the chamber bears several cup-marks. The upper part of the chamber walls is formed by thin sandstone slabs and is corbelled inwards, but the roof of the chamber has gone. Plundered in antiquity, only some bone fragments were recovered from the chamber.

The middle cairn is a ring-cairn, which was excavated in 1953. It takes the form of what can best be described as a doughnut of stones about 18m in diameter, bounded on the outer edge by a kerb of massive boulders and on the inner face by a wall of upright slabs. A low platform of stones encloses the outer kerb. There is no passage, which would suggest that the burial was placed in the centre of the ring, which was then infilled with stones. The whole structure stands within a circle of nine standing stones, three of which were linked to the central platform by radiating stone 'spokes'.

Like the NE cairn, the SW is a passage grave, its outer stone circle and platform disturbed by the modern road (one stone stands against the dyke on the S side of the roadway). The main cairn structure, passage, and central 4m-diameter chamber are well preserved. There are several cup-marked stones: on the S side of the passage; on the W side of the chamber at its entrance; and on the inner face of one of the stones of the enclosing circle.

The final element of the group, believed to be the remains of a small kerb-cairn, lies to the W of the central cairn. It takes the form of a small ring of boulders, 3.7m in diameter, which enclosed a pit containing an inhumation burial associated with several quartz pebbles.

3. **Castle Spynie**, *Broch (NH 542421). In forestry 4.5km SE of Beauly. Leave the A833 1km W of Inchmore and take the unclassifed road to Easter Moniack. At the junction after 0.5km turn left then first right (Moniack Castle). After some 350m turn left for Easter Clunes, then fork right after 1km. The broch lies in the woodland to the W of the road beyond the agricultural land.* **OS sheet 26.**

Together with the broch at Struy, this site represents the southern limit of the main area of distribution of monuments of this class. The broch crowns a rocky knoll, prominent on the skyline when viewed from the N, but with gentler slopes to the S and W. Although heavily overgrown, the site displays several interesting features, including the entrance passage in the SW sector. The wall is some 4.2m thick around a central area 10.8m in diameter. The remains of outworks around the broch are clearly visible, the N sector of walling being built of massive boulders.

4. **Corrimony**, *Clava cairn (NH 383303)*, Historic Scotland

signposted from the A831 Drumnadrochit-Cannich road, 7km E of Cannich. **OS sheet 26.**

This superb Clava style passage-grave stands on the broad gravel terrace on the S side of the River Enrick at the point where Glen Urquhart opens out towards its W end. In Clava tradition it stands in the centre of a ring of 11 standing stones with a diameter of some 21.3m. The cairn proper is not a true circle, its NW sector being somewhat flattened, giving it a diameter including its kerb of between 14m and 15m. The passage enters from the SW and is 7m long, most of it still roofed with massive lintels. The central chamber is circular, 3.6m in diameter, and still stands to a height of about 2m. The walls are slab-built in their upper sections and are corbelled inwards. The massive flat slab lying on the E side of the cairn, its exposed upper surface liberally peppered with cup-marks, is believed to have formed the final cap-stone over the chamber roof. The cairn was excavated in 1952, at which time the chamber was found to have had a floor of sand with an area of paving placed centrally. A considerable amount of charcoal was mixed among the flat slabs. On the slabs were the remains of a crouched inhumation burial accompanied by a burnt bone pin, probably representing just the last episode in the long functional life of the cairn.

5. Craig Phadraig, *Hillfort (NH 640452). On the summit of the wooded hill which dominates the western suburbs of Inverness, overlooking the Beauly Firth. Take the A862 Inverness-Beauly road. At the roundabout on the W side of the Caledonian Canal turn left (King Brude Road) , then 3rd left (Leachkin Road) and 3rd right again (Leachkin Brae). After a short distance turn right into the Forestry Commission car-park, from which a path climbs steeply to the hilltop.* **OS sheet 26.**

The fort itself is unplanted within the pine forestry which cloaks the flanks of the hill. The remains comprise the grass-grown ruins of two formerly timber-laced stone ramparts which enclose a roughly rectangular area some 80m long. No original entrances can be identified. The fort had been burned, producing extensive vitrification in the ramparts. Excavation in 1971 produced radiocarbon dates from the ramparts which pointed to construction in the 5th and 4th centuries BC. Trenching of the interior of the fort produced evidence for an important re-occupation of the site in the

Pictish period, the finds including sherds of imported pottery and a clay mould for the casting of decorative escutcheons for bronze hanging-bowls.

6. Dun Deardail, *Hillfort (NN 126702). In a clearing amongst forestry at the NW end of the Mamore ridge overlooking Glen Nevis, 4km SSE of Fort William. Take the track running W from Glen Nevis House and after 400m enter the forest. At the junction of the tracks after 150m turn right, and after a further 400m double back sharply to the left and follow the rising forestry track to its end. Climb steeply up the hillside from the head of the track, passing through a narrow conifer belt, to gain the summit of the hillock occupied by the fort.* **OS sheet 41.**

Difficult of access but a rewarding site – if only for the views. Massive vitrified ruins of a formerly timber-laced wall spread up to 15m in width, enclose an area of 45m by 27m. There is a single entrance in the NW side. The interior is subdivided by what appears to be a secondary cross-wall, but the remains of outerworks visible to the W and S may be contemporary with the main enclosure.

7. Dunearn, *Hillfort (NH 933406). On a thinly wooded hilltop 600m S of Bridge of Dulsie. Leave the B9007 Carrbridge-Nairn road 5km S of Ferness on the unclassified road to Bridge of Dulsie. After 1.3km the road bends sharply right. The fort occupies the wooded hill which rises above the bend.* **OS sheet 27.**

Shaped to fit the attenuated S-shape of the ridge which it crowns, the fort is an elongated enclosure measuring a maximum of 270m long by just under 50m wide. It has been defended by two walls, both now very ruinous, but the inner at least having originally been timber-laced and having produced evidence for vitrification. The outer rampart is reduced to little more than a scarped break in slope for much of its circuit. The interior, which was under cultivation until the early 20th century, is now featureless.

8. Dun Evan, *Hillfort (NH 827475). In a clearing in forestry some 2.5km SW of Cawdor. Take the unclassified road to Barevan from Cawdor village. Take the track to Achindown on the right of the road immediately before the bridge over the Allt Dearg. Fork right behind the buildings, then follow the footpath which climbs the ridge to the SW into the forestry.*

The path skirts along the SE flank of the unplanted summit occupied by the fort. **OS sheet 27.**

The rocky outcrop of Dun Evan commands magnificent views in all directions. Its summit is ringed by a ruinous wall which encloses an area of some 58m by 25m, spread to a width of up to 8m, broken only by the entrance at the NE. The interior is featureless, save for a circular depression which may mark the site of a rock-cut cistern. Traces of outer defences can be seen lower down the flanks of the outcrop, the most obvious being a tumbled stone wall which still rises to some 3m in height to the NW of the entrance. Traces of vitrification have been noted in the past.

9. Dun Grugaig *(Glen Beag), Dun (NG 851158). On a rocky outcrop above the gorge of the Abhainn a Ghlinne Bhig, to the S of the track from Balvraid to Suardalan, 750m SE of Balvraid.* **OS sheet 33.**

The defences of this site comprise a D-shaped enclosure measuring 14.3m by 11.5m. The defences on the W and S are slight, the precipitous gorge of the river affording protection, but on the E and N a massive wall, some 4.3m thick, rises sheer from the rocky outcrops. The site has not been excavated and the interior is heavily choked with rubble, but traces of mural passages or cells, and the remains of a scarcement round the inner face of the wall, can be traced. The entrance passage has checks for a timber door secured by a draw-bar.

10. Dun Telve and Dun Troddan, *Brochs (NG 829172 and NG 833172). Historic Scotland signposted sites in Glen Beag. Take the unclassified road at Shiel Bridge from the A87(T) Fort William to Kyle of Lochalsh road, signposted Glenelg and Kylerhea Ferry. Continue beyond Glenelg village on the Arnisdale road. After 1km, turn left before the bridge over the Abhainn a Ghlinne Bhig. The brochs stand roughly 500m apart some 2.5km up the glen.* **OS sheet 33.**

Commonly referred to as the Glen Elg brochs, these are the two finest examples of their class to survive on the Scottish mainland, both in terms of preservation and in the structural features displayed. Dun Telve is the first to be reached. It stands on the gravel terrace on the N side of the river in what can hardly be described as a defensive position. While two thirds of its wall have been reduced to its lower courses, the remaining third still stands over 10.1m in height. Rising from a largely solid base some 4m thick, the walls taper inwards in the distinctive 'cooling-tower' style best seen at Mousa in Shetland. Above the base the walls are divided into inner and outer skins, bonded together at intervals by courses of lintels to form galleries. Four of these survive in full and part of a fifth at the top. The entrance is in the W side. It is provided with one door check and the slot for a draw-bar, and a guard-chamber opens off it to the right. The passage opens into a central area some 9.75m in diameter. To the left of the entrance a doorway leads into a cell with a corbelled roof on the left, and the base of a stairway on the right. This rises for only seventeen steps, its upper section being lost in the fallen section of wall. On the surviving inner face of the wall are two scarcements. The lower supported the floor of the upper storey of the timber building ranged around the central area, while the upper – some 8.9m above ground, and a unique survival – may have carried the timbers of a roof which covered the whole of the internal space. The gallery level with the lower scarcement has carefully finished walls, possibly indicating that it was used for storage, while the upper galleries are rough and narrow. On the inner wall above the entrance are ladder-like voids formed by deliberate breaks in the stone, bridged by numerous lintels. This was probably intended to lessen the load borne by the lintel of the entrance, but may also have been used to ventilate the upper galleries.

Dun Troddan stands on a knoll on the N side of the glen 500m to the E. As at Dun Telve, roughly one third of its wall survives to considerable height above the base courses, rising in places to 7.6m. Three galleries survive in the thickness of the wall, the lowest one at first-floor level being finished to the same quality as at Dun Telve, probably being used for storage. The entrance passage, which lacks its roof, is provided with door checks, and a partly roofed guard-chamber opens to its left in the thickness of the 4.1m-thick wall. The central area measures 8.5m in diameter. A doorway in its NW quadrant opens to a corbel-roofed cell on the left, and to a stair on the right. This rises to a level passage which runs for 5.5m in the thickness of the wall, then begins to rise again, but only one tread remains, the remainder being lost in the fallen stretch of wall. A doorway from this stair probably opened on to the timber floor supported on the scarcement. Apertures in the wall, similar to those at Dun Telve, can be seen above the doorway leading to the stairs. Excavations in 1920 revealed a hearth in the middle of the central area, surrounded by the postholes of the timbers which carried the first floor of the buildings ranged round the inner face of the wall.

At both brochs there is evidence for continued occupation long after the brochs had become ruinous, or had been partly dismantled. At Dun Telve, traces of massively constructed outer buildings can be seen. Some may form part of an enclosing wall, but others appear to be considerably more modern.

11. Toum, *Round Cairn (NH 960217), immediately E of the steading at Toum, 0.5km from the A95 Aviemore-Grantown road up the farm track to Toum and Ouchnoire, 2km NE of Drumuillie.* **OS sheet 36.**

The finest surviving Bronze Age monument in Strathspey, the cairn occupies an elevated position overlooking the valley floor from the NW. The cairn, a massive mound of bare stones with traces of a cairn at its W side, still rises to over 4m in height.

MORAY

(see map on p.200)

1. Doune of Relugas, *Hillfort (NJ 003495), on a promontory above the River Divie in the private grounds of Relugas House, 9.25km SSW of Forres on the B9007 Logie-Carrbridge road.* **OS sheet 27.**

The great natural strength of this site has made it attractive for settlement over a long period from the 1st millennium BC into the late 1st millennium AD. At the centre of the defences are the remains of a timber-laced rampart which enclose an area 53m by 33m. This has been burned at some stage in its history, several large areas of vitrified stone being visible near the entrance on the E side. The rampart has also been heavily mutilated by construction of a terrace and dyke associated with the modern house. Outwith this inner core, there has been no need for additional defences on the E and S, but across the neck of the promontory to N and W are a massive earthen outer rampart and ditch.

2. Quarrywood Hill, *Henge(?), (NJ 185631), in a forestry clearing to the SE of the summit of Quarrywood Hill, 3km W of the centre of Elgin.* **OS sheet 28.**

On a gently sloping terrace above the steeper slopes overlooking the A96 are the remains of a henge-like enclosure. The site is defined by a heavily silted segmental ditch, 5m wide by between 1m and 1.5m deep, with the remains of an upcast bank on its outer lip. This encloses a roughly circular platform, 47m by 43m, at the SW quadrant of which are three remaining stones of a stone circle. There appears originally to have been a single entrance to the platform via a causeway across the ditch from the W.

3. Sculptor's Cave, *Ritual Site (NJ 175707), at the foot of steep cliffs immediately to the W of the coastguard tower, 1km W of Easter Covesea.* **OS sheet 28.**

Excavations in the 1920s produced a massive quantity of human bone, including the crania and cervical vertebrae, apparently severed by a sharp instrument, of several children. Along with these were found items of high quality late Bronze Age and later Pictish period metalwork. The metalwork appears to have been thrown into a pool of standing water at the rear of the cave, paralleling the ritual deposits of objects and victims known from elsewhere in Britain and Europe. The discovery of a group of lower jaws from child skulls in the vicinity of the cave entrance, in conjunction with several stakeholes for what has been interpreted as wooden racks, has led to the suggestion that the severed heads had been displayed on stakes until the flesh had rotted off and the jaws had detached, the skulls then being moved to the racks. It appears that the ritual importance of the cave continued into the Pictish period, when a series of symbols were carved into the ⌐ock around its entrance.

4. Templestones, *Stone Setting (NJ 068569). On grazing land behind private housing off the unclassified Rafford-Burgie road 3km SE of Forres. Permission should be obtained from the Steading.* **OS sheet 27.**

This tiny four-poster setting is a unique example in this area of a tradition more common in Aberdeenshire and upper Strathtay. It comprises four stones, the tallest some 1.4m high, positioned about 2m apart. The interior is occupied by a kerb cairn, the kerb-stones of which are best seen on the SE and SW sides.

5. The Deil's Stanes, *Stone Circle (NJ 289641), 1km N of Urquhart, immediately W of the unclassified Urquhart-Lochhill road, 75m N of the crossroads with the unclassified Elgin-Garmouth road.* **OS sheet 28.**

Five stones remain of a circle of nine recorded in 1526, which originally measured over 36m in diameter, four at the SE and one isolated at the NW. The stones appear to be graded in height, the tallest at 1.83m standing at the S. This, and 18th-century references to an 'altar', have led to suggestions that this was originally a recumbent stone circle, which would make it a remote outlier of that tradition.

Map 12: Orkney

ORKNEY

1. Brogar *(The Ring of Brodgar), Mainland, Henge and Stone Circle (HY 294134), on the isthmus between the Loch of Stenness and the Loch of Harray. Historic Scotland, signposted from the B9055 Barnhouse-Hestwall road 4.5km NE of Stromness.* **OS sheet 6.**

This is one of the most magnificent prehistoric sites in Scotland, occupying the SE end of what was probably a low-lying promontory jutting into a single, joined loch. Excavation has shown that the enclosing ditch, which may have originally had an upcast bank on its outer lip, was rock-cut to a depth of 3m and was up to 9m wide. Two causeways of unexcavated material lead across the ditch at the NW and SE to the central platform, which measures some 113m in diameter. The interior has not been excavated. Round the outer edge of the platform stood a ring of sixty stones, of which thirty-six remain, with only twenty-seven still standing. The stones, all sandstone slabs, range from between 2 and 4.5m in height.

2. Cuween Hill, *Mainland, Chambered Cairn (HY 364128). Historic Scotland, signposted from the unclassified road from Finstown to Kirkwall via Grimbister, 500m W of Grimbister, by farm-track and footpath.* **OS sheet 6.**

Commanding wide views over the Bay of Firth, this fine tomb occupies an elevated position on the NE flank of Cuween Hill. A passage entered from the E side of the cairn mound, which is 16m in diameter, leads to the rectangular central chamber. This rises to 2.3m in height, and has two small cells opening from each side. The W cell is divided into two compartments. Excavation revealed the remains of eight inhumations, with five human skulls placed on the floor of the central chamber in association with those of twenty-four dogs.

3. Grain, *Souterrain (HY 442116). Historic Scotland, signposted from the A965 Kirkwall-Finstown road on the W side of Kirkwall.* **OS sheet 6.**

Discovered by chance in 1827, the souterrain was re-sealed until 1857, when it was opened and excavated. Few details of the excavation remain, but these suggest that the souterrain was associated with a large surface settlement.

The souterrain proper is well preserved, largely on account of its deep burial below up to 2m of soil. The dry-stone-walled passage, which is roughly 4.5m long, was entered down a flight of stone steps. The passage slopes downwards and curves round to a kidney-shaped chamber. Throughout its length it is roofed at a height of 1.5m by flat slabs. The chamber is also roofed with slabs, the additional span being supported on four stone columns.

4. Gurness, *Broch (HY 382268). Located on Aikerness overlooking Eynhallow Sound on the NE side of the mainland, this Historic Scotland site is reached via a footpath from the car-park at the W end of the Sands of Ervie, signposted from the A966 200m E of Stenso.* **OS sheet 6.**

Excavations spanning several seasons from 1929 onwards made this one of the most important broch-sites in the Northern Isles. Its importance is reinforced by the high level of preservation of the broch structure and associated buildings, and by the range of artefacts recovered from the site. The broch stands in the centre of three rings of rampart, each with external quarry ditches. Each rampart is broken on its E side by a single entrance, aligned on the doorway of the broch itself. This, the most visible feature of the site, has an almost solid foundation with only guard-cells and short galleries to either side of the entrance passage. Between the innermost rampart and the broch are the foundations of a complex of houses and yards, representing several phases of building extending into the Pictish period. One house, believed to be of Pictish style and date, has been re-erected adjacent to the site museum.

5. Holm of Papa Westray *(south), Chambered Cairn (HY 509518). On the Holm of Papa Westray, a small island off the coast of Papa Westray.* **OS sheet 5.**

The Holm, which is believed to have been a promontory of its larger neighbour in prehistoric times, is now uninhabited but in the Neolithic supported a substantial agricultural community, which buried their dead in two large chambered tombs. The better preserved of these, the South cairn, is a chambered tomb of Maes Howe type, excavated in 1849. Excavation revealed the cairn material to be contained within a low revetment. A passage, roofed with large flagstone slabs, led to an elongated central chamber, subdivided at each end into smaller chambers entered through low-lintelled doorways. From the central chamber, three doors in each long side open into small cells, and three doors in each of the end chamber also open into cells. The tomb had been robbed in antiquity and no early remains were found, but the excavator noted that several of the stones in the chamber wall were decorated with a variety of motifs – zig-zags, inverted Vs, dots and arcs.

6. Isbister *(The Tomb of the Eagles), Chambered Cairn, South Ronaldsay (ND 470485). At the SE end of the island, 750m E of Cleat.* **OS sheet 7.**

Excavations in the 1980s have put this site at the forefront of Neolithic burial sites in Scotland. The cairn is a complex structure, comprising what appears to be a Midhowe type stalled chamber, but with three side cells opening from it after the fashion of Maes Howe. The main chamber is divided into compartments by four pairs of slabs, but only the pair at either end project significantly into the central space. As a consequence, the arrangement looks more like an elongated chamber with two smaller compartments at either end, rather than five separate compartments. Both end sections had flagged floors and flagstone shelves. The main chamber is unroofed, the roof having been removed when the tomb was infilled in antiquity.

The excavations revealed large quantities of bone, both human and animal, and artefacts, such as Unstan pottery, shell beads, flints and stone implements. The artefacts had been deliberately deposited as votive groups. The human bone belonged to 340 individuals, but all skeletons were disarticulated and incomplete, and the bones had clear signs of weathering, indicating that they had been excarnated (exposed to the elements to remove the flesh) before burial. The bones appear to have been deliberately sorted into groups according to type, e.g. skulls or long bones. Analysis of the bone has provided remarkable insights into the character of the Neolithic population, the remains being of both sexes and spanning all age groups.

The animal and fish bones from the tomb appear to represent offerings to the dead. Meat in particular appears to have been brought in as joints, but there were no butchery marks on the bones. Amongst the remains were the carcasses of ten white-tailed sea-eagles These, like the dog skulls from Cuween, may have been the totem of the people buried in the tomb.

7. Knap of Howar, *Settlement, Papa Westray (HY 483518).*
Historic Scotland maintained, on Papa Westray. **OS sheet 5.**

The excavated remains of one of the earliest Neolithic settlements in Orkney comprise two houses lying parallel to each other. Both are rectangular with rounded ends. The larger – and earlier – measures 9.7m by 4.8m internally, its dry-stone walls being up to 1.5m thick. It was subdivided internally by a partition of upright slabs and timber posts, which would also have supported the roof. A short passage leads from this house into the later structure, which also has an outside entrance. It measures 8m by 3m and is undivided, but has several cupboard recesses in its side walls. Radiocarbon dating showed the settlement to have been occupied between 3500 BC and 3100 BC, pottery from the site revealing that it had been the home of people of the Unstan tradition.

8. Maes Howe, *Mainland, Chambered Cairn (HY 318128).*
Access by footpath from the A965 Finstown to Stromness road, 3.5km W of Finstown. Historic Scotland maintained.
OS sheet 6.

Recognised, with considerable justice, as one of the finest prehistoric monuments in Europe, Maes Howe bears witness to the skills and sophistication of the Neolithic culture of Orkney. The type of site which lends its name to a distinctive classification of chambered tomb, it is a truly remarkable memorial to the technical achievements of the ancient population. The mound which covers the tomb stands on an artificially levelled platform enclosed by a bank and ditch, radiocarbon dating of samples from the latter indicating a construction date of shortly before 2700 BC. The mound itself, constructed from heaped peat, clay and stone, measures 35m in diameter and rises to 7m in height.

The entrance to the tomb is in the SW of the mound, and had been sealed with soil and stones at the ritual closing of the tomb. Some 3m into the mound is the entrance proper, opening into a stone-built passage some 9m long, its side walls incorporating some truly enormous single slabs. The passage opens into a central chamber 4.5m square and rising some 4m in height, although the upper part of the corbelled roof is modern. In each corner, massive pillarstones front supporting buttresses of coursed stone. In the centre of the SE, NE and NW walls of the chamber are the entrances to the side chambers. These are placed above ground level in the walls, and on the floor in front of them are the massive blocks with which the openings were formerly blocked.

When the tomb was investigated last century, no trace of Neolithic burials or artefacts were found within it. Indeed, it appears that it had been plundered and re-used on more than one occasion by subsequent settlers in Orkney. In particular, it had been entered several times during the Norse settlement of Orkney, the Scandinavian presence being marked by 24 runic inscriptions and several drawings.

9. Midhowe, *Rousay, Broch (HY 371308). Historic Scotland maintained site on the W side of Rousay. Access via footpath from the unclassified road from the B9064 at Westness to Wasbister.* **OS sheet 6.**

Coastal erosion has made Midhowe's promontory site yet more spectacular, but has also led to loss of considerable portions of the outer areas of the site. Defended on the landward side by a massive stone wall and two deep ditches, and by two natural geos on its flanks, this has been an immensely powerful site. The broch, unusually for Orkney, has had a gallery at ground level, but this appears to have led to instability in the structure since it was infilled in antiquity, with massive upright slabs placed against the outer wall as additional shoring. Only two small cells opening from the entrance passage – which is provided with checks for two timber doors – were left unblocked. A scarcement round the interior of the broch shows that there were originally timber buildings ranged against the inner wall, while a mural stair indicates that there were upper galleries.

The interior of the broch today is divided into two compartments by a partition of upright slabs. Both units were further subdivided and provided with hearths and water tanks, indicating that two separate families were resident in the old broch. Further buildings were inserted in the space between the broch and the outer wall, but only one complete structure survives in recognisable form. Excavation revealed considerable evidence for iron-smelting and the casting of bronze in workshops in this outer court.

10. Midhowe, *Rousay, Chambered Cairn (HY 372306). Some 100m SSW of the Broch of Midhowe. Access as above.* **OS sheet 6.**

One of the largest and finest of the surviving stalled tombs of Orkney. It comprises a 23m-long main chamber, subdivided by projecting slabs into 12 compartments, set within a large rectangular mound measuring some 30m by 15m. The entrance, which lay in the middle of the short S side, had been infilled with dry-stone walling at the end of the cairn's functioning life, at which time the roof had also been removed and the interior of the chamber filled with stones and soil. The fifth to eleventh compartments on the NE side are provided with low, slab-built benches, onto which were placed the 25 burials – 17 adult and six in the 14–20 age group. As at Isbister (see p. 213), the condition of the bones suggested that they had been exposed prior to burial to remove the flesh. Pottery recovered from the tomb was of Unstan type, and as at Isbister had been placed in a distinct heap in a cell midway along the passage. The cairn's outer wall has been of great sophistication, the stonework being laid in herringbone patterns, now best seen on the E side.

11. Quoyness, *Sanday, Chambered Cairn (HY 677377). Access by footpath from the B9069, 3.2km SSW of Roadside.* OS sheet 5.

This is one of the most spectacular of the Maes Howe type of chambered tomb after Maes Howe itself, and lies in an area of extensive Neolithic and Bronze Age burial activity. As at Maes Howe, the tomb comprises a central chamber reached along a 3.6m-long entrance passage, but the chamber has in this case six subsidiary cells opening from it. The main chamber is some 4m long by 2m wide and is built of coursed water-worn slabs. The walls are corbelled inwards and rise to some 4m in height. Excavation in 1867 produced evidence for burials in four of the cells, while a cist in the floor of the main chamber contained ten adult and four child inhumations. Artefacts recovered included polished stone and bone implements similar to forms found at Skara Brae. These, and radiocarbon dates from further bone recovered in subsequent excavations by Gordon Childe in the 1950s, pointed towards use in the early 3rd millennium BC.

The cairn, which like Maes Howe stood on its own kerbed platform, is of interesting construction, which the Historic Scotland consolidation of the site now stresses. Within the mound were three distinct built wall faces. The innermost encloses the chambers, while it and the middle wall contain the cairn material between them. The outermost wall, which blocks the entrance passage, was clearly built at the final sealing of the tomb.

12. Rennibister, *Mainland, Souterrain (HY 397126). At Rennibister farm, signposted by farm-track off the A965 Kirkwall to Finstown road, 4km E of Finstown.* **OS sheet 6.**

Found by accident in 1926 when a farm machine broke the roof of the main chamber. It comprised a narrow entrance passage, the first few metres of which had been blocked deliberately, leading to a small oval chamber measuring 3.5m by 2.5m, with five shallow recesses in its walls. Its roof of corbelled slabs was supported on four free-standing stone pillars. In the chamber were the incomplete skeletal remains of six adults and at least twelve adolescents, probably representing the re-use of the souterrain as a burial-place rather than any more sinister act.

13. Skara Brae, *Mainland, Settlement (HY 231188). At the S end of the Bay of Skaill. Access by footpath from the Historic Scotland car-park on the B9056 3km NW of Hestwall.* **OS sheet 6.**

This is without question the most famous Neolithic settlement site in Britain, and one which continues to fire the public imagination as well as to fuel academic debate. Radiocarbon dating has shown that it was occupied from *c.*3100 BC down to *c.*2450 BC, but the reasons for what appears to have been precipitate abandonment remain unknown. First discovered in 1850 when a storm stripped away part of its covering sand dunes, the site was first excavated in 1927 by Childe. Originally, it had lain well back from the shore, but erosion – which still threatens the site – probably removed much of the land to its W even in the prehistoric. The settlement comprises a cluster of sub-rectangular huts connected by passages. Seven huts, their walls built of coursed sandstone slabs, were cleared in 1927. The nature of the roofing is uncertain, corbelled stone has been suggested, as has turf and thatch supported on whalebone rafters. Only one hut has a window, otherwise the only external openings in the walls were the entrances. The buildings were enclosed within a mound of compressed midden material, probably dumped to provide added insulation against the Atlantic winds.

The huts are of two basic types: the first has a central hearth as the focus for each hut, bed spaces being provided in recesses in the walls; the second, which is later and larger, still has a central hearth, but the beds are free-standing boxes built out into the floor area. The beds, along with the so-called 'dressers' are the most remarkable features of the houses, representing in stone what was probably a timber-built tradition of furnishing elsewhere. The dressers are positioned to be seen directly from the entrance, and were probably used for displaying the household's fine pottery vessels. One building was unfurnished and may have served as a workshop.

The site has produced a remarkable assemblage of artefacts and organic materials, ranging from domestic refuse including bone and shells through to decorated stone and pottery. Several of the stones of the structures are also highly decorated. Small pots containing ochre residues might indicate that the occupants also painted their bodies.

From the organic material recovered, it has proven possible to reconstruct a good impression of the economy of the community. It was agriculturally based, growing cereal crops as well as raising cattle and sheep. Hunting provided added resources, while there is clear evidence that deep sea as well as inshore fishing and scavenging of stranded whale carcasses supplemented their diet.

14. Stenness, *Mainland, Henge and Stone Circle (HY 307125). At the S end of the isthmus between Loch of Stenness and Loch of Harray, signposted along the B9055 0.5km NW of Barnhouse on the A965 Finstown to Stromness Road.* **OS sheet 6.**

Only three massive uprights remain of the original twelve which stood on the central platform of this henge. The platform, measuring some 30m in diameter, is enclosed by a rock-cut ditch and is reached by a single causeway of uncut ground on the N side. In the centre of the henge, excavations revealed a rectangular setting of stones within which were deposits of cremated bone, charcoal and grooved ware pottery. Radiocarbon dates from this material indicated an early 3rd millennium BC construction for the henge.

15. Taversoe Tuick, *Rousay, Chambered Cairn (HY 426276). 1km W of the ferry pier, Historic Scotland signposted from the B9064.* **OS sheet 6.**

Notable chiefly for its unusual form, this monument consists of two stalled cairns built one on top of the other, both provided with their own entrances through the circular covering mound. The cairn is some 9m in diameter and stands on the N of a platform of flat stones extending over an area of some 3m by 7m. The lower chamber was entered by a paved passage in its S side, and was divided into compartments, provided with stone shelves, by three pairs of projecting slabs. The shelves were used to carry deposits of human bones. The lower tomb was cut into the bedrock of the hill, but the cut was lined with dry-stone walling. The slab-built roof, which forms the floor of the upper chamber, rests on the uncut bedrock rather than the walling. The upper chamber was entered from the N. The central chamber was divided into two compartments by slabs. Here, the burials comprised cremated remains of several adults and children in three slab-covered cists.

Some 7m S of the cairn is a smaller chambered tomb dug into the ground. Measuring only 1.5m by 1.3m, it had originally a lintelled roof supported on four slabs which divided it into five narrow compartments. It contained no skeletal remains, but three near-intact pottery bowls lay on the floor.

16. The Dwarfie Stane, *Hoy, Chambered Tomb (HY 243004). Historic Scotland. Access via footpath from the unclassified road from Quoys to Rackwick, 4km S of the ferry pier at Moaness.* **OS sheet 7.**

This huge sandstone block lies on the gentler slopes below the craggy outcrops of the Dwarfie Hamars, from which it had fallen in antiquity. Measuring some 8.5m long by 4.5m wide and 2m in height, it has been hollowed by the cutting of a passage in from its W face. Opening from the passage are two cells, separated from the entrance by raised kerbs. A large block of stone on the ground in front of the entrance was presumably the blocking for the passage.

17. Unstan, *Mainland, Chambered Tomb (HY 283118). On a headland projecting N into the Loch of Stenness, immediately E of Bridge of Waithes on the B965 Stromness to Finstown road.* **OS sheet 6.**

Excavation of this site in 1884 produced the pottery which is now named after the cairn within which it was found: Unstan ware. It is a fine example of a stalled cairn within a circular mound, constructed from concentric rings of walling. The long chamber was divided into five compartments, all of which held skeletal remains, while in a smaller chamber opening off the entrance passage there were two crouched inhumations.

18. Wideford Hill, *Mainland, Chambered Tomb (HY 409121). On the NW flank of Wideford Hill. Signposted from the unclassified road from Finstown to Kirkwall via Grimbister, access is via farm track and footpath from Haughhead. The monument lies 1.2km from the road.* **OS sheet 6.**

This splendidly sited cairn of Maes Howe type was excavated in 1849, at which time its covering mound of clay was removed to reveal its internal stone construction. The tomb proper is cut back into the hillside and is entered via a passage from the SW. Three cells – all empty at the time of excavation – open from the central chamber, that to the N being cut into bedrock. The chambers were enclosed within the innermost of three concentric rings of dry-stone walling.

ROSS AND CROMARTY

1. Ardvanie, *Chambered Cairn (NH 681874). In scrub on the N side of the old A93, 25km NW of Edderton, immediately adjacent to the track to Ardvanie.* **OS sheet 21.**

The cairn has been heavily plundered for stone and is somewhat overgrown, but several of its main features are clearly visible. The superstructure survives as a low, stony platform some 21m in diameter, with no clear evidence for a kerb. Towards the centre are the remains of a polygonal chamber roughly 3.3m long by 1.8m wide. The entrance passage was in the E side.

2. Cnoc an Duin, *Hillfort (NH 696769). On an outcrop at the S end of the massif of Cnoc an t-Sabhail above the deep valley of the Balnagown River. Access by track and footpath from Scotsburn House 4km NW of Kildary, or by track and footpath down Strathrory from the car-park at the bridge over the Balnagown River on the A836 3km N of Sittenham. The fort is approximately 3km distant from the road in either direction.* **OS sheet 21.**

This is one of the finest and clearest examples of an unfinished fort in N Scotland. The single wall which was originally intended to enclose an area some 220m by 75m was abandoned when little more than half of the circuit had been built. Two further lines of unfinished rampart with external quarry ditches can be traced at the W end.

3. Conon Bridge, *Henge (?) (NH 543551). Behind housing at the S end of Conon Bridge, on the E side of the A862.* **OS sheet 26.**

This is one of a group of three monuments in this area over which there are questions concerning their strict identification as henges (the others are at Contin, [3b] NH 441569, on level ground at the E end of Loch Achilty to the NW of the village, and at Culbokie, [3c] NH 594577, to the W of the B9169 between Duncanston and Culbokie, 1.5km SW of Culbokie). They conform generally to Class I form, but in all three cases the enclosing bank is unbroken, even at the single causeway across the ditch. It is possible that the gaps in the banks have been infilled at a later date, or that they represent an early stage in the development of henge monuments, but only excavation may help to elucidate an answer.

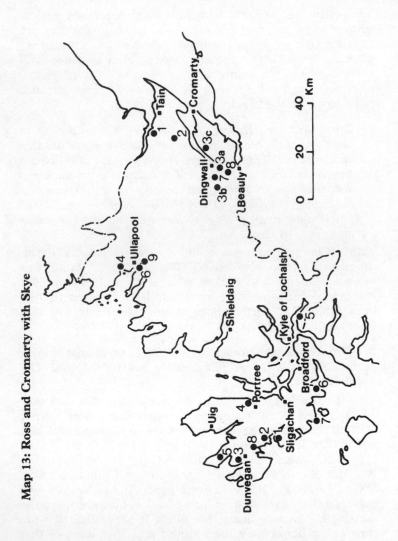

Map 13: Ross and Cromarty with Skye

4. Dun Canna, *Fort (NC 111008). Some 10.5km N of Ullapool on the A836, turn left onto the unclassified road to Blughasary. Park at road end (1.2km) and follow the track which crosses and re-crosses the meandering lower reaches of the River Kanaird. Roughly 300m after the third bridge, fork right and follow the track for a further 1.2km to its end below the fort.* **OS sheet 15.**

The tumbled ruins of this stone-walled fort occupy a high promontory at the N end of the sandy beach of the Camas Mor, backed to the N by the mountainous district of Coigach. The outline of the fort follows for the most part the lip of the rocky outcrop which it crowns. It is divided into two enclosures, the outer and larger being massively walled, while the inner, on the narrower promontory, has had a slighter wall. The original approach climbed the steep NE side of the promontory to a point where the wall of the fort diverged to form an overlap between which was the gate. This, however, is now largely obscured by tumble and thick heather growth. There is no clear break in the rampart of the inner enclosure to indicate where the gate into it lay.

5. Dun Grugaig, *Broch (NG 866251). In forestry on the S side of Loch Duich. The broch lies to the S of the footpath which runs W from the head of the track from Totaig, at the end of the unclassified road from Ratagan to Letterfearn, some 7km NW of Ratagan.* **OS sheet 33.**

This isolated site is well worth visiting, displaying a better state of preservation than other, more accessible, sites. It occupies a slightly levelled position on ground that slopes steeply to the N, its wall surviving up to 4m in height. The entrance passage, in the NE, is provided with door-checks, draw-bar slot and guard-chamber, while its outer opening is crowned by an enormous triangular lintel stone. There are two mural chambers opening from the central area, and a broken staircase rising now only to the remains of a gallery. The sloping interior means that the scarcement is, at the SW side of the interior, only some 71cm above the rocky floor, but at the NE lies at a height of some 2m.

6. Dun Lagaidh, *Fort and Dun (NH 142913). Leave the A835 Inverness-Ullapool road 1hm S of Inverlael on the unclassified road to Letters and Ardindrean. Continue to Loggie at the head of the road, then follow the track which drops down towards the lochside to the N to the fort.* **OS sheet 20.**

A long whale-backed rock outcrop above a sheltered anchorage on the W side of Loch Broom has attracted settlers for its defensive qualities from at least the earlier Iron Age. The earliest fortification on the site was a massive timber-laced rampart which occupied the W end of the hilltop. This enclosed an area some 90m by 35m, but whether the whole summit was protected by massive walling such as that traceable at the W end is unclear: the craggy N and S faces of the ridge show no signs of such defences. The summit area was subdivided by a transverse wall which now underlies the eastern end of the secondary dun which occupies the highest western portion of the site, and to the E of this wall was a slighter outer rampart, now largely obliterated by later lines of ditch. Exposed sections of vitrified material can be seen at the W and NW sectors.

The second phase of occupation at the site is represented by the dun which is still the most prominent feature of the remains. Described in some literature as a broch, the relative thinness of the walls suggests that this was not a tower of that class, but falls into the wider dun category. The structure is reduced largely to an amorphous heap of rubble, although the interior was largely cleared of debris in the course of modern excavations. Several of the main features of the dun were recognised in the excavations, but these were not consolidated and have been deliberately infilled to protect them. Thus, the main entrance in the E wall, and the mural chamber opening from its passage to the N, are not now visible. On the W side traces of a doorway leading into a short mural passage from which a stair leading up to the wall-head, of which about 15 treads remain, have been left open.

A final phase of occupation, possibly dating to the 12th century, is represented by the fragmentary remains of a small stone castle. A tower was erected on the rubble of the dun, while the W end of the site, roughly equivalent to the area of the first period fort, was enclosed by a wall of mortared stone to form a courtyard. Traces of this wall, built much narrower than the timber-laced rampart, run out from the dune to the N and S.

7. Knock Farril, *Hillfort (NH 504585). At the E end of the long, narrow ridge of Knock Farril overlooking lower Strathpeffer, 3.5km W of Dingwall. Access via footpath from the W end of Knockfarrel village, at the head of the* *unclassified road from the A835 (T) at Maryburgh to Ussie and Knockfarrel.* **OS sheet 26.**

What on the one hand appears to be a conventionally planned timber-laced fort has several unusual features which on the other render it a highly enigmatic monument. The main enclosure, its long axis running E and W, measures 129.5m by 38m within a single, heavily vitrified wall. From either end of this project long lines of vitrified walling of uncertain function, possibly representing walled entrance passages. Three later lines of banks and ditches cut across the fort.

8. **Muir of Ord**, *Henge (NH 527497). On the golf course at the SW end of Muir of Ord. Permission to visit the site should be obtained from the Club House.* **OS sheet 26.**

This Class II henge has had the dubious honour of being used as a green on the golf course, the surrounding bank and ditch offering an unusual obstacle to players, and part of the ditch at the NW having been filled in to ease access. The central platform measures roughly 25.5m by 19.5m within ditches up to 5.4m wide by 1.3m deep.

9. **Rhiroy**, *Broch (NH 149900). On the steep slopes overlooking Loch Broom from the W, between the townships of Rhiroy and Loggie. Access via the unclassified road to Letters running W from the A835(T) Inverness-Ullapool road. The broch is reached up a farm track on the W side of the road after some 6.5km.* **OS sheet 20.**

Rhiroy broch occupies the lip of a crag-edged terrace about 90m above the level of the loch. The edge of the crag has been subject to erosion and a considerable portion of the broch structure has fallen away, but on the uphill side the wall still rises in places to roughly 4m in height. Modern sheep-pens, in part built from broch material, abut its walls. The entrance was on the SE, but this has been built up. Internally, the broch has measured some 11.6m in diameter within walls 4.3m thick. The interior was cleared of rubble in the course of excavations in the 1970s, but most of the features in the thickness of the walls have been built up to protect them: 4m left of the entrance is a blocked doorway leading to a mural chamber and stairway. A doorway opened from a landing on the stairs into the timber gallery which would have been supported on the scarcement which still survives on the highest remaining portions of wall. The stair continued above the landing. There is a gallery at the highest level of the surviving structure. Due to the sloping nature of the interior floor, the scarcement is only 1.2m above ground on the uphill side, but would have been 2.5m above on the downhill. In the centre of the floor was a hearth, surrounded by a ring of posts which supported the timber buildings ranged against the inner face.

SKYE

(see map on p.222)

1. Dun Ardtreck, *Broch (NG 334358). On the W side of Ardtreck Point, 1.5km NW of Portnalong off the B8009 and unclassified road. Access difficult.* **OS sheet 32.**

The D-shaped enclosure of Dun Ardtreck stands on the cliff edge of a crag-girt outcrop rising sheer from the sea. Usually labelled a 'semi-broch', this is a galleried structure which bears many structural features similar to those associated with brochs proper. Excavation in the 1960s suggested construction in the 1st century BC for the main galleried wall, which encloses an area some 13m by 10m. The edge towards the sea was screened by a straight wall of quite slight construction. The entrance, which is raised above ground level, leads into a now roofless passage provided with door-checks, draw-bar holes and a guard-chamber. The mural galleries to right and left of the passage were entered from the courtyard. The primary occupation of the site ended with its burning. Re-occupation saw the partial dismantling of the walls and the construction of a house in the rubble-filled interior. There are traces of an outer enclosing wall round the lip of the landward crags, entered via a gateway in the S.

2. Dun Beag, *Broch (NG 339386). In moorland to the E of the A883 Sligachan-Dunvegan road 0.5km NW of Struanmore. Park in the lay-by on the W side of the road. The broch is clearly visible on the skyline to the E, access via the signposted gate.* **OS sheet 32.**

This well preserved site enjoys superb views W and S over Loch Bracadale and Loch Harport. It occupies the summit of a rocky outcrop, which lends additional defence. The interior, which has been cleared of rubble, measures some 11m in diameter, within walls up to 4.3m thick. The entrance passage in the SE has checks for a wooden door. In the thickness of the wall are a small bee-hive shaped cell, a long gallery and a chamber leading to the remains of the staircase to the vanished upper levels.

3. Dun Fiadhairt, *Broch (NG 231504). Crowning a rocky outcrop in the centre of the headland on the W side of Camalaig Bay, roughly 2km NW of Dunvegan Castle.* **OS sheet 23.**

The inner and outer faces of this superb little site were left exposed following excavation in 1914, allowing a better impression to be gained of its original appearance. The interior measures 9.5m in diameter within walls 3.6m thick. The entrance was on the W via a passage provided with guard-chambers to either side. Opening from the courtyard on the N are two mural chambers, that to the E containing a staircase. There appears to have been a second entrance to the E, but its outer end has been blocked. Opening from the D side of its passage is a narrow mural gallery that runs round most of the S side of the broch.

4. **Dun Gerashader**, *Fort (NG 489453). To the SE of the A855 Portree-Staffin road, 1.5km N of Portree.* **OS sheet 23.**

Crowning a rocky outcrop above the River Chlacaig are the remains of a substantial fortification. The only easy line of approach to the summit, from the S, is screened by a massive rampart, some 4m thick. Thinner walls on the remaining sides enclose an area some 51.8m by 30m. The S defences are strengthened additionally by two lines of boulders, akin to chevaux de frise, set some 18m and 24m in advance of the wall.

5. **Dun Hallin**, *Broch (NG 256592). 700m ENE of Hallin in Waternish in NW Skye. The easiest access is from the N across rough ground S of the unclassified road from Hallin to Gillen.* **OS sheet 23.**

Crowning a knoll on the NW ridge of Beinn na Mointeich, Dun Hallin commands extensive views S and W over Loch Dunvegan. The broch is well preserved, its outer walls rising free from accumulated debris and still standing nearly 4m high. The entrance passage on the SE was flanked by guard-chambers, but the wall is most heavily damaged in this sector. The walls themselves are 3.4m thick around a central courtyard some 11m in diameter. Remains of mural galleries and a stair can be traced in the debris of the wall at the SW. The broch has stood within an irregularly-shaped walled enclosure measuring some 46m by 38m. The enclosure wall is heavily ruined, but sections of its outer facing can be traced around the N and E perimeter.

6. **Dun Ringill**, *Dun (NG 561170). On the E coast of the Strathaird peninsula overlooking Loch Slapin. Access by*

footpath on the N side of the Abhainn Cille Mhaire, opposite Kilmarie. **OS sheet 32.**

This wonderfully atmospheric site occupies a rocky promontory rising above the pebbly shore of Loch Slapin. A massive wall screens three sides, leaving only the E open. The wall is up to 4.5m thick, and shows signs of successive phases of building around the entrance on the NW side. It encloses an area some 22m by 17.5m, which contains the remains of a rectangular structure of early medieval date. The entrance passage is well preserved, complete with door-checks, draw-bar hole and slot. There is a mural gallery on the S side which leads to a large cell measuring some 5.5m by 1.5m, its inner wall still rising to over 4m in height. The rectangular foundations to the W of the dun appear to mark the site of its successor settlement.

7. Rubh' an Dunain, *Chambered Cairn (NG 393163). On the N side of Loch na h-Airde at the SW extremity of the promontory on the S side of Loch Brittle. Access via footpath running for some 5.5km SW along the lochside from the Glen Brittle campsite.* **OS sheet 32.**

The headland of Rubh' an Dunain is rich in archaeology. The footpath runs at first through the remains of an abandoned township, patches of cultivation as well as house sites clearly visible through the blanket of heather. Towards the end of the path a transverse dyke cuts off the last kilometre or so of the headland, defining the territory of a second township whose substantial remains line the hillside to the NE of Loch na h-Airde. The loch itself is tidal, the channel at its S end having been canalised to power a tidal mill and to provide safe access for boats to be drawn up into noosts. In addition, the imposing remains of a galleried dun straddle a rocky headland to the E of the tidal channel.

The chambered cairn is a fine example of a Hebridean style passage grave within a circular cairn. It has been plundered for stone for dyke-building in the past, but survives to about 20m in diameter by some 3.4m in height. Excavation in 1931–2 cleared the forecourt of blocking material to reveal a facade of slabby uprights linked by stretches of dry-stone walling. Left unconsolidated, these have slumped forward in places. From the centre of the facade the still lintelled passage leads to a polygonal chamber, roughly 2.2m across at its widest point and rising to 2m in height. The walls are constructed from massive uprights linked, like the facade, by stretches of dry-stone walling. The upper levels of the chamber are coursed but had not been corbelled, the roof instead being of basalt slabs is now missing. The excavations revealed several burials representing two phases of use, the earlier in the Neolithic, the later in the Early Bronze Age, both associated with pottery.

8. **Vatten**, *Chambered Cairns (NG 298440). Immediately to the W of the A863 Sligachan-Dunvegan road 1km NW of Caroy.* **OS sheet 23.**

The two cairns at Vatten are unexcavated but appear to be of Hebridean type. Both appear to have been built on low platforms edged by kerbs, but slippage of cairn material has obscured this. At the more southerly of the two, which measures 27m in diameter and rises to some 6m in height, traces of a boulder kerb can be seen on the E side.

SHETLAND

1. Clickhimmin, *Mainland, Fort and Broch (HU 464408).*
On a promontory at the S end of Loch of Clickhimmin at the
W side of Lerwick. Access by footpath from the A970 Lerwick
to Sumburgh road. **OS sheet 4.**

One of the finest prehistoric monuments in Shetland, the
fort and broch at Clickhimmin display a remarkable
sequence of development from the later Bronze Age through
into the later 1st millennium AD. The promontory occupied
by the site was formerly an islet in a tidal inlet opening off
Brei Wick, access to which was along a causeway from the S.
The site was consolidated following excavation in the 1950s,
and the full development of the settlement can be seen
clearly. The earliest phase, dating from *c.*700 BC, is
represented by the low walls of an oval, stone-built house
with a central hearth. This early settlement seems to have
relied on its island site for defence, but in the later 1st
millennium BC it was massively redeveloped with a substantial
stone wall round the perimeter of the island, and an
elaborate entrance through a free-standing blockhouse. This
was a two-storey structure, its walls galleried and provided
with stairs to reach the upper level. The entrance passage is
provided with checks for a timber door, slots for a draw-bar,
and a guard chamber. Against the inner face of the
blockhouse, and ranged round the interior of the enclosing
wall, were timber buildings, possibly of at least two storeys.

In the centre of this enclosure, work appears to have been
commenced on a massively built inner defence soon after
completion of the blockhouse. While work was still at an
early stage, it was decided instead to construct a broch
partially superimposed over the inner defensive circuit. The
broch displays a number of unusual features, including two
entrances and a cell placed immediately over the entrance
passage and provided with a 'viewing-slot' which would have
allowed a defender to stab intruders from above! In the 1st
millennium AD, the broch appears to have fallen into disuse
and a wheelhouse was built in its central courtyard. Several
other huts were built into the space between the broch and
the outer wall.

2. Jarlshof, *Mainland, Settlement, Broch etc. (HU 398095).*
On the shore of West Voe of Sumburgh, immediately S of
Sumburgh airport. **OS sheet 4.**

Map 14: Shetland

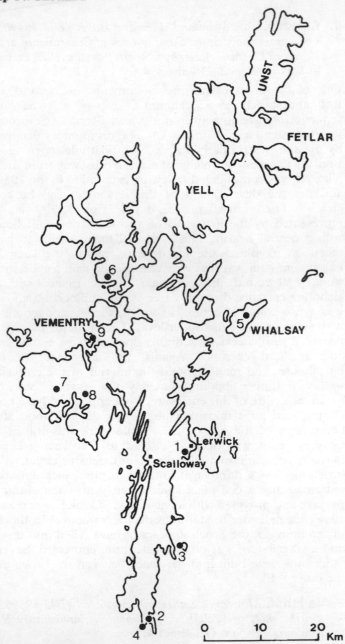

With Skara Brae in Orkney, this is one of the most famous archaeological sites in Scotland, representing over 4000 years of settlement on one site. Here can be seen, remarkably well preserved, remains stretching from the earlier Bronze Age through to the early 17th century AD. The earliest surviving remains – it is uncertain how much of the original settled area has been eroded away by the sea – lie at the E end of the site. Here are the remains of a series of circular and oval stone-walled houses, divided internally by projecting walls. There is evidence for prolonged use and changes of function in these buildings, some having been converted into workshops and what appear to have been cattle byres.

Following a phase of abandonment in the early 1st millennium BC, the site was re-occupied and a broch with attendant courtyard and outbuildings built to the W of the Bronze Age settlement. Only half of this survives, the remainder having been washed away by the sea. The broch had undergone alteration, including the insertion of an aisled roundhouse into its outer court. This itself had been plundered for building stone for two wheelhouses in the middle of the 1st millennium AD. Two other well preserved Iron Age huts lie at the W perimeter of the site.

The Iron Age settlement was itself superseded in the later 1st millennium AD by a Norse settlement, the remains of which lie to the N of the earlier structures. This was in turn succeeded by a medieval farmstead, possibly including the church of Dunrossness. The final element on the site is the early 17th-century laird's house which lies between the broch and the Norse settlement. It was to this ruin that Sir Walter Scott gave the name 'Jarlshof', using it as one of the main scenes of action in his novel *The Pirate*, which has since been applied to the whole site.

3. **Mousa**, *Mousa, Broch (HU 457236). On the island of Mousa off the E side of the S Mainland. Access by ferry (subject to weather conditions) from the Wick of Sandsayre, some 20km S of Lerwick.* **OS sheet 4.**

The best preserved example of a broch, Mousa was for long taken as the model for reconstructing the original appearance of these structures, but is now recognised as an exceptional example of its class rather than the norm. It is, nevertheless, a spectacular monument to the technical skills of its Iron Age builders, still forming a major landmark on the E side of Mousa sound. Looking like a stone-built cooling tower, its tapering walls rise featureless to a height of 13.3m, broken only by a single doorway at its base. This leads through a passage 1.2m wide and 4.9m long to the central courtyard. Midway along its length are the checks for a timber door, beyond which the passage widens to 1.5m. The central court is 6.1m in diameter within walls 4.5m thick on average, but it has been later reduced in extent by the insertion of a wheelhouse in the early 1st millennium AD. Opening off the court are three doorways leading into elongated cells within the thickness of the wall-base. Two scarcements ring the interior wall, one at 2.1m above the ground-level, the upper at 3.7m.

4. **Ness of Burgi**, *Mainland, Fort and Blockhouse (HU 388085). On the W side of the long, narrow promontory of Scat Ness. Access by unclassified road running S to Brecks and Scat Ness from the A970 W of Sumburgh airport, and thence across rough ground to the S.* **OS sheet 4.**

One of the most spectacularly sited and better preserved of the many promontory forts which stud the Shetland coastline. Two rock-cut ditches cut off the promontory from the mainland. Between them is a massive stone-faced rampart, 6.4m thick and up to 2.1m high. Behind this triple defence, built on the inner lip of the second ditch, is a massive blockhouse. Originally more than 22m long – its S end has fallen away due to cliff erosion – and some 6m wide, it has been substantially restored following excavation, but had survived up to 2m high in places and with several lintel stones of its passages in position. It is pierced at approximately its middle by a single entrance aligned on a gap in the outer rampart. This leads into a passage provided with door-checks and slots for a draw-bar. There are cells in the thickness of the wall to either side of the passage, and the remains of a third can be seen in the fallen S end.

5. **Pettigarths Field**, *Whalsay, Settlement (HU 587652). On the island of Whalsay, by ferry from Laxo Voe on the Mainland to Symbister on Whalsay.* **OS sheet 2.**

Two Neolithic houses, known locally as 'the Standing Stones of Yoxie' and 'the Benie Hoose', lie in the area of the island known as Pettigarths Field. Both are of similar plan, comprising an outer court linked by an entrance passage to the main house. The Standing Stones of Yoxie structure is two-roomed, the Benie Hoose has only one, but in both cases the main chambers have been further subdivided.

6. Punds Water, *Mainland, Chambered Cairn (HU 324712). In open moorland N of Mangaster, off the A970 2.5km N of Mavis Grind.* **OS sheet 3.**

A well preserved example of a Shetland heel-shaped cairn. Built of white quartzite boulders, the cairn measures only 15m in diameter. It has a rounded 'back' while the 'front' is extended into projecting horns set on either side of a curving façade. In the centre of the façade a narrow entrance leads through into a trefoil-shaped chamber, now roofless, but with walls still standing up to 1.4m in height. Excavation in 1930 showed that the floor of the chamber was of red water-worn pebbles set into clay.

7. Scord of Brouster, *Mainland, Settlement (HU 255516). In open moorland to the N of the A971 Bridge of Walls-Melby road, 0.5km NW of Bridge of Walls.* **OS sheet 3.**

The hillside at Scord of Brouster is covered with the remains of one of the best preserved and most extensive Neolithic settlements and attendant field-systems in Scotland. Excavation in the 1970s uncovered three oval houses positioned within their own fields, with several other fields outlined by walls and banks of cleared stone extending to some 2 ha. The largest house measures 7m by 5m internally within its carefully faced wall, and was subdivided internally by four large projections or pillars around a central hearth.

8. Stanydale, *Mainland, 'Temple' and House (HU 285502 and HU 288503). In open moorland to the N of Gruting in the W mainland. Signposted from the A971 1km W of Effirth, access via footpath from the unclassified road to Sefster and Gruting.* **OS sheet 3.**

The moorland to the S of Stanydale carries the extensive remains of Neolithic settlement and field systems. The principal feature of the landscape is the monument usually referred to as the Stanydale temple. This is a massively built structure which appears to have stylistic affinities with the distinctive heel-shaped Shetland cairns. Its scale suggests that it is more than simply a burial-place, and it has been suggested that it was either a communal meeting house or, indeed, a temple. The walls are up to 4m thick and enclose an oval chamber some 12m long by 9m at its widest, entered by a single door in the middle of the E end. At the broader W end stone-built piers project into the central chamber to form a small recess in the wall face. Two stone-lined postholes on the long axis once held massive timber uprights which supported a ridged roof.

Several houses can be seen on either side of the path leading to the temple. The one excavated example shows these to be of a form typical to Shetland – similar to those at Pettigarths Field – comprising a single oval chamber within a thick stone wall, with recesses in the inner face of the wall. A small cell opens off one end of the main chamber.

9. Vementry, *Vementry, Chambered Cairn (HU 295609). On the small, uninhabited island of Vementry at the W end of Swarbacks Minn. Access by privately hired boat from West Burrafirth.* **OS sheet 3.**

Despite the difficulties of access, the island of Vementry is well worth the effort of visiting. In addition to the superb cairn which crowns Muckle Ward, the highest point of the island, there is a well preserved Neolithic house on the S side of the Maa Loch, and a second chambered cairn on the W shore of Northra Voe. At Swarbacks Head at the N end of the island there are the remains of a gun battery which protected the entrance to Swarback Minn, the main anchorage in World War I for the Northern Cruiser Flotilla. The cairn on Muckle Ward, however, is the chief monument on Vementry and is one of the finest and best preserved chamber tombs in Shetland. The main cairn structure is circular, 7.9m in diameter, rising from a heel-shaped platform with a façade of stone blocks. The platform measures 11.3m across the façade by 10m. The chamber, which is entered via a 3.6m-long entrance passage, is trefoil-shaped, the N lobe still preserving its roofing lintels.

WESTERN ISLES

1. Barpa Langass, *North Uist, Chambered cairn (NF 838657). On the NE flank of Ben Langass, clearly visible on the skyline 200m S of the A867 Clachan-a-Luib to Lochmaddy road.* **OS sheet 18.**

The magnificent cairn of Barpa Langass is one of the most impressive prehistoric monuments in the Outer Isles. It is truly massive, measuring some 25m in diameter and rising to 4m in height over the lintelled passage-grave. The entrance lay in the centre of a forecourt on the E side, but this still contains the blocking placed there at the end of the tomb's use. The outer part of the passage is not visible through this, but stones have been removed behind the line of the façade to reveal a length of passage, through which it is possible to crawl into the chamber. The chamber is a polygon some 4m by 1.8m, constructed from seven upright slabs with stretches of dry-stone walling in the spaces between them, and roofed by three massive slabs. Traces of an enclosing kerb of boulders can be seen through the slipped rubble tail from the cairn at various places around its circumference.

2. Callanish, *Lewis, Stone Circle and Chambered Cairn (NB 213330). At the S end of Callanish township, signposted W off the A858 Stornoway to Carloway road, 2.5km S of Breasclete.* **OS sheet 13.**

Perhaps the most atmospheric, and certainly one of the most impressive prehistoric monuments in Britain. The standing stones of Callanish lie on the spine of the long ridge which extends N from a rocky knoll towards the S end of a blunt promontory between Loch Ceann Hulavig and Tob Breasclete. They do not occupy the highest portion of the ridge, but still form a prominent skyline feature. The main element of the monument is a ring of thirteen slender stones, flattened somewhat on its E side to form an enclosure some 13m by 11m in diameter, the tallest of the stones rising to 3.5m. In the centre of this ring is a single shaft of stone rising to 4.75m in height. Between this stone and the E edge of the ring is a small passage-grave, which is now recognised as part of the original scheme of the monument rather than a later insertion. It was first explored after its discovery through peat-stripping in 1857. Extending N from this ring is an avenue of stones 8m wide and extending for over 80m

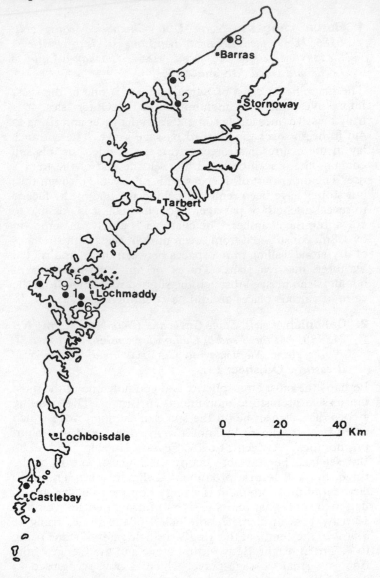

down the spine of the ridge. On the E, W and S of the ring, alignments of stones project like radiating spokes, the longest at the S extending for 27m. The passage-grave was set within a small cairn, some 7m in diameter. Its E side joins the circumference of the stone circle, one of the rings forming the N portal stone of its entrance. The short passage led into a now dilapidated two-compartment chamber. Excavations at the site in the 1970s revealed that it had been constructed on what was a previously cultivated landscape.

3. Dun Carloway, *Lewis, Broch (NB 189412). On a rocky outcrop overlooking Loch an Duin, to the N of the unclassified road (signposted Historic Scotland) running W from the A858 2km SW of Carloway.* **OS sheet 8.**

The most substantial broch ruin in the Western Isles, Dun Carloway dominates the skyline above the modern township at the foot of its rocky perch. The doorway in the NW opens onto an entrance passage through the 3.6m-thick walls. Opening from the S side of the passage is a guard chamber. The interior of the broch measures some 7.6m in diameter, and opening from it are entrances to three other mural chambers. Above the level of the higher door lintels is the scarcement which supported the timbers of the buildings ranged around the interior. From the SE cell, directly opposite the entrance, a staircase gave access to the upper levels. The walling of the S side of the broch survives to over 9m in height.

4. Dun Bharpa, *Barra, Chambered Cairn (NF 671019). Leave the A888 700m N of Borve on the unclassified road to Craigston. At the head of the road strike uphill for 0.5km (climbing some 75m) to gain the bealach between Beinn Mhartainn and Grianan. The cairn stands towards the centre of the ridge.* **OS sheet 31.**

The relative isolation of this site has ensured a high degree of preservation, although the cairn does appear to have been disturbed in the recent past. Measuring some 26m in diameter, the cairn was originally bounded by an intermittent kerb of massive uprights, some up to 2m in height. A series of slabs revealed on the edge of the E side probably marks the line of the passage. The position of the chamber is marked by the massive capstone lying on the top of the mound. This is nearly some 3m long, 1.75m wide and 0.3m thick.

5. Dun Torcuill, *North Uist, Dun (?) (NF 888737). On an islet towards the SW end of Loch an Duin, roughly 6km NW of Lochmaddy. Leave the A865 Lochmaddy-Grenitote road 5.5km NW of Lochmaddy on the unclassified road to Lochportain. The loch is on the N side of the road after 500m.* **OS sheet 18.**

This is a well preserved example of a class of monument typical to the Western Isles, to be seen on a grander scale at Dun an Sticer 4km to the N near Newtonferry. The entrance on the NW faces out onto the causeway which links the islet to the shore, and opens onto the entrance-passage. The walls vary in thickness between 2.3m and 3.8m around a central court some 11.6m in diameter, and contain a mural cell at the SW. On the S side the walls still stand to over 3m in height.

6. Pobuill Fhionn, *North Uist, Stone Circle (NF 842650). On the SW side of Ben Langass, slightly over 1km SE of the chambered cairn at Barpa Langass. The easiest access is via the track to Langass Lodge running SE from the A867 Lochmaddy to Clachan-a-Luib road, 3km NE of Clachan-a-Luib. Follow the track and footpath from the Lodge SE for 250m to the stone circle.* **OS sheet 18.**

The hillside overlooking Loch Langass has been cut into and the excavated material piled on the downslope side to form a terraced position for an elliptical setting of irregularly shaped stones. The stones define an area measuring some 37m by 30m in diameter, the arcs at the NW and SE ends surviving best.

7. South Clettraval, *North Uist, Chambered Cairn, Wheelhouse and Standing Stone (NF 749713 and NF 750712). Take the track running E from the A865 opposite the junction with the unclassified road to Tigharry and follow this to the gates at the foot of the steeper section of track leading to the radar station on the summit of the hill. The chambered cairn lies to the S of the road some 35m below the summit.* **OS sheet 18.**

The magnificent views S and W over the machair land on the Atlantic coast of North Uist amply repay the effort in climbing to this site. The cairn was severely robbed for stone in antiquity and its elongated wedge outline is obliterated, but its surviving passage and chamber show it to have been a Clyde type tomb and therefore unique in this area. The S side of the façade is recognisable as a line of slightly displaced slabs extending from the E end of the passage. Some kerb-stones can also be traced on this side. Two massive upright slabs at the W are the remains of the end compartment. Excavation of the site in 1934 produced large quantities of Neolithic and Beaker pottery, but little remained of the actual burials.

The chief reason for the ruinous state of the cairn lies towards its W end at a slightly lower level than the chamber. Standing on and built of robbed material from the elongated tail of the cairn is an Iron Age roundhouse. The walls are severely tumbled, but parts of the inner face can be seen on the N side. There, too, can be seen the remains of at least three radial 'spokes' of walling, forming compartments around the open central area, showing this to have been a wheelhouse. Some 150m SSE of the cairn and wheelhouse is a single standing stone.

8. Steinacleit, *Lewis, Settlement (NB 396540). Signposted S from the A857 opposite the junction with the unclassified road to Shader.* **OS sheet 8.**

There has been much speculation about the nature of this site, which is unexcavated, with identification ranging from denuded chambered cairn to domestic site. The latter is now the more favoured option, particularly in view of the large enclosure appended to its N side, which offers some parallels with the early settlement at Scord of Brouster in Shetland. The dominant feature of the site is a circular structure surviving as a kerb of massive stones some 16m in diameter. The enclosure, an oval area defined by a low wall of stones, measures some 82m by 55m.

9. Unival, *North Uist, Chambered Cairn and House (NF 800668). This site lies in remote moorland on the S flank of Unival. All approaches involve at least 2km of walking across the boggy moors, but the shortest approach is from the head of the track which runs NE from the A865 at Claddach Illeray, some 200m SE of the school.* **OS sheet 18.**

The site development here follows closely that displayed nearby on South Clettraval. The most obvious feature is the group of upright stones which mark the position of the chambered tomb. This lies at the heart of a denuded cairn, a low square of stones some 16m across bounded by a kerb composed of uprights linked with sections of dry-stone walling. The uprights of the SE face increase in height towards the centre, where the short, narrow passage runs into the central chamber. This, now roofless, is a polygonal compartment measuring 1.8m by 2.2m formed by a series of massive uprights. It was excavated in 1935 and 1939 when the remains of two inhumations, a large quantity of Neolithic pottery and implements of stone and flint were recovered. An amorphous hollow at the NE corner of the cairn marks the position of a two-compartment Iron Age house. The occupants of the house appear to have used the earlier burial chamber as a cooking pit.

SELECT BIBLIOGRAPHY

Davidson, H.E., *The Lost Beliefs of Northern Europe* (London, 1993)

Greene, K., *Archaeology: an Introduction* (London, 1995)

Hayes, A., *Archaeology of the British Isles* (London, 1993)

Hedeager, L., *Iron-Age Societies* (Oxford, 1992)

Kinsella, T. (trans.), *The Tain* (Portlaoise, 1986)

Laing, L., *Celtic Britain* (London, 1979)

MacSween, A. and Sharp, M., *Prehistoric Scotland* (London, 1989)

Megaw, J.V.S. and Simpson, D.D.A., *Introduction to British Prehistory* (Leicester, 1979)

Piggott, S., *Scotland Before History* (Edinburgh, 1982)

Ritchie, A., Prehistoric Orkney (London, 1995)

Ritchie, G. and Ritchie, A., *Scotland. Archaeology and Early History* (Edinburgh, 1991)

Wickham-Jones, C.R., *Scotland's First Settlers* (London, 1994)